Managing Your Money:
An Investment Guide for
Professionals and Entrepreneurs

Managing Your Money

An Investment Guide for Professionals and Entrepreneurs

PAUL A. RANDLE

PHILIP R. SWENSEN

LIFETIME LEARNING PUBLICATIONS • Belmont, California

A division of Wadsworth, Inc.

Editing, design, production supervision: Brian K. Williams
Editing: Sylvia Williams
Cartoons: Phil Frank
Illustrations: Carl Brown
Composition: Graphic Typesetting Service

Printed in the United States of America

2 3 4 5 6 7 8 9 10—83 32 31 80

Library of Congress Cataloging in Publication Data

Randle, Paul A
    Managing your money.
    Includes bibliography and index.
    1. Finance, Personal. 2. Investment.
I. Swensen, Philip R., joint author. II. Title.
HG 179.R323   332'.024   79-12669
ISBN 0-534-97996-3
ISBN 0-534-97994-7 pbk.

CONTENTS

> For the layman, finance can be a bewildering maze of rules of thumb, hot tips, and blind faith. Only by understanding the foundation of finance—the concepts of time and money—can one begin to evaluate financial decisions objectively and rationally.

> The cash flow: the most elementary and perhaps most resisted principle of finance. But it is impossible to make good financial decisions about your business, household expenditures, or particular investments without knowing where and when the money comes from and where and when it goes.

> A retirement plan is like taking money out of your left pocket, deducting it from your taxable income, then putting the money back in your right pocket. By funding a personal retirement plan you can significantly reduce your current income tax liability because contributions to the plan are tax deductible. Moreover, earnings on retirement-plan investments are excmpt from income taxes until withdrawals when you retire.

> An essential part of the corporate pension or profit-sharing plan, as well as other fringe-benefit programs, your professional corporation can heap employee benefits on you—if you play by the rules. Failure to play by the legal rules of corporate practice, however, and the IRS will slap your hand—hard.

"If a risk exists, insure against it" seems to be the rule the insurance industry would have us follow. Actually, the contrary is true. You should insure against catastrophes such as open-heart surgery while assuming the costs of runny noses out of your own pocket.

Next to housing, life insurance premiums may be your largest personal expenditure. Yet the odds are you are grossly under-insured and your family will be inadequately provided for in the event of your death. Why? Because the only life insurance product shown you is so expensive you can't afford all you need. Less expensive policies are explained as subjecting you to dangerous risks. Baloney.

When we select investments, a high return almost always looks more appealing than a lower return. When relative riskiness is considered, however, the safety and liquidity of corporate securities make them vital to an investment portfolio.

Cattle feeding, oil drilling, shopping centers, tax shelters—sometimes these types of investments work out. Often they do not. The results are dictated by an iron-clad law: When potential return is high, risk is high.

The principal requirement of pension plan investment is described in one word: prudence. Because of the tax-deferred status of the plan, it is possible to invest very conservatively and still accumulate a fortune. Ignore prudence and it's possible to go to jail.

Use your own money? Borrow from the bank? Lease the asset? These are all alternative ways to finance investment in an asset. But there is always one decision to make before you arrange the financing: Is the asset a profitable addition to your portfolio?

An estate plan is a strategy, not a set of legal documents. The strategy works only if you follow it. Plot the strategy early, follow it faithfully, and preserve your estate for your heirs instead of for the IRS.

Chapter 13. Inflation and Your Financial Plan   193

Inflation will undoubtedly be with us in the foreseeable future. To ignore its important effects on your financial plans could lead to disappointment, if not disaster.

PREFACE

Countless times we have been told that people such as yourself, practicing in one of the professions or forms of entrepreneurship, cannot be made to understand even the most rudimentary principles of finance. Your lack of business training, the many demands on your time, your lack of interest in things so mundane as finance, all require that you delegate your financial affairs to attorneys, accountants, advisors, and insurance men—or so we continually hear.

Our long experience, however, tells us that your answer to this widely held misconception would be a resounding, *Baloney!* Indeed, we have found that you are a well-educated, very intelligent person, with an intense interest in understanding your personal financial affairs. Contact with thousands of people like yourself has proved that you easily grasp basic principles that lesser lights find difficult. And, furthermore, once you understand these principles, you also understand the absurdity of the rule-of-thumb world inhabited by many of those who advise you.

After you have read this book, you will understand what the great financial benefits of a well-designed retirement plan are and how it may well be your surest hedge against inflation. You will have a good idea as to whether your practice or business should be incorporated, as well as some of the essential requirements of sound estate planning. You will be able to unravel with confidence some of the investment schemes that constantly confront you, whether they be a blue-chip stock or a blue-sky oil drilling operation. The thoroughly intimidating tangle of insurance planning will become clear to you as you understand the costs and benefits of all types of insurance coverage.

Your understanding of these essential financial issues will not be based on easy rules of thumb or glib generalities, but rather on your mastery of several fundamental principles of all financial analysis. With this understanding, you can formulate the objectives and establish the strategy for your financial future. Without it, you cannot. It's that simple.

Because your time is more productively spent in practicing your profession than in any other endeavor, what you read here is not a do-it-yourself guide. You will frequently seek legal and accounting advice in implementing your plans. You are the person, however, who should be formulating strategy, establishing objectives, and giving the orders. And when things do not seem to be going as they should, when strategies are not accomplishing desired objectives, when an investment appears to be turning sour, you should be able to ask tough questions.

For you, then, there's a bottom line that has three steps:

- Make a plan,
- Give the orders,
- And be able, always, to ask the right questions.

You must meet that bottom line. And we're dedicated to seeing that you do.

Paul A. Randle
Philip R. Swensen

Managing Your Money:
An Investment Guide for
Professionals and Entrepreneurs

PART One

Using Cash Flows to Build Your Framework

CHAPTER 1

What This Book Will Do for You

This book deals with the planning for and the analysis of financial decisions—*your* financial decisions. Our experience has shown that as people like you prepare for their selected professions, their training seldom includes a sound, practical framework to assist them in making day-to-day financial decisions. We want to stress the word *framework*, for providing a framework is the objective of this book. We do not anticipate that you will become an expert financial analyst; in fact, we do not recommend it, for your time will be more profitably spent pursuing your own career. We do know, however, that this book will provide central concepts that apply universally to sound financial decisions. If you have these concepts well in mind—that is, if you really understand them—you won't be fooled by attempts to get you to part with your hard-earned dollars. Even more importantly, this understanding will allow you to take the offensive: to direct your team of advisors as they follow the strategy you devise.

Making financial decisions: the importance of a framework

Defining Your Objectives: What Do You Really Want?

In applying what you read to your own financial situation, recognize that setting financial objectives is a highly personal and individualistic exercise. Neither we nor anyone else can exercise the prerogative of defining your goals and objectives. We can, however, help strip away some of the mysteries of finance:

Your goals are YOUR goals

- We can put to rest rules of thumb that are not only inaccurate but dangerous.
- We can help you evaluate what kinds of risk you have the ability to assume.
- We can explain ways to cut taxes, save money, evaluate investments, borrow money, buy insurance.

But after you have finished reading the book, it will still be up to you to examine carefully your own personality, resources, and family needs and then to decide realistically what you want your financial

Ask yourself tough questions

future to look like. We suggest you and your spouse spend a quiet moment or two discussing financial objectives, ranking each as to its relative importance in your lives. Ask tough questions about yourselves: How do I feel about assuming large amounts of financial risk? What provision do I want to make for my family should I die? Will I support the kids in college or let them pay their own way? How much money do I need in my retirement years? Do I have the disposition and knowledge to manage my own retirement fund? How much discretionary income is available to fund retirement benefits and purchase insurance? We think the answers to these types of questions will come into clear focus as you read and digest the chapters that follow.

By all means you be the one to answer the questions and let those answers become the primary input to your personal financial plan. Don't, as happens with so many professional people, merely coast—living, as it were, from day to day, with no clear-cut financial plans or objectives. By all means don't let your plans be formulated by salesmen of financial products and services. Remember, they have a strong vested interest in selling those products—that is how they make their living. While their advice may be excellent, you have no way to judge unless you yourself have previously defined your objectives.

Then start with two objectives

Now, contrary to our own advice and with the temerity of authors, we urge you to consider at least two specific financial objectives: We think prudence dictates that you provide a comfortably adequate retirement income for your retirement age, and at the same time provide financial security for your family should your death occur while they are still financially dependent on you. We think provision for these two needs is of paramount importance—particularly for the self-employed professional who does not participate in employer-provided retirement and insurance programs.

When you have solved these two problems, you can take your financial plan in any one of a thousand directions, depending on your desires, whims, personality, and resources.

> Be conservative in planning for the two objectives that really count: your retirement income and your family's security should you die. Fly as high as you would like with the resources left over after these two objectives are met. But don't ever gamble with your own or your family's security.

We've suggested that your personality—particularly how you view risk—will largely determine the direction of your evolving financial strategy. But if you are to maintain the balance we've just described, there's an overriding consideration: The ultimate limitation must always be the amount and availability of discretionary income. While this seems obvious, we are frequently amazed at the numbers of professionals who have no idea of their income or their expenditures. Our theory is that when receipts are high, professionals tend to overlook expenditures such as office overhead, taxes, and equipment purchases that must be made before receipts become spendable income. The consequence for many is a dramatic and disastrous overspending.

The first step, then, in any financial plan is to formulate a good, old-fashioned budget. It need not be formal; in fact, we have purposely not included a budget form lest you develop a slavish devotion to an accounting regimen. And it must be flexible: Don't make your life miserable by exacting spartan demands required by inflexible budgetary constraints. But do write it down, identifying explicitly all revenues and expenditures. Make it an information-producing device that provides the data necessary to your financial plan.

You're going to need a budget

The Tools of Financial Planning: How to Get What You Want

Practically all of the financial decisions you make—at least those of significant consequence—have one major common ingredient—TIME. By this we mean that decisions regarding retirement planning, insurance, home ownership, pension plans, estate planning, portfolio management, asset acquisition, and so forth, all involve either the commitment or receipt of money over an extended time period.

You have to know how time relates to money

To understand the economic consequences of such decisions, *it is absolutely essential that you understand the fundamental relationships between time and money.* Herein lies the major difference between this book and all other personal finance books presently available. Rather than simply discussing the elements of budgeting, checking accounts, careful purchasing, and the like, we provide a framework within which all major financial decisions can be made with confidence.

No corporate controller would think of making financial decisions with any other tools but those discussed in this book. And the beauty of these tools is that they are infinitely more applicable to your problems than they are to those of General Motors.

A Word About Each Chapter

Chap. 2, "Time and Money: The Foundation." We shall start in the next chapter with the most important and gut-level concept of finance—*the time value of money.* You need not be intimidated by this material. Even though we are convinced that it is not widely understood, the ideas are simple and they fit together in an amazingly

Money has time value

logical way. On the other hand, you must thoroughly understand Chapter 2 before most of the remaining chapters will make sense. So dig into the next chapter with resolve. Go through it several times if you must, until you clearly understand the time value of money. After that, you will easily understand decisions regarding such important matters as life insurance and pension plans as we strip away the magic and confusion that now surrounds them.

Chap. 3, "Making Sure the Cash Flows Flow." In the final analysis, the value of any financial transaction must be measured in the amount of cash that flows into your pocket—or the quality of services rendered by those dollars that flow out. Because of various accounting practices, your bottom-line reported income each year may vary markedly from the cash in the till. In Chapter 3 you will learn why this is so, and how to ferret out the relevant items for constructing a picture of the actual cash flows associated with your personal, business, or practice income—or from a particular investment project. Once the cash flows are properly organized, you can easily determine their net economic impact on your resources. Only by measuring these cash flows can you determine whether any given investment will merit your consideration.

Cash flows should determine your investments

Chap. 4, "Selecting the Right Retirement Plan: The Only Way to Have Your Cake and Eat It." With Chapters 2 and 3 safely under your belt, you can decipher the entire spectrum of investment alternatives. Chapter 4 examines a very important investment decision, especially for self-employed people—namely, the construction of an appropriate retirement plan. There are many complex legal and actuarial requirements of plan construction that will require the services of an attorney. This chapter will, however, help you understand these requirements so that you can discuss them intelligently with the professionals who assist you.

A retirement plan is crucial for the self-employed

Chap. 5, "The Pros and Cons of Professional Incorporation: Play by the Rules and Win Big." Closely allied to the problems of retirement planning—particularly for professionals—is the need for incorporation. In spite of the many advantages to the corporate form of organization, there are costs as well as benefits you should be aware of. Chapter 5 presents a detailed picture of the pro's and con's of incorporation to help you decide if this step is for you.

And incorporation may be, too

Chap. 6, "All About Insurance: Insure for Surgery but Pay for Runny Noses." Chapters 6 and 7 may be just about the most useful material you will ever read. Of all the financial decisions you confront, some of the most important are in the area of insurance—especially life insurance. Yet our experience shows that there is a great deal of confusion surrounding the topic of insurance—confusion not only as to the myriad of products available, but also as to what insurance is and how

Insurance—what it is

much is needed. Chapter 6 outlines the fundamentals of insurance so that you can understand the crucial difference between insurance protection and the investment attributes of many insurance policies.

Chap. 7, "Determining Your Life Insurance Needs: How to Have Enough Without Going Broke." Chapter 7 follows with a careful analysis of life insurance; you'll learn how to decide on the amount of life insurance you need and what particular insurance products are available to meet that need. We are convinced that careful insurance planning can save you substantial amounts of money while simultaneously providing you with more appropriate coverage than you currently have.

Your insurance—how much and what kind you need

Chap. 8, "The Conventional Investments: If You Opt for Safety." Chapters 8, 9, and 10 acquaint you with the alternative investment possibilities available as you accumulate excess funds. The conventional investments, characterized by lower levels of risk and profitability, are discussed in Chapter 8. You will also learn of the various types of risk that all investment ventures are subject to. These risks should be recognized and assumed only in the proportion consistent with your preferences and your investment goals.

How to judge investment ventures

Chap. 9, "The High Fliers: If You Thrive on Risk." If you are a gunslinger who loves to assume risk for potentially huge returns, go straight to Chapter 9. The high fliers such as cattle feeding and oil drilling are discussed. These can be exciting ventures but you must recognize them as truly speculative: You may lose your shirt; but if you hit it big, you'll be rich.

Chap. 10, "Investments in a Pension Plan: A Time for Prudence." One of the most important investment programs you will initiate will be your pension plan. It should also be the most conservatively managed. You may wish to employ professionals to manage this fund or you may choose to get personally involved in the management. In either case, Chapter 10 is intended to acquaint you thoroughly with the in's and out's of pension fund portfolio planning and administration.

Your pension fund

Chap. 11, "How to Finance Your Investments: Choosing the Best Way to Build Your Portfolio." As investment opportunities come to your attention, it is one thing to analyze them for investment value, but quite another task to decide how to finance those that appear to be profitable. For example, once you decide an investment is desirable, should you borrow money or finance it from some other source? Chapter 11 examines this issue and details how the financing decision can greatly affect the yield on your personal dollars.

How to finance your investments

Chap. 12, "Estate Planning: A Strategy You Can Master." With the passage of the Tax Reform Act of 1976, the problems of estate planning have assumed new dimensions. Chapter 12 makes specific recom-

How to plan your estate

mendations that can save you enormous headaches if your estate plan is properly constructed *as you accumulate assets,* rather than at the end of your life. Here again, you will need to consult your attorney for specifics, but this chapter will allow you to discuss the available alternatives intelligently.

How to deal with inflation

Chap. 13, "Beating Inflation: A Challenge You Must Face." In books like ours, the problem of inflation is generally dealt with as an investment risk and dismissed in a few short paragraphs. Because this problem has become so serious and pervasive in the last decade, we feel it deserves more attention than it generally receives. Chapter 13 describes what inflation is, why it exists, what the prospects are for the future, why it hurts, and how to deal with it.

You will undoubtedly not be able to assimilate all the material in these thirteen chapters in the first reading. There are chapters you will want to refer back to as the materials have more relevance to your personal situation. We have found, however, that almost all professionals face each of the financial problems outlined in this book at some point in their lives. Many such problems occur almost daily. We hope that this book can assist you in making sense out of these financial decisions, all of which are crucial to your welfare. If so, you can gain some peace of mind—and probably save a few bucks along the way. These are our objectives.

The Importance of Examples

You'll have simple examples for important concepts

In the chapters that follow, many examples are presented to illustrate the point under discussion. To enhance your understanding of important concepts, we have purposely made the examples extreme simplifications of typical real-life situations. Let us be quick to add, however, that the examples differ from the real world only in the degree of detail they contain, not in concept.

Remember, it is our intention to provide you with a conceptual framework within which you can understand the nature of financial decisions, not to turn you into a financial analyst. You are, or should be, assisted by an accountant, attorney, retirement plan actuary—and perhaps a financial planner—each of whom assists you with specific problems. These individuals are well qualified to add the appropriate detail you need to the illustrations in this book. Your understanding of the problem, however, will insure that your interests are accurately represented.

Many of our examples and illustrations refer to physicians and dentists, simply because much of our experience has been with those professions. It is not our intention to imply that they are the only professionals in need of this material—or even those in greatest need. The elements of financial analysis we discuss are applicable to every individual regardless of occupation, age, sex, or financial status. To the extent we can all learn a few basic concepts of finance, our financial decisions can be made with more confidence and we can be better prepared to deal with this important area of our lives.

So, let's roll up our sleeves and get on with it. . . .

CHAPTER 2

Time and Money: The Foundation

It is the purpose of this chapter to acquaint you with the fundamentals of the time value of money and to explain how this concept is crucial to sound financial decisions. After you have read this chapter, you will understand:

- How the profitability of an investment is affected by time.
- That the price you can pay for an investment is the value of its future economic returns to you.
- How to compute that value.

The Importance of Compound Interest

The concept of *compound interest* is central to sound financial decisions.

> If you thoroughly understand the simple mathematics of compound interest, you will be able to analyze the financial consequences of your decisions regarding insurance, taxes, estate plans, pension plans, personal investments, equipment acquisitions, and virtually every other decision laying claim to your financial resources.

The going in this chapter may get tough from time to time, but do not be discouraged. We want you to understand the concepts discussed here. Quick and dirty rules of thumb are effective only for salesmen trying to get your wallet. The only intelligent way for you to make sound financial decisions is based on the principles developed in this chapter. If you stick with it, you may find it not only fun but also the most profitable thing you have ever learned.

You can understand compound interest

A word about calculators

All of the computational work you are about to do in this chapter can be done instantly with sophisticated yet inexpensive preprogrammed financial calculators. These invaluable devices make the analysis of very complex financial decisions quite literally as easy as pushing buttons.

A word of caution, though: It is essential that you understand the material in this chapter before using these marvelous machines. Failure to heed this warning will turn you into a highly skilled button pusher, completely in the dark about what you are doing. First gain a conceptual understanding of the material that follows; then the calculator will become an indispensable tool.

We hesitate to recommend one brand over another, but two calculators are noteworthy because of the completeness of their excellent user manuals; these manuals are almost minifinance courses, presented in easy-to-understand formats. They are Hewlett Packard (HP 22) and Texas Instruments (MBA). Either of these fine machines will greatly simplify the types of financial decisionmaking discussed in this chapter.

What Makes a Good Investor

The entire notion of the time value of money stems from one fundamental financial principle that can be summed up as follows: Given that you have one dollar today, there are only two things you can do with it: You can consume it by purchasing goods and services, or you can invest it for the purpose of consuming it at some future date. Since the decision to invest requires a delay in consumption, such a decision requires a profit sufficient to entice you to forego current consumption in favor of consumption at some future date. This profit is known as the rate of interest, and it manifests itself in all forms of financial decisions.

What you can do with a dollar

As long as a rate of interest exists, we can be sure that investment will take place. The particular type of investment that will be selected, however, is dependent upon the financial resources and preferences of each individual investor. Although each investor will differ markedly in such preferences, all rational investors should have these three characteristics in common:

Characteristics common to all good investors

- For any given sum, investors will prefer early returns to later returns. That is, given a choice of $50 now or $50 at some future time, you will always prefer the $50 now.
- For any given rate of return, investors will prefer less risk to more risk. That is, if two investment alternatives present the same rate of return but differing probabilities of default, you will always select the alternative that presents the lower probability of losing your money.
- For any given level of risk, investors will always prefer higher returns to lower returns. If two investments are equally risky, you will always select the one with the highest return.

The latter two of these assumptions are reasonably self-evident and reflect accurately the propensities of all of us. The first assumption embodies the principle of compound interest and will constitute our primary focus in this chapter.

The Compounded Value of a Sum

If you read through this section carefully, you will see how a sum invested now can grow, through time, to large future values. The notion is really very simple; yet it appears in various forms throughout all of financial analysis—so let's take a minute and step through it slowly.

Suppose you have $1,000 available to invest in a savings account yielding a 6 percent annual return. You see no immediate need for the money and thus you expect to leave it undisturbed for 5 years and simply let the interest accrue each year. The question you would now like answered is: How much will I have at the end of that 5-year period?

Let's take it a year at a time to see how this type of problem is solved. First, some definitions and notation. Let

PV (present value) = the value of your investment at the present time, or $1,000;

FV (future value) = the value of your investment at some future point in time;

i = the prevailing rate of interest, or 6 percent in this example;

n = the number of years over which the compounding takes place—5, in this case.

To determine the value of your $1,000 investment at the end of the first year we can see that

$$FV_1 = PV + PV \times i,$$

An example: future value after 1 year

which simply states that the future value at the end of the first year (FV_1) will be equal to the original principal (PV), plus the interest earned on that principal $(PV \times i)$. Numerically,

$$FV_1 = \$1,000 + \$1,000 \,(.06) = \$1,060.$$

Or, even more simply if you remember how to factor from high school algebra:

$$FV_1 = \$1,000 \,(1 + .06) = \$1,060.$$

But how much will you have at the end of the second year, assuming you allow the entire $1,060 to remain on deposit?

You know that

$$FV_2 = FV_1 + FV_1(.06),$$

or

Future value after 2 years

$$FV_2 = FV_1(1 + .06).$$

But remember that

$$FV_1 = PV(1 + .06),$$

so

$$FV_2 = PV(1 + .06)(1 + .06)$$

or even more simply,

$$FV_2 = PV(1 + .06)^2 = \$1,123.60.$$

Notice that during the second year the interest earned amounted to $1,123.60 − $1,060.00 = $63.60, whereas it was only $60 the first year. The source of the higher interest earnings in the second year was the interest earned on the interest of year 1. Thus, if a sum is deposited and left undisturbed, the interest accumulation will accelerate due to this compounding effect.

You could continue to compute the future value for each year, but actually, you only need the relationship

$$FV_n = PV(1 + i)^n.$$

Future value after any number of years
With that general statement you can now compute the value for any future year without computing intermediate values. For our original example, the value at the end of year 5 is

$$FV_5 = \$1,000(1 + .06)^5 = \$1,338.23.$$

Thus, the compounded (future) value of $1,000, invested for 5 years, at a rate of interest of 6 percent, is $1,338.23.

Finding Variables Other Than Future Value

In this section you will see how to solve precisely the same problem but phrased in a slightly different way. Many times a need for money at some future time can be anticipated now. Further, it is often wise to invest some amount now to accommodate a future need. The sum invested now to guarantee a future amount is called the *present value* of that future sum.

Now let's look at precisely the same problem, but phrase it in a slightly different way. Suppose you can foresee a need 5 years from now for an office machine that will cost $1,338.23 at that time. You have some extra cash available now that you would like to invest for that eventuality. If you had an investment opportunity yielding 6 percent, how much would you need to invest now to be sure of having the $1,338.23 available? Remember, the formula for compounding a sum was

$$FV = PV(1 + i)^n.$$

However, your problem is now such that *FV* is known and you must determine the present value of that future required amount.

A minor manipulation of the formula yields

Present value of a future sum
$$PV = \frac{FV}{(1 + i)^n},$$

which allows you easily to compute that present value *(PV)*. Solving the example,

$$PV = \frac{\$1,338.23}{(1. + .06)^5} = \$1,000.00.$$

That is, if you now invest \$1,000 at 6 percent annually, it will grow to \$1,338.23 at the end of 5 years.

You now see how easily you can compute the compounded future value of some given present investment—or, alternatively, the present value necessary to compound into some predetermined future sum.

The solution to such problems can be greatly facilitated by the use of the tables found at the end of this chapter. Notice again that the future-value problems always take the following form:

$$FV = PV(1 + i)^n.$$

Use our tables

The quantity $(1 + i)^n$ can be computed for any values of n and i and presented in tabular form as in Appendix A.1 (page 26). For example, if $n = 5$ and $i = 6$ percent, you can compute $(1 + .06)^5 = 1.3382$. This interest factor *(IF)* can be applied to any principal amount *(PV)* and yield the future value of that principal amount as it was allowed to grow at 6 percent annually for 5 years. The table of Appendix A.1 computes an array of these interest factors for periods ranging from 1 to 30 years and interest rates ranging from 1 to 20 percent and is thus a handy tool for solving compound-interest problems.

For example, suppose you invest \$500 at 14 percent for 12 years. How much will you have at the end of that 12-year period? A general statement for the problem is

Investing \$500 at 14 percent

$$FV = PV \times IF_1,$$

where IF_1 is simply the interest factor obtained from Appendix A.1. We find that the interest factor corresponding to a 12-year investment at 14 percent is 4.767. Hence, our solution is

$$FV_{12} = \$500(4.767) = 2,383.50.$$

That is, your original \$500 investment will have compounded to \$2,675 under the prescribed conditions. Appendix A.1 has eliminated the repetitive use of a rather cumbersome formula and also eliminates the task of raising a number to a power.

If, on the other hand, you wish to compute the present value of some known future sum, you have seen that the appropriate formula is

$$PV = FV \times \frac{1}{(1 + i)^n}.$$

The quantity $1/(1 + i)^n$ can easily be computed for any values of i and n, and efficiently presented in tabular form. In fact, Appendix A.2 is just such a table. For interest rates ranging from 1 percent to 20 percent, and periods ranging from 1 to 30 years, this appendix presents the interest factor to be employed in determining the present value of any known future sum.

For example, suppose you desire to provide a fund of $16,000 to put your new son through college when he starts 18 years from now. If your current investment opportunities yield 7 percent, how much must you invest now to realize the $16,000 when it is needed? From the table of Appendix A.2 we find that the interest factor associated with a 7 percent annual yield for 18 years is equal to .296. The solution to the problem is now greatly simplified, and is equal to

$$PV = \$16,000 \times .296 = \$4,736.$$

The present value of $16,000 received 18 years from now is $4,736. If this latter amount is invested now at a 7 percent annual rate, it will grow to $16,000 in 18 years. Similar present-value problems can easily be solved with the information in Appendix A.2.

To be certain that these principles are understood, see if you can work through a number of simple examples.

Example 1. You look forward to retirement in 30 years and desire to deposit one lump sum that will grow to be equal to $250,000 at that time. If you can invest at an annual rate of 9 percent, how much do you need to deposit now to reach that goal?

Solution. We know $FV_{30} = \$250,000$, $i = .09$, $n = 30$, but we do not know the present value *(PV)*, the amount we need to invest today. Remembering the formula

$$PV = FV(IF_2),$$

where, again, IF_2 is a shorthand way of noting the appropriate interest factor obtained from Appendix A.2, where we find that the interest factor corresponding to 30 years with an interest rate of 9 percent is equal to .075. Solving:

$$PV = \$250,000 \times .075 = \$18,750.$$

That is, $18,750 must be invested today at 9 percent to yield $250,000 in 30 years.

Example 2. Property values in the area where your office building is located are increasing at the rate of 4 percent a year. If your building is presently worth $150,000, what will it be worth in 7 years?

Solution. We know $PV = \$150,000$, $i = 4\%$, and $n = 7$. We need to determine the future value *(FV)* in 7 years:

$$FV_7 = PV \times IF_1.$$

From Appendix A.1 we find $IF = 1.316$. Solving:

$$FV_7 = \$150,000 \times 1.316 = \$197,400.$$

Example 3. You need to amass $90,000 in the next 10 years to meet a balloon payment on your building. You now have $41,700 available for investment. What annual interest rate must be realized in order to amass the required amount?

Solution. Here again is a slightly different twist to a now familiar problem. The information we do know is

$$PV = \$41,700,$$
$$FV_{10} = \$90,000,$$
$$n = 10 \text{ years},$$

and it is now our task to determine the interest rate, or compute i. Again, the tables are of great help in solving this problem. Setting up the equation

$$FV_{10} = PV \times IF_1,$$

or

$$\$90,000 = \$41,700 \times IF_1,$$

so

$$IF_1 = \frac{\$90,000}{41,700} = 2.158.$$

We now know that with n equal to 10 and the interest rate unknown the interest factor must equal 2.158. Turning now to Appendix A.1, go down the left-hand column until you find the row corresponding with year 10. Then follow horizontally along that row until you find the interest factor close to 2.158. You will find such a number under the 8 percent column. Therefore, you have determined that $41,700 will grow into $90,000 after 10 years only if it is invested in an alternative yielding an 8 percent annual rate of return.

Example 4. A potential oil-field site has been currently appraised at $27,910, but it has been appreciating at 20 percent a year. If this rate continues, in how many years will this land be worth $100,000?

An oil-field site

Solution. In this final example we again have a little different twist. We know the following facts:

$$PV = \$27,910,$$
$$FV = \$100,000,$$
$$i = 20 \text{ percent}.$$

But we need to determine the number of years *(n)* it will take $27,910 to grow into $100,000 if it compounds at a 20 percent annual rate. We know

$$FV_n = PV \times IF_1$$

or

$$\$100,000 = \$27,910 \times IF_1,$$

so

$$IF_1 = \frac{\$100,000}{\$27,910} = 3.583.$$

Turn to Appendix A.1 again, and follow along the top row until you come to the 20 percent column. Then move down the column until you find an interest factor very close to or equal to 3.583. You will find this number corresponds to a period of 7 years, so $27,910 will grow into $100,000 in 7 years if it compounds at a 20 percent annual rate.

Consider alternatives at a common point in time

What These Examples Show. These concepts give you the capability to compare financial values that occur at different points in time. It is difficult, for example, to know whether $10,000 received 8 years from now is better than $5,000 received today. To make the proper decision you must compare these values at a common point in time. If you know the prevailing rate of interest available to you, or the rate you expect to earn on such investments, you can either compute the future value of $5,000 (which you receive today) compounded for 8 years, or the present value of $10,000 (which you receive 8 years hence). Either computation will allow you to make a sound financial decision, although the latter procedure is more commonly used. The reason for the more common usage of present value is that time period zero (today) is common to every investment alternative, irrespective of how many years it produces income.

Just for fun, you may wish to try your hand at present-value analysis: Which is the most valuable, the $5,000 received today, or the $10,000 you can receive 8 years from now, if the interest rate is 10 percent?

The Compound Value of an Annuity

An annuity is a flow of cash

Now that you have examined the compounding characteristics of a single lump-sum payment, we can turn our attention to a potentially more useful tool: the effects of compounding on a flow, or stream, of income. Such a flow of income is called an annuity.

> An annuity is a payment (or receipt), usually of a fixed amount, made periodically at stated, predetermined intervals. Most commonly, each payment is made at the end of the payment period and is thus referred to as an *ordinary annuity*, or *annuity in arrears*.

An annuity due

A common example of this type of payment stream is the monthly payment on an amortized mortgage loan. Each payment pays the interest accrued during the previous period and reduces the principal balance by a slight amount. If the payment is required at the beginning of the period, such as a retirement-annuity-benefit payment, it would be referred to as an *annuity due*. Practically all of the annuity problems with which we shall deal are of the ordinary-annuity type—that is, the payment is assumed to be received at the end of the period.

Determining the value of annuities

Annuities are a common characteristic of literally thousands of financial contracts and investments. Home mortgages, installment loans, pension plans, retirement benefits, and insurance settlements are only a few examples of financial arrangements in which annuities figure prominently. The question is, how can their value be determined?

Suppose that by some set of fortuitous circumstances you become the recipient of $1,000 a year for each of the next 7 years. Your first payment will come to you 1 year from today, and you will continue to receive $1,000 at the end of each year until the final payment is made at the end of the seventh year. Further, you see no immediate need for this money and as a result, you decide to make annual deposits in a secure savings account that yields 7 percent per year. How much will you have at the end of the seventh year just as you receive the final payment? You can see from your understanding of the compounding of a single sum that it would be possible to compute the future value of this flow by treating each individual payment separately. To clarify the problem, Figure 2.1 illustrates it diagrammatically.

An annuity after 7 years

Figure 2.1 is like a time picture of your savings account. Notice the time frame extends from year zero, which we will take as today, to the end of year 7, which coincides with the final payment date. With the help of Appendix A.1, you can compute the future value of each one of the payments as they are deposited to yield 7 percent annually.

A time picture of your savings account

The initial payment, which is received 1 year from now, is immediately put on deposit and remains on deposit throughout the entire period, that is, until the end of year 7. As a result, it is on deposit for a total of 6 years. The future value of that single deposit can be computed by finding the interest factor in Appendix A.1 corresponding to an interest rate of 7 percent for 6 years, a value of 1.501. Applying that interest factor to the $1,000 principal amount you see that the deposit will grow to $1,501 by the end of year 7.

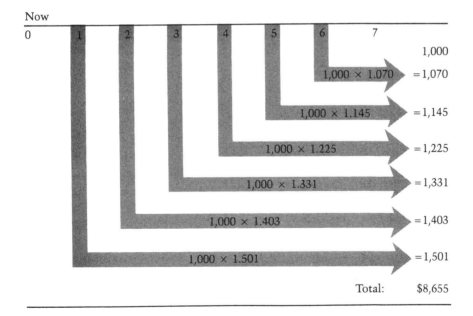

Figure 2.1 The future value of a savings program: invest $1,000 annually at 7 percent per annum.

In a similar manner, the second payment you receive will immediately be deposited and left for the remaining 5 years, and will compound to equal $1,403 in that time.

Further, you can compute the future value of each of the $1,000 payments as they are received and immediately deposited. Notice that the last payment comes to you at the end of year 7, and thus does not earn interest as our other six payments. You can now arrive at the total value of the 7-year annuity simply by adding up each of the compounded seven annual payments—an accumulation of $8,655—at the end of the seventh year.

What you will receive

To summarize, an annuity of $1,000, received at the end of each of the next 7 years, will grow to a total value of $8,655 by the time you receive your last payment.

Now that you can graphically conceptualize what takes place in the compounding of a future value of an annuity, let's examine the same problem in a slightly different way. Table 2.1 solves, in tabular form, the value of this savings account.

Table 2.1 The Future Value of a Savings Program: Invest $1,000 Annually at 7 Percent per Annum

End of year	Amount invested		Interest factor, Appendix A.1, at 7%		Future value
1	$1,000	×	$1.501	=	$1,501
2	1,000	×	1.403	=	1,403
3	1,000	×	1.311	=	1,311
4	1,000	×	1.225	=	1,225
5	1,000	×	1.145	=	1,145
6	1,000	×	1.070	=	1,070
7	1,000	×	1.000	=	1,000
		Totals	$8.655		$8,655

Note that you could greatly simplify the problem by multiplying the periodic annuity amount by the sum of the interest factors taken from Appendix A.1. Even more conveniently, Appendix A.3 gives an interest factor that is equivalent (except for a possible small rounding error) to that sum, but for any interest rate and any period of time. This table also allows us to state a general solution to this particular annuity problem.

Use Appendix A.3

The future value of any annuity is

$$FV = PMT_n \times IF_3,$$

where

FV = the future value of the annuity,

PMT_n = the amount (periodic payment) of the annuity for n periods,

IF_3 = a future-value interest factor (given i and n) from Appendix A.3.

Look again at the example to see how this useful table speeds up a solution. To restate the problem, you receive an annuity of $1,000 at the end of each year, for 7 years. Each of these payments will be quickly invested to yield a 7 percent annual rate of return. The appropriate interest factor for 7 years, at 7 percent, is 8.655. Multiplying this interest factor by your $1,000 annuity payments, you quickly find the future value of the annuity stream to be equal to $8,655. The future value of any stream of payments may be similarly found.

After you stretch—and perhaps swear a bit—spend some time with the two examples that follow to make sure you understand this important concept.

Example 5. You plan to retire in 20 years. To provide for that retirement you initiate a savings program of $8,000 per year in an investment yielding 9 percent. The first payment will be deposited 1 year from now, and the last at the end of year 20. What will be the value of the fund at the end of year 20?

Saving to retire

Solution. With the use of Appendix A.3 you can easily obtain the solution. Your last payment into the retirement fund will be made at the end of year 20. Simply scan down the far left-hand column of Appendix A.3 until you reach period 20, and then horizontally until you come to the 9 percent column. The interest factor is 51.160. Multiplying this interest factor by the $8,000 annual contribution, you compute the future of your retirement fund to equal $409,280.

Example 6. Take the more modest example of a situation where you put aside only $1,000 per year for 30 years into an investment yielding an 8 percent annual rate of return.

Investing for 30 years

Solution. The interest factor from Appendix A.3 is equal to 113.283. Applying this interest to your $1,000 annual payments yields a future value of $113,283 at the end of the thirtieth year.

This example dramatizes the impact of compounding on regular contributions. Even modest contributions can grow to significant amounts if those contributions are made faithfully and regularly. The reason for this growth is, of course, that the early contributions earn interest over many compounding periods. The first payment, for example, is earning interest for the entire 30 years—an important point of pension-plan development. It is to your advantage to develop a program as early in your career as possible so that compounding can have this dramatic influence on the growth of the fund through time.

The dramatic influence of compounding

The Present Value of an Annuity

Let us emphasize again that many financial decisions are characterized by a stream, or flow, of cash that accrues throughout each of several future periods. In this section you will learn how to appraise, or value, those annuities. Consider the following example:

Suppose you are about to enter into a financial contract that will provide an income of $500 at the end of each year for the next 10

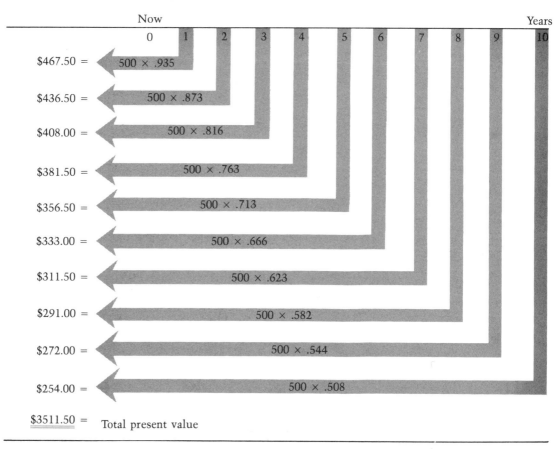

Figure 2.2 The present value of an income flow, $500 per year for 10 years, at 7 percent.

Learn to value your annuities

years. If the prevailing rate of interest is 7 percent, what is the present value (that is, the worth today) of that entire stream of receipts? Figure 2.2 illustrates the time diagram of this important problem and computes the present value of the investment. A more concise solution is contained in Table 2.2, which also shows that the problem could more easily be solved simply by multiplying the amount of the annuity ($500) by the sum of the present-value factors from Appendix A.2.

What you did in Table 2.2 is appraise the value of this investment. Wanting to earn 7 percent, you have determined that you could pay $3,511.50 for the investment and still earn your desired return.

Fortunately, you do not need to go through all the work shown in Table 2.2, since Appendix A.4 gives an interest factor equal to what you tediously computed by adding factors from Appendix A.2. Turn to Appendix A.4 and verify that the present value of an annuity of $1 per year, for 10 years, at 7 percent, is indeed equal to 7.023.

Follow this example

With this last tool, it is possible to state the present value of an annuity as being equal to

$$PV = PMT_n \times IF_{4,}$$

Table 2.2 The Present Value of an Income Flow, $500 per Year for 10 Years, at 7 Percent

Year	Annual Receipt		Present value factor from Appendix A.2, at 7%		Present value
1	$500	×	.935	=	$467.50
2	500	×	.873	=	436.50
3	500	×	.816	=	408.00
4	500	×	.763	=	381.50
5	500	×	.713	=	356.50
6	500	×	.666	=	333.00
7	500	×	.623	=	311.50
8	500	×	.582	=	291.00
9	500	×	.544	=	272.00
10	500	×	.508	=	254.00
	Totals		7.023		$3,511.50

where

PV = the present value of annuity stream,
PMT_n = the periodic annuity amount,
IF_4 = a present value interest factor (given i and n) from Appendix A.4.

You can now see how easy it is to solve the last example:

$$PV = \$500_{10} \times 7.023 = \$3,511.50.$$

By employing the interest factors of Appendix A.4, you can easily calculate the present value of any annuity stream, for any rate of interest, throughout any range of payment periods. Test your knowledge of this important tool by solving the following examples.

Example 7. You are contemplating the purchase of an office machine that has an expected lifetime of 12 years. It is estimated that this piece of equipment will save you $12,000 in annual expenses that you would otherwise incur. Further, you have alternative uses for your money that will earn 16 percent a year. What is the maximum price that you should be willing to pay for this piece of equipment?

Solution. This question is simply a sly, alternative way of asking for the present value of a $12,000 annual income stream, discounted at 16 percent, for 12 years. With the help of Appendix A.4 you can solve the problem quickly. The interest factor from the appendix corresponding to 12 payment periods at an interest rate of 16 percent is equal to 5.197. Multiplying the 5.197 interest factor times $12,000 yields the present value of the promised flow, and is equal to $62,364. Thus, the maximum amount you should be willing to pay for the asset is the present value of its expected flow, or $62,364. If this is the price that is actually paid, you will in fact receive a 16 percent rate of return on your investment.

Purchasing office machines: another example

Drawing from a retirement fund

Example 8. You are presently building up a retirement fund. By the time you retire, it is expected that you will have accumulated $150,000. If the fund is then invested to yield an 8 percent annual return, and you are expected to live an additional 20 years, how much can you withdraw each year so that by the end of year 20 the fund will have just been liquidated?

Solution. Notice in this example that the present value, the number of periods, and the interest rate are known. However, you would like to discover the annuity payment. Algebraically, you can see that

$$PV = PMT_{20} \times IF_4$$

or

$$PMT_{20} = \frac{PV}{IF_4}.$$

Again, Appendix A.4 reveals that the interest factor for 20 years at 8 percent is 9.818. Taking the initial value of the fund, $150,000, and dividing that present value by 9.818, indicates that the annual benefit that can be withdrawn is equal to $15,278.06.

Receiving an inheritance

Example 9. You have just received an inheritance of $50,000 cash. The fund is invested to yield 10 percent, but you desire to draw $6,000 per year from the fund to supplement your annual income. For how many years can you withdraw the annual $6,000 before the fund runs out?

Solution. In all such problems, you must know three of the four variables of our compound interest equations so that you are left to solve for the single remaining unknown. In this problem, the present value of the fund is given at $50,000. The annual annuity is $6,000 and, finally, the annual rate of return is 10 percent. You can now proceed with this information and solve for n, the number of periods over which this annuity can be realized. Remember that if you divide the present value by the annuity payment, you will obtain a figure equal to the interest factor, 8.330 in this example. Turning again to Appendix A.4, follow down the 10 percent column until you find an interest factor very nearly equal to 8.330. The interest factor in the table which most closely corresponds to 8.330 is found on the row indicating 19 years. Thus, you can be sure that your fund of $50,000 earning 10 percent will be depleted in approximately 19 years if you make $6,000 annual withdrawals from the fund.

Computing the interest rate on your office building

Example 10. Your new office building was recently constructed for $325,000 and financed for 25 years. Your annual payment is equal to $27,887.42. What is the annual interest rate of that 25-year mortgage?

Solution. The unknown variable in this problem is the rate of interest. Notice that the present value of the mortgage, $325,000; the mortgage period, 25 years; and the mortgage payment, $27,887.42, are all known factors. You need to solve, therefore, for the remaining unknown variable—that is, for the annual rate of interest. By dividing your payment of $27,887.42 into your mortgage value, $325,000, we know that the interest factor must be equal to 11.654. Refer now to Appendix A.4 and come down the left-hand column until you come to period 25, then scan across until you find an interest factor very nearly equal to 11.654. Such an interest factor is found in the 7 percent column, indicating that the annual interest rate on the mortgage is very close to 7 percent.

Summary

You should now be familiar with the application and usefulness of the tables found in the appendixes to this chapter. You should also be familiar with their use in solving problems dealing with the compound interest of lump sums as well as the compound interest of annuity flows. In future chapters, we will show you how these concepts are not only tremendously useful in solving daily problems but, indeed, are the very foundation upon which life insurance, pension plan, investment plan, and estate-planning decisions are made.

Compounding and discounting: the foundation

Let us stress again, however, the purpose of this chapter. It is not to turn you into a financial analyst—you are much better off doing whatever it is you do best. Rather, it is to give you a conceptual understanding of finance. This understanding is the stuff of which financial decisions are made. When sales people are trying to sell you a product, and glibly recite the benefits of their product, ask them to put it in the context of this chapter. If they cannot do it (and 99 and 44/100 percent—Ivory Soap purity—cannot), you know they may be trying to pull the wool over your eyes. On the other hand, they may have a superior product but simply lack the knowledge to place it in the context of what we have been discussing.

In the first case, your sales people are crooks and you don't want anything to do with them. In the second case, they are ignorant of the most elemental tools of financial decision making so that regardless of their sincerity, they could lead you into a financial disaster. It strikes us that you can do without either type of advisor. Unless you can deal intelligently with the subject, however, you will never know. And that has been the purpose of this chapter.

Be able to deal with advisors

BIBLIOGRAPHY

Clayton, Gary E., and Spivey, Christopher B. *The Time Value of Money.* Philadelphia: W. B. Saunders, 1978.
An excellent little paperback devoted solely to this important topic. All aspects of discounting and compounding are considered in a readable and easily understood format.

Kroncke, Charles O.; Nemmers, Erwin E.; and Grunwald, Alan E. *Managerial Finance: Essentials.* 2d ed. Minneapolis: West Publishing Co., 1978.
  Chapter 9 of this text is entitled, "The Mathematics of Finance" and is an excellent presentation of the same basic principles presented in this chapter. The notation is slightly different than that we have used, but it should pose no problem.

Weston, J. Fred, and Brigham, Eugene F. *Essentials of Managerial Finance.* 4th ed. Hinsdale, Ill.: Dryden Press, 1977.
  Chapter 10 provides an excellent presentation of the relationships between time and money for one who would like greater depth than is herein presented.

INTEREST TABLES

Appendix A.1 The Future Value of $1

Period	1%	2%	4%	6%	7%	8%	9%	10%	11%	12%	14%	16%	20%
1	1.010	1.020	1.040	1.060	1.070	1.080	1.090	1.100	1.110	1.120	1.139	1.160	1.200
2	1.020	1.040	1.082	1.124	1.145	1.166	1.188	1.210	1.232	1.254	1.297	1.346	1.440
3	1.030	1.061	1.125	1.191	1.225	1.260	1.295	1.331	1.368	1.405	1.478	1.561	1.728
4	1.041	1.082	1.170	1.262	1.311	1.360	1.412	1.464	1.518	1.574	1.683	1.811	2.074
5	1.051	1.104	1.217	1.338	1.403	1.469	1.539	1.611	1.685	1.762	1.917	2.100	2.488
6	1.062	1.126	1.265	1.419	1.501	1.587	1.677	1.772	1.870	1.974	2.183	2.436	2.986
7	1.072	1.149	1.316	1.504	1.606	1.714	1.828	1.949	2.076	2.211	2.487	2.826	3.583
8	1.083	1.172	1.369	1.594	1.718	1.851	1.993	2.144	2.305	2.476	2.833	3.278	4.300
9	1.094	1.195	1.423	1.689	1.838	1.999	2.172	2.358	2.558	2.773	3.226	3.803	5.160
10	1.105	1.219	1.480	1.791	1.967	2.159	2.367	2.594	2.839	3.106	3.675	4.411	6.192
11	1.116	1.243	1.539	1.898	2.105	2.332	2.580	2.853	3.152	3.479	4.186	5.117	7.430
12	1.127	1.268	1.601	2.012	2.252	2.518	2.813	3.138	3.498	3.896	4.767	5.936	8.916
13	1.138	1.294	1.665	2.133	2.410	2.720	3.066	3.452	3.883	4.363	5.430	6.886	10.699
14	1.149	1.319	1.732	2.261	2.579	2.937	3.342	3.797	4.310	4.887	6.185	7.988	12.839
15	1.161	1.346	1.801	2.397	2.759	3.172	3.642	4.177	4.785	5.474	7.045	9.266	15.407
16	1.173	1.373	1.873	2.540	2.952	3.426	3.970	4.595	5.311	6.130	8.024	10.748	18.488
17	1.184	1.400	1.948	2.693	3.159	3.700	4.328	5.054	5.895	6.866	9.139	12.468	22.186
18	1.196	1.428	2.026	2.854	3.380	3.996	4.717	5.560	6.544	7.690	10.409	14.463	26.623
19	1.208	1.457	2.107	3.026	3.617	4.316	5.142	6.116	7.263	8.613	11.856	16.777	31.948
20	1.220	1.486	2.191	3.207	3.870	4.661	5.604	6.727	8.062	9.646	13.504	19.461	38.338
25	1.282	1.641	2.666	4.292	5.427	6.848	8.623	10.835	13.585	17.000	25.888	40.874	95.396
30	1.348	1.811	3.243	5.743	7.612	10.063	13.268	17.449	22.892	29.960	49.626	85.850	237.376

Appendix A.2 The Present Value of $1

Period	1%	2%	4%	6%	7%	8%	9%	10%	11%	12%	14%	16%	20%
1	.990	.980	.962	.943	.935	.926	.917	.909	.901	.893	.878	.862	.833
2	.980	.961	.925	.890	.873	.857	.842	.826	.812	.797	.771	.743	.694
3	.971	.942	.889	.840	.816	.794	.772	.751	.731	.712	.677	.641	.579
4	.961	.924	.855	.792	.763	.735	.708	.683	.659	.636	.594	.552	.482
5	.951	.906	.822	.747	.713	.681	.650	.621	.593	.567	.522	.476	.402
6	.942	.888	.790	.705	.666	.630	.596	.564	.535	.507	.458	.410	.335
7	.933	.871	.760	.665	.623	.583	.547	.513	.482	.452	.402	.354	.279
8	.923	.853	.731	.627	.582	.540	.502	.467	.434	.404	.353	.305	.233
9	.914	.837	.703	.592	.544	.500	.460	.424	.391	.361	.310	.263	.194
10	.905	.820	.676	.558	.508	.463	.422	.386	.352	.322	.272	.227	.162
11	.896	.804	.650	.527	.475	.429	.388	.350	.317	.287	.239	.195	.135
12	.887	.788	.625	.497	.444	.397	.356	.319	.286	.257	.210	.168	.112
13	.879	.773	.601	.469	.415	.368	.326	.290	.258	.229	.184	.145	.093
14	.870	.758	.577	.442	.388	.340	.299	.263	.232	.205	.162	.125	.078
15	.861	.743	.555	.417	.362	.315	.275	.239	.209	.183	.142	.108	.065
16	.853	.728	.534	.394	.339	.292	.252	.218	.188	.163	.125	.093	.054
17	.844	.714	.513	.371	.317	.270	.231	.198	.170	.146	.109	.080	.045
18	.836	.700	.494	.350	.296	.250	.212	.180	.153	.130	.096	.069	.038
19	.828	.686	.475	.331	.277	.232	.194	.164	.138	.116	.084	.060	.031
20	.820	.673	.456	.312	.258	.215	.178	.149	.124	.104	.074	.051	.026
25	.780	.610	.375	.233	.184	.146	.116	.092	.074	.059	.039	.024	.010
30	.742	.552	.308	.174	.131	.099	.075	.057	.044	.033	.020	.012	.004

Appendix A.3 The Future Value of an Annuity of $1 per Year

Period	1%	2%	4%	6%	7%	8%	9%	10%	11%	12%	14%	16%	20%
1	1.000	1.000	1.000	1.000	1.000	1.000	1.000	1.000	1.000	1.000	1.000	1.000	1.000
2	2.010	2.020	2.040	2.060	2.070	2.080	2.090	2.100	2.110	2.120	2.139	2.160	2.200
3	3.030	3.060	3.122	3.184	3.215	3.246	3.278	3.310	3.342	3.374	3.436	3.506	3.640
4	4.060	4.122	4.246	4.375	4.440	4.506	4.573	4.641	4.710	4.779	4.914	5.066	5.368
5	5.101	5.204	5.416	5.637	5.751	5.867	5.985	6.105	6.228	6.353	6.597	6.877	7.442
6	6.152	6.308	6.633	6.975	7.153	7.336	7.523	7.716	7.913	8.115	8.514	8.977	9.930
7	7.214	7.434	7.898	8.394	8.654	8.923	9.200	9.487	9.783	10.089	10.697	11.414	12.916
8	8.286	8.583	9.214	9.897	10.260	10.637	11.028	11.436	11.859	12.300	13.184	14.240	16.499
9	9.369	9.755	10.583	11.491	11.978	12.488	13.021	13.579	14.164	14.776	16.017	17.519	20.799
10	10.462	10.950	12.006	13.181	13.816	14.487	15.193	15.937	16.722	17.549	19.243	21.321	25.959
11	11.567	12.169	13.486	14.972	15.784	16.645	17.560	18.531	19.561	20.655	22.918	25.733	32.150
12	12.683	13.412	15.026	16.870	17.888	18.977	20.141	21.384	22.713	24.133	27.104	30.850	39.581
13	13.809	14.680	16.627	18.882	20.141	21.495	22.953	24.523	26.212	28.029	31.871	36.786	48.497
14	14.947	15.974	18.292	21.015	22.550	24.215	26.019	27.975	30.095	32.393	37.301	43.672	59.196
15	16.097	17.293	20.024	23.276	25.129	27.152	29.361	31.772	34.405	37.280	43.486	51.660	72.035
16	17.258	18.639	21.825	25.673	27.888	30.324	33.003	35.950	39.190	42.753	50.531	60.925	87.442
17	18.430	20.012	23.698	28.213	30.840	33.750	36.974	40.545	44.501	48.884	58.555	71.673	105.931
18	19.615	21.412	25.645	30,906	33.999	37.450	41.301	45.599	50.396	55.750	67.694	84.141	128.117
19	20.811	22.841	27.671	33.760	37.379	41.446	46.018	51.159	56.939	63.440	78.103	98.603	154.740
20	22.019	24.297	29.778	36.786	40.995	45.762	51.160	57.275	64.203	72.052	89.960	115.380	186.688
25	28.243	32.030	41.646	54.865	63.249	73.106	84.701	98.347	114.413	133.334	179.048	249.214	471.981
30	34.785	40.568	56.085	79.058	94.461	113.283	136.308	164.494	199.021	241.333	349.829	530.312	1181.882

Appendix A.4 The Present Value of an Annuity of $1 per Year

Period	1%	2%	4%	6%	7%	8%	9%	10%	11%	12%	14%	16%	20%
1	.990	.980	.962	.943	.935	.926	.917	.909	.901	.893	.878	.862	.833
2	1.970	1.942	1.866	1.833	1.808	1.783	1.759	1.736	1.713	1.690	1.649	1.605	1.528
3	2.941	2.884	2.775	2.673	2.624	2.577	2.531	2.487	2.444	2.402	2.326	2.246	2.106
4	3.902	3.808	3.630	3.465	3.387	3.312	3.240	3.170	3.102	3.037	2.920	2.798	2.589
5	4.853	4.713	4.452	4.212	4.100	3.993	3.890	3.791	3.696	3.605	3.441	3.274	2.991
6	5.795	5.601	5.242	4.917	4.767	4.623	4.486	4.355	4.231	4.111	3.899	3.685	3.326
7	6.728	6.472	6.002	5.582	5.389	5.206	5.033	4.868	4.712	4.564	4.301	4.039	3.605
8	7.652	7.325	6.733	6.210	5.971	5.747	5.535	5.335	5.146	4.968	4.654	4.344	3.837
9	8.566	8.162	7.435	6.802	6.515	6.247	5.995	5.759	5.537	5.328	4.964	4.607	4.031
10	9.471	8.983	8.111	7.360	7.024	6.710	6.418	6.145	5.889	5.650	5.237	4.833	4.192
11	10.368	9.787	8.760	7.887	7.499	7.139	6.805	6.495	6.207	5.938	5.475	5.029	4.327
12	11.255	10.575	9.385	8.384	7.943	7.536	7.161	6.814	6.492	6.194	5.685	5.197	4.439
13	12.134	11.348	9.986	8.853	8.358	7.904	7.487	7.103	6.750	6.424	5.869	5.342	4.533
14	13.004	12.106	10.563	9.295	8.745	8.244	7.786	7.367	6.982	6.628	6.031	5.468	4.611
15	13.865	12.849	11.118	9.712	9.108	8.559	8.061	7.606	7.191	6.811	6.173	5.575	4.675
16	14.718	13.578	11.652	10.106	9.447	8.851	8.313	7.824	7.379	6.974	6.298	5.668	4.730
17	15.562	14.292	12.166	10.477	9.763	9.122	8.544	8.022	7.549	7.120	6.407	5.749	4.775
18	16.398	14.992	12.659	10.828	10.059	9.372	8.756	8.201	7.702	7.250	6.503	5.818	4.812
19	17.226	15.678	13.134	11.158	10.336	9.604	8.950	8.365	7.839	7.366	6.587	5.877	4.843
20	18.046	16.351	13.590	11.470	10.594	9.818	9.129	8.514	7.963	7.469	6.662	5.929	4.870
25	22.023	19.523	15.622	12.783	11.654	10.675	9.823	9.077	8.422	7.843	6.916	6.097	4.948
30	25.808	22.396	17.292	13.765	12.409	11.258	10.274	9.427	8.694	8.055	7.049	6.177	4.979

CHAPTER 3

Making Sure the Cash Flows Flow

After you have read this chapter, you will understand:

- What an income statement is and how it relates to flows of cash.
- How to differentiate between cash and noncash expenses and understand their importance in determining cash flows.
- What the advantage is of accelerated depreciation.
- How to apply the concepts developed in Chapter 2 in valuing cash flows.

In Chapter 2, you analyzed the value of an investment by bringing its annual benefits to present value, at your desired rate of return, and comparing that value with the purchase price of the investment. These inflows and outflows of cash—benefits and costs, if you wish—are referred to as the *cash flows* associated with an investment. The essential ingredient in evaluating any financial transaction is the ability to formulate clearly all of the cash flows associated with the transaction so that the flows can be valued.

The Importance of Cash Flows

In analyzing any financial transaction, the most important thing to remember is that the final objective of the transaction must be to increase your personal wealth. In the context of Chapter 2, the value of the cash benefits coming from the investment must exceed the cost of the investment. In more elementary terms, the investment must make a profit. While this appealing idea is, in fact, the foundation on which investment value is built, it is extremely easy for the unwary investor to be persuaded toward other financial objectives.

Your cash flows determine value

A good example of this concept is illustrated by the desire of many high-income individuals to decrease their tax liability through use of so-called tax shelters. Given some level of income, all that can reduce tax liability is an increase in business expenses or investment

Be wary of tax shelters

losses. Thus, although taxes can easily be reduced, the number of dollars left in the bank account will be less than if the higher tax bill had been paid. Why?

In a 50 percent tax bracket, it takes $1.00 in expense to effect a $0.50 tax saving. Since the cash inflow (the tax saving) is significantly less than the cash outflow (the expense that resulted in the tax saving), this strategy does not make economic sense.

Fortunately, there are many legal and economically sound practices that can reduce your tax burden; but, like all financial decisions, they must be analyzed carefully to make sure they are economically sound. We will examine the nature of cash flows—cash benefits and costs—so that you can correctly analyze various strategies. These in turn will enable you to examine financial alternatives and select the ones that offer the greatest potential for success.

The Income Statement

Your income statement is the starting point

As you are well aware, your year-end income statement is of great interest to you and to the Internal Revenue Service. As its name implies, the income statement is designed to show the revenues and expenditures of business operations or personal transactions over a period of time.

The standard accounting format for the construction of an income statement is to begin with total sales, or operating revenues, and then subtract from that figure all expenses of the operating period. The final figure of the income statement is called net, after-tax income, or net accounting income.

Table 3.1 is an example of an income statement for a hypothetical professional practice. Without going into great detail, you can see the straightforward organization of the income statement. The initial entry is total revenue received during the calendar year. From this total revenue figure are deducted various kinds of expenses, such as cost of supplies used, office staff and general administrative expense, lease payments, depreciation expense, and interest paid on various kinds of liabilities. After all of these expenses have been deducted, the federal and state income tax liability is calculated and deducted from before-tax income to arrive at the bottom line—that is, net after-tax income to be distributed among the owners of the practice.

The Nature of Cash Expense. It is essential, from a financial planning standpoint, to understand clearly the nature of these expenses. Some of the expenses just itemized—the cost of supplies used, office staff and general administrative expense, lease payments, and interest

There is cash expense

Table 3.1 ABC Clinic, Inc., Income Statement, 1977

Total revenues from services rendered	$1,200,000
Cost of supplies used	− 450,000
Gross profit	$ 750,000
Operating Expenses:	
Office staff and general administration	− 40,000
Lease payment on office building	− 50,000
Gross operating income	$ 660,000
Depreciation expense	− 180,000
Net operating income	$ 480,000
Other income:	
Dividends	10,000
Gross income	$ 490,000
Interest expenses:	
Interest on accounts payable	− 8,000
Interest on first mortgage	− 34,000
Net income before tax	$ 448,000
Federal income tax (at 45%)	− 201,600
Net after-tax income	$ 246,400
Plus depreciation expense	180,000
Net cash flow	$ 426,400

payments—are cash expenses. That is, they are expenses that will result in an actual cash outflow from your bank account.

The Nature of Depreciation Expense. There is one additional very important expense item, however: depreciation. Depreciation differs from other expense items in the income statement in that it does not constitute an actual cash outflow during the accounting period. To be sure, you had to pay for the asset, but the Internal Revenue Service will not let you write its cost off all at once. Rather, you depreciate it, or amortize its cost over its useful life. Thus, depreciation is a legitimate expense item representing the use of the fixed asset throughout its lifetime, *but is not a cash outflow.*

And there is depreciation expense

Because of this, the net after-tax income shown in Table 3.1 is really understated. We subtracted $180,000 in depreciation expense, but that $180,000 never left the practice. To state your true cash position, or net cash flow, it is appropriate to add back the $180,000 to net income. The amount of cash that came in, and stayed in, this practice is $426,400. At this point you may scratch your head and ask, "If I really made $426,400, where is it? It isn't there." That is probably true, and reflects the fact that other expenditures must be made from that pot of cash—expenditures that do not show up on the income statement. It is from this pot of cash that you must make all personal expenditures, buy the groceries and shoes for the kids, and buy the asset that resulted in the depreciation expense.

How to find your true cash position

Your cash flow on the bottom line must be positive

If you wonder where you have just been, let's sum it up: The important line on the income statement is the bottom one. If cash flow is not positive—sooner or later—the financial transaction is not doing what you want it to do. This is not to say that a profitable investment must have a positive cash flow in every year. An apartment building might have large losses in its first several years of operation, with positive cash flows after the start-up period, and a large profit 10 years downstream when the building is sold. In spite of the losses in the early years the investment may prove to be eminently profitable. The only way profitability can be determined, however, is through analysis of the project's cash flows.

Your pot of cash: a test of spending

A Test of Your Spending Habits. A very good test of whether your spending is in control is how much is left in that pot of cash. If it is always negative, the deficit must be made up by borrowing.

> Debt can be a very profitable way to finance an investment (as we will see in Chapter 11). Whenever debt is incurred to finance current consumption, however, it quickly becomes burdensome, greatly increasing the cost of your consumption. The presence of this type of debt is a signal that you are spending more than you make and inviting problems that can lead you into serious trouble if not soon checked.

Depreciation Expense

The treatment of depreciation expense in financial planning is extremely important in that it has a significant impact on the after-tax net cash flows. This expense must be examined carefully, since it is the source of much confusion.

There are a number of ways to depreciate an asset. The easiest method of depreciation is simply to take the purchase price of the asset, subtract from that purchase price an estimated salvage value, and divide the difference by the number of years of its estimated lifetime. Such a depreciation method is termed *straight line*, as equal amounts of depreciation are taken each year throughout the life of the asset.

Accelerated depreciation works for you

Other methods of depreciation are allowed by the Internal Revenue Service, however, and these result in larger proportions of depreciation being claimed in the early years of the asset lifetime. When larger depreciation expenses are claimed in early years, the depreciation is said to be accelerated. In most cases, it is to your advantage to depreciate an asset as rapidly as possible. Even though the total amount of depreciation taken—and thus the total amount of tax savings that results from depreciation—will be the same regardless of the depreciation method, by accelerating the depreciation, larger tax savings accrue in earlier years. From Chapter 2 you know that benefits (in this case, tax savings) received earlier are preferred to those received later, since they have a higher present value. To illustrate this important concept, let's look at a simple example.

Example 1. Suppose you require a piece of equipment that costs $20,000 and has an estimated 5-year lifetime with a zero salvage value at the end of that 5-year period. The machine qualifies for accelerated depreciation and you could elect the *double declining balance* method.* You know that you could also depreciate this machine over its 5-year life utilizing straight-line depreciation should you choose. Your tax rate is 40 percent, and you feel you should use an interest rate of 8 percent in evaluating your investment in this new machine. Table 3.2 shows the present value of the tax savings resulting from depreciation under each of these alternatives.

The double declining balance

Solution. Since the depreciation will be deducted as an expense from your pretax income, it will reduce your total tax bill. The exact amount of the annual tax reduction is found by multiplying your marginal tax rate by the amount of the annual depreciation expense.† Table 3.2 makes it abundantly clear that the total amount of depreciation taken and the total tax saving resulting from the depreciation expense are exactly the same whether or not depreciation is accelerated. The crucial financial question now is, which stream of tax benefits is to be preferred? That question can be analyzed with the present-value tools developed in the previous chapter, and this analysis is also shown in Table 3.2.

Notice that the present value of the tax savings is nearly $500 greater—$6,878.40 versus $6,388.80—when accelerated depreciation techniques are employed as compared to the straight-line method. This benefit accrues because the larger early benefits resulting from faster depreciation have relatively larger present values than do the larger benefits of straight-line depreciation methods, which occur late in the life of the asset. Thus, given the time value of money, you can see the net financial advantage of accelerated depreciation.

---

*Double declining balance depreciation is computed at twice the straight-line rate. For example, if the life of an asset is 10 years, the straight-line rate would be one-tenth (or 10 percent) of the asset value per year. The double declining rate would be twice this, or 20 percent per year of the asset value that remains after the previous year's depreciation is deducted.

† A taxpayer's marginal tax rate is the rate applied to the last dollar of income earned. If, for example, you had taxable income of $50,000, the tax table might read "tax is $14,060 plus 50 percent of everything over $44,000." Thus, your marginal tax rate is 50 percent although your average tax rate (total tax divided by total taxable income) is only 34 percent. In analyzing investment decisions, it is the marginal tax rate that is important since the investment is made at the margin. That is, the investment income (or loss) is added to the already existing income of the investor and hence is subject to taxation at the marginal rate.

Table 3.2 Computation of Annual Depreciation and the Present Value of the Tax Savings

	Cost of machine	= $20,000
	Expected life of machine	= 5 years
	Expected salvage value	= 0
	Tax rate	= 40%
	Discount rate	= 8%

	Straight line			Double Declining Balance				
Year	Annual depreciation $20,000 \div 5 = \$4,000$	× Tax rate	= Tax saving	Annual depreciation	× Tax rate =	Tax saving	× Present value factor[b]	= Present value of tax savings
1	$4,000 × 40%$		$= \$1,600$	$\frac{\$20,000}{5} × 2 = \$8,000$	$× 40% =$	$\$3,200$	$× .926$	$= \$2,963.20$
2	$4,000 × 40%$		$= 1,600$	$\frac{\$20,000-\$8,000}{4} × 2 = \$6,000$	$× 40% =$	$2,400$	$× .857$	$= 2,056.80$
3	$4,000 × 40%$		$= 1,600$	$\frac{\$20,000-14,000}{3} × 2 = \$4,000$	$× 40% =$	$1,600$	$× .794$	$= 1,270.40$
4	$4,000 × 40%$		$= 1,600$	$\frac{\$20,000-18,000}{2} × 2 = \$2,000$	$× 40% =$	800	$× .735$	$= 588.00$
5	$4,000 × 40%$		$= 1,600$	0	$× 40% =$	0	$× .681$	$= 0$
Totals	$\$20,000$		$\$8,000$	$\$20,000$		$\$8,000$		$\$6,878.40$

Present value of straight-line depreciation tax savings $\$1,600_5 × 3.993^a = \$6,388.80$ Present value of DDB depreciation tax savings

[a] From Appendix A.4
[b] From Appendix A.2

Estimating Cash Flows

Cash flow estimates should determine investment decisions

The most important task in evaluating the potential profitability of an investment is the estimation of the future cash flows that should result from that investment. The final result of an investment decision is only as good as the accuracy of your cash flow estimates, and therefore, time should be spent in thoughtfully preparing estimates of all cash income and outflows related to the investment alternative.

> We express the benefits expected to be derived from an investment in terms of cash rather than in terms of accounting income because it is cash that is central to all decisions of a financial nature.

Your only purpose for investing cash now is the hope of receiving cash returns of a greater amount in the future. Only cash receipts can be reinvested or used for consumption purposes. As you saw in the previous section, cash flow, not income, is of central importance in personal financial decisions.

Example 2. To see why this cash flow analysis is important, let's look at a specific example. Suppose you are contemplating the purchase of a new X-ray machine that has an initial cost of $15,000 and an expected life of 5 years. At the end of its 5-year life, you expect it will be completely worn out and will have no salvage value.

Purchase of equipment as an example

Further assume that this machine will generate an additional $4,500 in revenues each year during its lifetime. Your marginal tax rate is 45 percent, and you have alternative investment strategies that would yield a 7 percent annual rate of return. You thus feel that your investment in this machine must do at least that well. For simplicity, depreciate the asset on a straight-line basis. The question now becomes: Is the present value flow of cash benefits resulting from the purchase of this machine at least equal to its purchase price?

Solution. The first step to the solution of this type of a problem is to determine the cash flows generated by the asset as accurately as possible. This is done as shown in tables 3.3 and 3.4.

Table 3.3 Information Needed to Estimate Cash Flows

Price of asset = $15,000	Marginal tax bracket = 45%
Useful life of asset = 5 years	Interest rate = 7%
Annual revenues generated = $4,500	Annual depreciation = $3,000

Table 3.4 Computation of Net Cash Flow

Increase in revenues	$4,500
less depreciation	−3,000
Increase in taxable income	$1,500
taxes (1500 × .45)	−675
Increases in after-tax earnings	$ 825
plus depreciation	3,000
Net cash flow	$3,825

Now you must determine if an annual benefit of $3,825 for 5 years is sufficient to warrant an outlay of $15,000. Utilizing the table Appendix A.4 at the end of Chapter 2, you can find the present value of the benefit stream as follows:

$$PV = \$3,825 \times 4.100 = \$15,682.50.$$

(The figure 4.100 is taken from Appendix A.4—5 years, 7 percent.)

If the present value of the benefit was exactly equal to the $15,000 cost, the rate of return on the investment would be exactly 7 percent. Since the present value of the benefit stream exceeds the purchase price, it is clearly to our benefit to purchase the asset. That is, since the flow of benefits received, discounted to the present at 7 percent, exceeds the $15,000 purchase price, we can therefore be sure that our annual rate of return on the investment in this machine is in excess of 7 percent. (As a matter of fact, the true rate of return is just slightly less than 9 percent.)

Example 3. Suppose that a medical-dental building complex comes up for sale in your city, and you are wondering about its purchase as a possible investment. This prompts you to do some fact-finding, which reveals the following data: There are 32 offices in this complex and they have been leased at $850 per month each. Recent records indicate that the administrative expense to maintain and run the complex has averaged approximately $5,000 a month. The interest on the mortgage, which you would be assuming, is $2,000 per month. Finally, the depreciation that can be claimed each year equals $75,000. The expected lifetime of the complex is another 20 years. Again your marginal tax bracket is 45 percent, and on an investment of this type you feel you should earn at least 12 percent. What price should you be willing to pay for this building complex?

Purchase of a building complex as an example

Solution. Of course, the answer to this question depends upon an analysis of the cash flow that would result from the purchase of the building. The price should certainly not exceed the discounted flow of benefits that are forecasted to be realized over the 20-year life of the project. Table 3.5 illustrates.

Table 3.5 Computation of Cash Flows—Medical-Dental Office Building

Annual revenue (32 × $850 × 12)	$326,400
Administrative expense ($5,000 × 12)	−60,000
Interest expense ($2,000 × 12)	−24,000
Depreciation expense	−75,000
Before-tax earnings	$167,400
Tax ($167,400 × .45)	−75,330
After-tax earnings	92,070
Plus depreciation	75,000
Net cash flow	$167,070

Again, if on an investment of this type you require at least a 12 percent return, you should be willing to pay no more than the present value (PV) of the expected benefit stream discounted at 12 percent:

$$PV = \$167,070 \times 7.469 = \underline{\$1,247,856}.$$

(The figure 7,469 is taken from Appendix A.4—20 years, 12 percent.)

Thus, the maximum price you would pay is $1,247,856. If that amount were paid, and the expected revenues were realized, you would make a 12 percent annual return on the project.

Evaluation of Real Estate Investments

Example 3 illustrates an important concept regarding real estate investment. Many of the limited partnership investment alternatives available to professionals and other high-income individuals are of a real estate nature. The purchase price necessarily requires appraisal of the property. There are basically three ways that appraisals can be made:

1. The appraiser can go in and (figuratively) count the bricks, mortar, shingles, wood, and furnishings of the building, and then compute replacement cost. That is, the value of the building is then appraised at what it would cost to replace the building at today's prices.
2. The appraiser can compare the property with recently sold property with similar characteristics. The reasoning here is that if properties A and B are similar and A just sold for $175,000, B must also be worth $175,000.
3. The appraiser can analyze the flows of cash—both the benefits and the costs—that the investment yields and then find the present value of this cash stream over the expected lifetime of the asset.

As you might expect, these alternative appraisal methods may yield vastly different results. However, from a personal investment standpoint, the third method is far superior to the first two. Remember, your concern is to earn a desired rate of return on your invested dollars. The discounted cash flow method of appraisal will determine a value (if you can buy the asset for that price) that will yield your required rate of return.

Use the discounted cash flow method of appraisal

Too many times the asking price of an asset far exceeds the value of the discounted cash flows; then other reasons are given to justify the purchase: "Well, be realistic. You couldn't begin to replace this building for less than . . ." Or, "You say the property is only worth $100,000, but the identical building right next door just sold last week for $175,000."

In a very real sense it is completely unimportant what someone else paid (or would pay) for an asset; or how much it would cost to build it from scratch. All an investment is worth to you is the value of the income it will produce. From an investment standpoint, therefore, if you pay one cent more for it you are making a serious mistake.

What Is a Tax Shelter?

As you are now aware, it is extremely important for you to distinguish carefully between cash expenses and noncash expenses. Cash expenses are manifested in the form of salaries, interest, lease payments, administrative costs, overhead, and so forth, while depreciation is the most frequently encountered noncash expense.

You will be approached throughout your professional career by many sales people extolling the merits of a particular tax-sheltered investment. The large majority of these have received widespread and rapid acceptance because they do reduce income tax liability. At all times, however, the investment should be examined carefully to determine the relevant cash flows and to see exactly why income tax liability is being reduced.

Reduced tax liability may cost you cash

> If your tax liability is lower due to the payment of some cash expense such as interest or general partner fees, the so-called tax shelter is purely illusory. While it is true that you may indeed pay lower income taxes, you did so only because taxable income was reduced by the payment of a cash expense. The money is gone from your wallet just as certainly as if you had paid it to the federal government for taxes. As a result, you find yourself worse off than you would have been had the investment not presented itself.

When a tax shelter is worthwhile

On the other hand, if the tax shelter comes as a result of some noncash expense, such as depreciation, and if the investment produces an economic return at some point in the future, the investment may be worthwhile. The final decision still must be based on an analysis of the cash flows—including tax savings—produced by the investment. The following example might best illustrate this important point.

Comparing two tax shelter investments

Example 4. Consider two tax shelter investments that are proposed to you. Investment A allows you a depreciation expense of $15,000, while investment B has no depreciation but has a tax-deductible interest expense of $15,000. Either investment produces gross income (in addition to the tax shelter) of $10,000, which will be added to your normal taxable income of $50,000. Table 3.6 illustrates the cash flows resulting from no investment at all compared to cash flows with the addition of each of these tax shelter investments.

As the example clearly illustrates, both the depreciation expense and interest expense will result in reduction of a tax liability. That is, your tax burden will decline to $20,250 (from $22,500) with either investment A or B.

Solution. Notice, however, that only the depreciation expense of investment A resulted in a higher net cash flow. Clearly the so-called tax shelter of investment B is a costly one. In fact, you would have been better off with no tax shelter at all than with the tax shelter provided by the interest expense of investment B. Again, it is the net cash flow, or dollars in your pocket at the end of an investment period, that ultimately determines investment value.

Table 3.6 Comparison of Tax Shelter Investments

	Normal income	Normal income plus investment A	Normal income plus investment B
Taxable income	$50,000	$60,000	$60,000
depreciation (A)	0	−15,000	0
interest (B)	0	0	−15,000
Taxable income	$50,000	$45,000	$45,000
tax (at 45%)	−22,500	−20,250	−20,250
After-tax income	$27,500	$24,750	$24,750
Plus depreciation	0	15,000	0
Net cash flow	$27,500	$39,750	$24,750

Summary

The point that should be absolutely clear by now is that the ultimate value of any investment undertaking is dependent on the associated stream of cash. Only after you have constructed a picture of the expected cash flows can you determine whether the investment has merit—that is, whether it will achieve the objective of increasing your wealth.

Construct a picture of your cash flows

Further, you must be extremely careful to differentiate between cash and noncash expenses when reconstructing the cash flows from standard accounting statements.

Be wary of tax shelter schemes. Tax shelters are a legitimate and useful investment alternative, but tax reduction that results from a reduction of your cash position is, in fact, no benefit to you at all.

Finally, once the cash flows are clearly in mind, you can easily compute the present value of these returns, using the techniques of Chapter 2, to determine if the investment promises to yield the return you require.

We are confident that there is no practice that will save you more headaches, or more dollars, than to undertake the following two-step analysis before each investment:

The two-step financial analysis

- Construct the cash flows.
- Compute the present value of the flows, using your required return.

If such an analysis reveals you are getting a good buy, then jump in—that is how people make money.

BIBLIOGRAPHY

Bierman, Harold, Jr., and Smidt, Seymour. *The Capital Budgeting Decision.* 4th ed. New York: Macmillan, 1975.
This is an excellent reference for an in-depth study of the use of cash flows in evaluating investments; see Chapter 6.

Kronce, Charles O.; Nemmers, Erwin E.; and Grunwald, Alan E. *Managerial Finance: Essentials.* 2d ed. Minneapolis: West Publishing Co., 1978.
Chapter 11 contains a discussion of determining cash flows and provides a framework for organizing cash-flow analysis and forecast. This book also contains an excellent glossary of financial terms.

Schall, Lawrence D., and Haley, Charles W. *Introduction to Financial Management.* New York: McGraw-Hill Book Co., 1977.
This textbook of corporation finance has a discussion on determination of cash flows in Chapter 7.

PART Two

Planning Your Financial Course
as a Professional

Selecting the Right Retirement Plan: The Only Way to Have Your Cake and Eat It Too

After reading this chapter, you will understand:

- Exactly what a retirement plan is and how it can be designed to accomplish your specific objectives.
- The available types of retirement plans—both corporate and noncorporate—and the advantages and disadvantages of each.
- Ways to minimize the costs and maximize the benefits of your retirement plan.

Beginning in this chapter, we are going to apply the concepts we have discussed to your personal and business financial problems so that you can build the framework we spoke of in Chapter 1. Let's begin with retirement plans.

The years have a way of creeping by unnoticed, and perhaps the most tragic thing we see is individuals who are approaching retirement age and recognize that they have failed to make provision for their "golden" years. By the time they face up to the facts, it is frequently too late to do anything: time has quite literally run out. We can help you plan now.

By now you are sufficiently familiar with the principles discussed in Chapter 2 so that you understand the effect of time on the growth of money. Nowhere is this effect felt more strongly, however, than in the area of your personal pension and/or profit-sharing plan. It is simply a question of retiring on the banker's money or on your own.

Retire on your own money

At 7 percent interest, money doubles approximately every 10 years. This means that $1 contributed to a retirement plan at age 35 will grow to $2 by age 45, $4 by age 55, and $8 by age 65. Looking at the problem from the other end, a $1 withdrawal from the plan at age 65 requires a deposit of only 13 cents at age 35; the other 87 cents is interest. A more costly (to you) alternative is to start the retirement

It costs more if you're 55

plan at age 55. Then you must contribute 50 cents for every dollar you want to withdraw at age 65. Small stretches of the imagination will let you design even worse alternatives.

> The point: The essential ingredient in making compound interest work for you is time. Unless there is sufficient time to let interest accrue and to let more income be earned on previously earned interest, compound interest simply does not have time to work its magic. Start the plan early, fund it faithfully.

Your Retirement Plan and the Pension Reform Act

The entire area of pension and profit-sharing plans was made immensely more complex by the passage of the so-called Pension Reform Act of 1974. The initial reaction of many professionals was a combination of confusion and outrage: outrage because of the large number of new regulations imposed on these plans as well as the complex and costly legal and accounting services required to bring plans in compliance with the law; confusion because the sheer mass of regulation supporting the act is overwhelming at times and almost always confusing.

Corporate or Keogh: your golden opportunity

Now that the dust has settled, however, one thing is crystal clear: The tax-qualified pension plan—whether it is a corporate pension or profit-sharing plan, a Keogh plan, or an Individual Retirement Account (IRA)—is a golden opportunity for the professional person to accumulate large numbers of dollars for retirement. At the same time, a retirement plan can significantly reduce federal income tax liability during the working years. There is little question that the benefits exceed the cost—in spite of the complex requirements of the new law.

What the law says a retirement plan is

You should keep in mind what retirement plans are and what they are not. The law is clear in defining the purpose of the retirement plan: It is to accumulate a fund of assets that, in turn, can provide a retirement annuity. Retirement plans have no other purpose.

Assets for retirement must be your prime objective

To establish a plan because it is a tax shelter, or because it is a slick way to accumulate a lot of money, or so you can play the stock market, or any one of a hundred other reasons will only get you into trouble. Of course, there are tax advantages because of the deductibility of the plan contribution. Naturally a fund of assets will accumulate that will require investment. But these are only natural outcomes of such a plan. The primary objective remains, once and for all, formation of a retirement fund. If that is not your objective as you consider creating a plan, you should forget the whole idea.

With this proviso clear, however, we believe that if you do not presently have a retirement plan, you need one. Unless you are independently wealthy, retirement years could be very cold and hungry without the asset accumulation such a plan will build for you. If you are independently wealthy, you could significantly reduce current income tax liability by consuming present wealth through funding a retirement plan with a large portion of your present income.

First you must decide whether you should select a Keogh plan, one of the corporate plans, or an IRA. If you already have a Keogh plan, you must decide whether you want to incorporate so you can form a pension plan, a profit-sharing plan, or both, or to adopt an IRA. If you already have a corporate plan, you want to determine whether or not that plan is doing all it should be doing. If not, the plan can be amended to increase your personal benefits, or to reduce its cost.

To accomplish these ends, we want to compare for you specific plan features such as participation, contribution, and vesting. This comparison highlights the similarities and differences of corporate and noncorporate plans. Because of the fairly high probability of your becoming lost in the maze of the many available alternatives, we have summarized the three types of retirement plans, and their available options in Table 4.1. Since this table makes a side-by-side comparison of the features available in the various types of retirement plans, we think you will find it worthwhile to spend a few moments with it before reading the rest of this chapter.

You need to compare plans

Table 4.1 A Comparison of Alternative Retirement Plans

The important questions	Individual Retirement Account (IRA)	Self-employed retirement plan (Keogh plan)	Corporate retirement plans
How much may be contributed to my account?	$7,500, or 15% of your practice income, whichever is less	$7,500 or 15% of your practice income, whichever is less	$25,000 or 25% of your salary, whichever is less[a]
Is a pension option available?	Yes	Yes	Yes
Can it be a defined-contribution pension plan?	Yes	Yes	Yes
Can it be a defined-benefit pension plan?	No	Defined-benefit Keogh plans are allowed by the law, but are not a practical reality	Yes
Is a profit-sharing option available?	Yes	Yes	Yes
What qualifications must employees meet in order to participate?	Only you participate	As a condition of participation, employees may be required to • Work at least three years • work more than 1,000 hours per year	As a condition of participation, employees may be required to • work at least one year • work more than 1,000 hours per year • be over 25 years of age
How rapidly do monies in employees' accounts vest?	Immediately	Immediately	Immediately

[a]This is a general rule, but these limits can be exceeded for a number of reasons that will be explained in this chapter.

Table 4.1 (continued)

The important questions	Individual Retirement Account (IRA)	Self-employed retirement plan (Keogh plan)	Corporate retirement plans
Can the plan be integrated with Social Security	No	The law provides for integration of Keogh plans, but it is not a practical reality	Yes
What is the allowable retirement age?	Not before age 59½	Not before age 59½	Flexible—established by the trust instrument, and may be amended to fit your needs
Can I borrow from the plan?	No	No	An employee borrowing agreement allows you (as well as other plan participants) to borrow from the plan if such loans are deemed prudent by the trustee of the plan assets
Who can be trustee of the plan?	You must designate a corporate trustee—bank, insurance company, mutual fund, etc.	You must designate a corporate trustee—bank, insurance company, mutual fund, etc.	You may designate anyone you wish, including yourself, to serve as trustee

What About Individual Retirement Accounts?

The old IRA pension plan

In 1974, through the Pension Reform Act, Congress created a new type of retirement-funding vehicle called the Individual Retirement Account, or IRA. The intent of such a plan was to allow individuals who do not have access to a pension plan through their employers to create a special savings account for retirement purposes. The 1974 law allowed such individuals to contribute 15 percent of their income, to a maximum of $1,500, to such an account. The law stipulated that such plans were tax qualified—that is, the contributions constituted a tax-deductible expense, and plan earnings were free from taxation until retirement withdrawals were made.

While the idea has some appealing merits (for example, as a self-employed professional you could contribute to such a plan for yourself but would not be required to contribute for your employees—though that's not a good way to build a trusted staff), the modest contribution of $1,500 per year was inadequate to build the size of retirement annuity required by most professionals. If a new physician or dentist started making maximum contributions the day he started practice at age 28 and made the maximum contribution faithfully until retirement at age 65, he would accumulate approximately $240,000. While this seems like a great deal of money, it would provide a retirement annuity of only $22,700 per year—a figure grossly inadequate to supply the standard of living to which most professionals become accustomed.

Since the preceding explanation of IRAs is in the past tense, you may by now be muttering, "Why so much time talking about what was?" Why indeed. To help you see, as strongly as possible, the contrast between what was and what is. In the Revenue Act of 1978, Congress increased the limits on IRAs, making it possible to contribute the greater of 15 percent of income, or $7,500. This step very clearly makes the IRA a more viable retirement-funding alternative than the old Keogh plan for those professionals who do not feel they wish to include their employees' participation in their retirement plan.

A simple example illustrates the net effect of this new and important change in the law: Suppose you have for years been making contributions to a Keogh plan for you and your employees. Your salary is $50,000, and the combined salary of three auxiliaries who participate in the plan is $30,000, and 10 percent of compensation is contributed to the plan ($5,000 for yourself, and $3,000 for employees). By terminating Keogh participation and forming an IRA for yourself, you immediately save the $3,000 previously contributed for employees. You could, in fact, increase your own contribution to $7,500, the $2,500 increase being funded from the savings you achieve by eliminating employee participation.

The new IRA has attractive features

You can increase your own contribution

In short, if you have been using a Keogh plan, and your income does not allow the greater contributions allowed by corporate retirement plans, you may seriously want to consider the benefits of adopting a new Individual Retirement Account.

Pension Versus Profit Sharing: Understanding the Options

If a Keogh or corporate plan is selected instead of an IRA, there are two options under which contributions can be made. You may select either a pension plan or a profit-sharing plan (or both). While either of the two can satisfy your needs for the accumulation of retirement assets, the legal requirements surrounding the two plans are quite different.

The Pension Option The pension option requires you as the employer (you are the employer of yourself as well as your employees) to define in advance the manner in which retirement benefits will be accumulated. The employer—you if you are unincorporated, or your corporation if you are—then commits to fund the pension plan by making the agreed-upon contributions. The important thing about a pension plan is *the contributions must be made.* You are not afforded the luxury of making a contribution if you want to and then passing it up in another year because funds are short. The contributions are mandatory, and failure to make a plan contribution disqualifies the plan. The funding formulas—that is, the manner of determining the size of the plan contribution for each employee—will be discussed later in this chapter.

The pension plan: you must contribute

Profit-sharing Plans A profit-sharing plan, on the other hand, allows you somewhat greater flexibility in that annual plan contributions are elective. In fact, profit-sharing contributions must be made out of prof-

Profit-sharing plans are more flexible

its (or retained earnings). While such flexibility is nice, the disadvantage to profit-sharing plans lies in this very flexibility: If employees of your practice (including you) are depending on the accumulations in this plan for retirement income, failure to make the plan contributions scuttles their (and your) retirement plans. The beauty of a pension plan is the "schoolmaster" effect of the mandatory contributions.

What You Can Contribute to Your Plan

Depending on the plan you elect, the amount that can be contributed to it annually is carefully spelled out by law.

> As a general rule, you may make substantially greater contributions to a corporate plan than to a Keogh plan. This makes the corporate plans a more desirable option if you want to save lots of bucks.

Limitations of the Keogh plan

Keogh Plans Remember, you may use either the pension or profit-sharing option in a Keogh plan. Under either of the two alternatives, however, the total amount that can be contributed to any individual's account in any given year is $7,500, or 15 percent of income, *whichever is less*. This may be an adequately large contribution in many cases. Frequently, though—particularly for high-income professionals or for individuals starting this process late in life—the amount results in an inadequate asset accumulation by retirement age. For example, a physician starting the program at age 55, and contributing the maximum $7,500 each year, would only accumulate (at 7 percent) $103,623 by age 65. And this would provide a retirement income of only $11,377 per year.

Corporate Plans The annual contribution that can be allocated to an individual's account in a corporate pension or profit-sharing plan is somewhat more complicated than for Keogh plans. Generally, the 1974 law allows a contribution of the lesser of $25,000 (adjusted annually by a cost-of-living escalator), or 25 percent of the participant's income. But this depends on whether the plan is a pension plan, a profit-sharing plan, or both—and even depends on the type of pension plan used. For now we will say that if only a pension plan is used, the total contribution limits of 25 percent or $25,000 would apply. If only a profit-sharing plan is used, the deductible contribution limit is reduced to 15 percent or $15,000, whichever is less. If a combination (both pension and profit-sharing) of these two plans is used, the total contribution again becomes 25 percent or $25,000, whichever is less, with the stipulation that no more than 15 percent or $15,000 be allocated to the profit-sharing plan.

The impact of the higher contributions allowed in corporate plans, as opposed to the 15 percent Keogh contributions, is dramatic. Table 4.2 shows both the potential asset accumulations and retirement benefits that may be achieved at several contribution levels and differing numbers of years of participation. Given the difference in the amounts accumulated in a Keogh plan versus a corporate plan, it is clear that an individual wishing to have a larger retirement annuity must rely on the corporate alternatives.

You accumulate larger funds with corporate plans

Table 4.2 Retirement Fund Accumulations and Retirement Annuities at 7 Percent

Annual contribution	Contributions made for 5 years		Contributions made for 15 years		Contributions made for 25 years	
	Accumulation	15-year retirement annuity	Accumulation	15-year retirement annuity	Accumulation	15-year retirement annuity
$ 3,000	$ 17,252	$ 1,894	$ 75,389	$ 8,277	$ 189,747	$ 20,833
7,500	43,130	4,735	188,467	20,692	474,367	52,082
10,000	57,506	6,313	251,290	27,590	632,490	69,443
15,000	86,260	9,470	376,935	41,385	948,735	104,065
20,000	115,013	12,627	502,580	55,180	1,264,980	138,887
25,000	143,766	15,783	628,225	68,975	1,581,225	173,608

There are even pension plans (we will look at these in a few pages) that allow us to disregard the general $25,000 or 25 percent rule. This type of plan, called a defined-benefit pension plan, allows contributions of whatever size may be necessary in order to fund a predefined retirement benefit. With this plan, contributions far in excess of the usual annual ceiling are possible.

In any kind of plan, Keogh or corporate, you should keep in mind that the primary constraint on size of plan contributions is available income. The income generated by a professional practice is directly attributable to the professionals in the practice. Normally whatever is left over after payment of expenses becomes the salary of the professional. This means, of course, that any retirement plan contribution must come from a reduction in your paycheck.

Available income is the primary constraint

> Whatever you do, do not mandate a plan contribution so large it makes normal living impossible.

Participation Standards: Spelled Out by Law

Participation standards, which define when an employee must participate in a plan, are very clearly spelled out by law and regulation and are scarcely subject to misinterpretation. In spite of this clarity, the

Eligible employees must participate

desire of many employers is to lower plan cost by excluding as many employees as possible from plan participation. Our advice, however, is to avoid the temptation to find ways to exclude employees. Anything that might be interpreted by either the Internal Revenue Service or the Labor Department as being discriminatory could result in disqualification of the plan. The rule is simple: If an employee is eligible for participation, he or she should participate.

Employee participation in a Keogh plan

Keogh Plans There are three standards governing participation in a Keogh plan: (1) length of employment with the firm, (2) number of hours worked per year, and (3) age. An employee must generally satisfy each of the tests before participation is required.

Generally, as soon as an employee has been with the firm for three years, that person is eligible for participation in the Keogh plan of the employer. While that is the basic rule, the exact waiting period is determined by the length of time the business operated prior to establishing the Keogh plan.

Length of employment

For example, suppose a new doctor opens a dental practice, initiates a Keogh plan on exactly the same day, and begins participating in the Keogh plan himself. The standard of participation has been set as no waiting period, and any employees joining the dental practice in the future must also be accorded immediate participation in the plan. The only way our doctor could require future employees to remain outside of the plan for 3 years would be to defer formation of the plan until 3 years after opening the practice.

Number of hours worked per year

In order to be accorded participation in a Keogh plan, an employee must also be employed by the firm more than half-time, which is defined to be 1,000 hours per year. This requirement can be a source of confusion leading to unjust exclusion of an employee from participation. Sometimes an employer is tempted to hire someone full-time, then fire the employee before 1,000 hours have been worked and claim the employee did not meet the 1,000-hour test. If such action was taken purposely to exclude an employee from plan participation, it could be held to be discriminatory—so don't do it. This requirement is specifically designed to exclude part-time employees only, not to reduce the cost of employee contributions by playing turnover games with employees.

Years of age

The third requirement for participation in the Keogh plan is that the employee be 25 years of age or more. Specifically, the rule requires that if the employee is 24½ on the first day of the plan year, that person must be accorded participation in that year. However, if the business is owned by one or two individuals who also participate in the plan—as is normally the case—this restriction may not apply. Thus, participation in Keogh plans must usually be accorded irrespective of age; and if you have any doubts in a given situation, by all means ask your attorney.

Corporate Plans Although participation requirements for corporate plans are much like those for Keogh, there is one minor difference: the length of time a worker must be employed by the firm prior to plan participation.

Whereas Keogh participation requires three years of employment, the maximum waiting period for entry into a corporate plan is one year unless vesting is immediate. (This requirement is more academic than real since, as we have pointed out, immediate participation must usually be accorded.) For a corporate plan, the problem is a practical one, caused by the fact that most professional practices have operated for some time prior to incorporation. Since the principal reason for incorporation is to allow formation of a pension or profit-sharing plan, and since the plan is formed as soon as the incorporation takes place, and since the officers of the corporation afford themselves immediate participation, the standard is thus set. The only means by which a corporation could hold its employees outside the plan for a year would be for the officers of the corporation to defer their own participation for that period of time. Since this is seldom done, there is usually no waiting period in a corporate plan.

Employee participation in a corporate plan

Why there is seldom a waiting period

Given these circumstances, you can see that it pays to plan ahead. If financial resources do not allow formation of a pension plan today but will two years from now, it would be a good idea to plan the incorporation to take place a year before adoption of the pension plan. Then, when the plan is adopted, all employees will have been employed by the corporation for one year so that a one-year waiting period can be adopted for new employees. The age 25 restriction may be also applied for corporate plans.

Vesting Protects You and Your Employees

Vesting refers to the rate at which pension contributions accumulated in an employee's account *permanently* accrue to the benefit of the employee. One of the primary goals of the 1974 Pension Reform Act was to eliminate abuses in this area. Prior to passage of the act it was conceivable for an employee to participate in a plan for many years and then be terminated shortly before retirement with almost complete loss of retirement benefits. Such a case was possible because many pension plans were slow to vest benefits in the employee.

How funds permanently accrue: a vesting schedule

Historically, some of the greatest abusers of vesting have been small pension and profit-sharing plans such as those found in professional corporations. Where the corporation is closely held, it is easy for the officers to terminate employees periodically, causing unvested contributions made to accounts of the terminated employees to be forfeited and allocated to the accounts of the other participants. Since the officers make up the greatest number of permanent employees of the corporation, they are also the principal beneficiaries of such forfeitures.

Keogh Plans In the Keogh plan the vesting schedule is extremely simple and straightforward: Vesting is full and immediate. This means the instant a contribution is made to an employee's account, it vests to

Vesting of a Keogh plan

that account. If the employee terminates employment with the company the day after the contribution is made, that person is nonetheless entitled to terminate participation in the plan and withdraw all amounts in the particular account, principal plus interest.

While primarily designed to protect the participating employee, such a vesting schedule frequently invites turnover, inasmuch as an employee can only gain access to assets accumulated in the Keogh account by quitting. This plan therefore has an extremely high cost, particularly in medical and dental practices where there is some tendency to hire many young, low-skilled employees who turn over frequently anyway.

Pension and Profit-sharing Plans The law is explicit in defining several permissible vesting schedules for corporate pension or profit-sharing plans, although it does not specify which schedule must be adopted by the corporation.

Vesting of corporate plans

One example of a schedule suggested by the law is the 5- and 15-year rule, which states that an employee must be 25 percent vested after 5 years of service, and 100 percent vested at the end of 15 years. Another is the 10-year rule, which states that an employee must be 100 percent vested after 10 years of service. Still a third, called the rule of 45, states that an employee with 5 or more years of service must be at least 50 percent vested when the sum of age and years of service totals 45. The remainder of the account must vest at the rate of 10 percent per year over the next 5 years.

Age formulas may not apply to a professional corporation

While these formulas are convenient, unfortunately none of them, as a practical matter, seems to apply to the professional corporation. The Internal Revenue Service apparently holds that these types of schedules were specifically designed for larger corporations with far larger work forces and more stability than are usually found in a professional practice. For this reason, the types of schedules the IRS tends to approve for the professional corporation require vesting in a much shorter period of time—frequently as short as 100 percent vesting in 5 years.

While longer vesting schedules have been approved in some instances, it is the opinion of many attorneys and actuaries that anything that might, in the future, be interpreted by the IRS or the Labor Department to be discriminatory could easily result in disqualification of a plan. For this reason such attorneys frequently do not attempt qualification of vesting schedules more rigorous than 100-percent vesting in 5 or 6 years.

An IRS qualification letter

Parts of a qualification letter received from the IRS are reprinted below. This letter shows the fact that a plan, although approved, may lose qualification if future audit reveals its vesting schedule to be discriminatory in favor of corporate officers or highly paid employees. It is clear that while the IRS may qualify a plan with, say, a 10-year vesting schedule, the plan is in trouble if future performance proves the vesting schedule to be discriminatory.

Dear Applicant:
Based on the information you supplied, we have made a favorable determination on your application.

Continued qualification of the plan will depend on its effect in operation under its present form. The status of the plan will be reviewed periodically. [There are] some events . . . that would automatically nullify this determination without specific notice from us.

A high rate of service separations may leave relatively few of the lower paid employees, but practically all of the office-shareholders and highly compensated employees in the plan. If employee turnover results in the allocation of forfeitures principally to the benefit of officers, shareholders, and highly compensated employees a favorable determination letter will not apply.

A Look at Funding Alternatives

While there are many funding methods, a look at two of them illustrates the basic approaches to funding. These two are *defined-contribution plans* and *defined-benefit plans*.

Two ways to fund a plan

In a defined-contribution plan, an annual contribution equal to some percentage of the participant's salary is made to the plan each year. The total amount that accumulates in a particular employee's account will determine the size of the pension annuity at the time of retirement—a case of "what you have is what you get." A defined-benefit pension plan, on the other hand, defines in advance the size of the desired pension benefit. Annual plan contributions must then be made in an amount sufficient to supply the desired retirement annuity.

The difference between the two

While both funding methods are theoretically available to both corporate pension plans and Keogh plans, the defined-benefit option is, for all practical purposes, impossible in Keogh plans. If you want a defined-benefit plan, you are looking at incorporation.

Defined-Contribution Plans The contributions that may be made annually to a defined-contribution corporate pension plan is 25 percent of the employee's compensation from the corporation. The corresponding maximum for a Keogh plan would be 15 percent of the employee's income.

For any individual, it is therefore easy to determine precisely the amount that will be in the employee's account at the time of retirement. For example, suppose your compensation from either an unincorporated or incorporated practice is $50,000 per year and you desire to make a defined contribution of 15 percent per year. Further, assume that you have 25 years until retirement at age 65, and that the plan will earn 6 percent per annum. The estimated value of the retirement plan at the age of 65 is merely the future value of an annuity of $7,500 per year for 25 years, as shown in Table 4.3.

Calculated growth of defined-contribution plan

Table 4.3 Computation of the Value of Your Retirement Account:
Defined-Contribution Plans at 15 Percent

*How the value of a
defined-contribution
plan is computed*

Facts:

Employee compensation	=	$50,000
Plan contribution	=	7,500 (15% of $50,000)
Years until retirement	=	25
Earnings on plan assets	=	6%

$FV = \$7,500_{25} \times 54.865^{a}$

$FV = \$411,487.50$

[a] From Appendix A.3.

Given the length of time an individual has to work until retirement and the estimated return on the plan assets, the only limiting factor on the size of the individual's retirement annuity is the size of the annual contribution. If we assume that an individual has 15 years to live after retirement, Table 4.4 shows the retirement annuity that can be provided from the account value computed in Table 4.3. The available benefit is merely the annuity that has, at 6 percent, a present value of $411,487.50.

Table 4.4 Computation of Your Retirement Annuity

Facts:

Accumulated value in your account	=	$411,487.50
Length of retirement annuity	=	15 years
Earnings on plan assets	=	6%

$\$411,487.50 = PMT_{15} \times 9.712^{a}$

$PMT_{15} = \dfrac{\$411,487.50}{9.712}$

$PMT_{15} = \$\ 42,368.98$

[a] From Appendix A.4.

Clearly, an individual who has both a sufficiently long time to work until retirement and sufficient income to make a large contribution has the opportunity to build an extremely comfortable retirement benefit via a defined-contribution plan.

*The disadvantage of a
defined-contribution
plan*

This kind of plan, however, can seriously discriminate against employees who have a relatively short period of time to work until retirement. As Table 4.5 shows, employee A, who is 55 years of age and who has only 10 years to work until retirement, will be entitled to a retirement benefit of only $10,178.90—less than half the $23,902.70 employee B will receive, even though B makes a salary of only $10,000 per year. This discrimination is, of course, caused by the simple mathematical fact that B has 30 years longer to work than does A.

Table 4.5 Computation of Comparative Retirement Benefits for Two Employees: Defined-Contribution Plan

Facts	Defined-contribution plan	
	Employee A	Employee B
Employee compensation	$50,000	$10,000
Plan contribution (15% of compensation)	7,500	1,500
Years until retirement	10 years	40 years
Length of retirement annuity	15 years	15 years
Earnings on plan assets	6%	6%
Plan values at retirement (Future values of the annual contributions)	$FV = \$7,500_{10} \times 13.181^a$ $FV = \$98,857.50$	$FV = \$1,500_{40} \times 154.762^a$ $FV = \$232,143.00$
Annual retirement benefits (The retirement annuity that has a present value equal to the value of the plan account at age 65)	$\$98,857.50 = PMT_{15} \times 9.712^b$ $PMT_{15} = \$10,178.90$	$\$232,143.00 = PMT_{15} \times 9.712^b$ $PMT_{15} = \$23,902.70$

[a] Interest factor from Appendix A.3.
[b] Interest factor from Appendix A.4.

Defined-Benefit Plans Defined-benefit plans are designed to remove the discrimination illustrated in Table 4.5 by providing a retirement benefit that is based on the preretirement salary of the employee—not on the length of time to work until retirement. That is, the retirement benefit, not the plan contribution, is defined in advance. Given the size of the defined-retirement benefit and the life expectancy of an individual after retirement, it is an easy matter to compute the size of the annual plan contribution necessary to fund the plan. Of course an individual with a short period of time to work until retirement must have substantially greater contributions allocated to an account than the individual having many years to work.

A defined-benefit plan works for those with fewer years

In order to determine the exact size of plan contributions, it is first necessary to define the retirement benefit desired under the plan. For purposes of illustration let us again look at employees A and B from the previous example. This time, however, let us define the desired retirement benefit to be 50 percent of salary during the three years prior to retirement. This would entitle A and B to pensions of $25,000 and $5,000, respectively, based on their present salaries.

Table 4.6 computes first, the amount that must be in each employee's account at retirement; and second, the annual plan contribution necessary to accumulate those amounts. As you can see, the retirement benefits are in proportion to salaries received during working years instead of being distorted in favor of employees with many years to work until retirement.

In addition to providing a retirement benefit that is proportional to preretirement salary, defined-benefit plans also have the distinct advantage of providing a professional person, who is 40 to 55 years of

Table 4.6 Computation of Comparative Retirement Benefits for Two Employees: Defined-Benefit Plan

	Defined-benefit plan	
Facts	Employee A	Employee B
Employee compensation	$50,000	$10,000
Defined benefit (50% of compensation)	25,000 per year	5,000 per year
Years until retirement	10 years	40 years
Length of retirement annuity	15 years	15 years
Earnings on plan assets	6%	6%
Required accumulations at retirement (The present value of the retirement annuity)	$PV = \$25,000_{15} \times 9.712^a$ $PV = \$242,800$	$PV = 5,000_{15} \times 9.712^a$ $PV = \$48,560$
Required annual contribution (The annuity that will accumulate the required plan value by age 65)	$\$242,800 = PMT_{10} \times 13.181^b$ $PMT_{10} = \$18,420.45$	$\$48,560 = PMT_{10} \times 154.762^b$ $PMT_{40} = \$313.77$

[a]Interest Factor from Appendix A.4.
[b]Interest Factor from Appendix A.3.

You can make large contributions to a defined-benefit plan

age but has never participated in a retirement plan, the privilege of making annual contributions considerably in excess of the general limitation of $25,000 per year. Specifically, any size contribution can be made as long as it is necessary to fund the defined benefit and as long as the defined benefit does not exceed $75,000, or 100 percent of annual income in the highest three consecutive years prior to retirement.

Thus, an individual at age 55, who is making $75,000 per year, could conceivably construct a pension plan that would pay a retirement benefit of $75,000 per year for 15 years. In order to do this, the individual must accumulate a sufficient block of assets to provide $75,000 retirement annuity, and has only a 10-year period of time in which to make that accumulation. Try your hand at the computations, and then compare the results with Table 4.7. Be certain to note that if this employee is the owner-employee of a professional corporation, he must take a substantial salary cut in his remaining 10 years in order to fund the retirement benefit. Since the professional is the source of income to the corporation, the corporation cannot continue to pay a $75,000 salary and also make a $55,000 plan contribution.

Minimum-funding Standards The excitement over the easily seen potential in a defined-benefit plan must be tempered by the requirement that *minimim-funding standards* must be met on such plans. What this means, in layman's language, is that adjustments of plan contributions must be made periodically in order to maintain the actuarial integrity of the plan. Thus, as employees' salaries are raised, the defined benefit goes up (50 percent of the new wage is more than 50 percent of the old), requiring an increase in plan contributions to fund the higher benefit.

Minimum-funding standards drive contributions up

Table 4.7 Computation of the Plan Contribution Required to Fund a Retirement Annuity of $75,000 for 15 Years

Required accumulation at retirement (The present value of the retirement annuity)	$PV = \$75{,}000_{15} \times 9.712^a$ $PV = \$728{,}400$
Required annual contribution (The annuity that will accumulate the required plan value by age 65)[c]	$\$728{,}400 = PMT_{10} \times 13.181^b$ $PMT_{10} = \$55{,}261.00$

[a]Interest factor from Appendix A.4.
[b]Interest factor from Appendix A.3.
[c]Earnings on plan assets = 6%.

Furthermore, the law requires that an actuarial analysis of the plan be performed periodically to determine if the accumulation to date is sufficient to meet the requirements of the plan. If, because of reverses in the securities markets or other investment losses, the value of the fund is not sufficient to meet the actuarial needs of the plan, the deficit must be amortized over the subsequent 15-year period.

For example, consider a medium-sized pension plan in a clinic, which should have asset accumulations of $300,000 but has only $250,000 because of poor investment performance. It will be necessary to increase the amount of the annual contribution by $2,148 per year for each of the next 15 years in order to amortize this deficit. (The figure $2,148 is the annuity that will grow to $50,000 in 15 years at 6 percent—try it!) A similar amortization is required if the asset value of the fund is greater than the amount required to meet the actuarial requirements of the plan. This means if superior investment performance causes the value of the fund to be greater than is needed, plan contributions must be reduced until the surplus is amortized.

These requirements can hit a small professional corporation particularly hard unless common sense is used as a plan is adopted. It might be very foolish, for example, for a new physician to adopt a defined-benefit plan paying 100 percent of salary as a retirement annuity. As the doctor's income increases with a growing practice, the required contributions may make it impossible to fund the plan.

Be sure you can fund your plan

Similarly, in a small corporation where the entire income of the corporation is attributable to one individual—as is frequently the case in a medical or dental practice—the demands of the loss-amortization requirement may be unbearable. A severe decline in the market value of assets in the plan could increase required contributions to the point where there is insufficient income available to meet the living needs of the individual physician or dentist.

Integration of Benefits

The law allows corporate plans—and theoretically, Keogh plans—to be integrated with the retirement benefits received under the Social Security system. Integration means that all employees in such plans are assumed to receive retirement benefits from two sources: first, from the Social Security annuity; and second, from the corporate retirement plan. The purpose of integration is to remove the discrimination against high-income employees that is caused by the Social Security system.

An example will illustrate the nature of this discrimination. A relatively low-income employee earning $15,000 per year, could retire with an annuity of about $4,800 per year from Social Security. An executive officer in the same corporation, with an annual income of $100,000 per year, would be entitled to approximately the same Social Security benefit. This means the low-income employee receives a retirement benefit equal to 32 percent of salary, while the employer receives a retirement annuity of only 5 percent of salary. The purpose of plan integration is to partially alleviate this discrimination. While there are numerous ways to integrate a pension plan (and even a profit-sharing plan), a look at two types of integration will illustrate the effect of plan integration on allocation of plan contributions to participants.

Integration can work to your advantage

Integration of Defined-Contribution Plans A defined-contribution plan can be integrated by allocating plan contributions to participants in two stages: first, some percentage (up to a maximum of 7 percent) of the employee's salary in excess of the integration level; with second, the remainder of the total plan contribution being allocated to all the employees according to the ratio of individual compensation to total compensation of all participants.

How integration works with a defined-contribution plan

Although the process sounds a bit formidable, a simple example will make it clear. Table 4.8 shows a professional corporation with a physician and four auxiliaries. The pension plan is a 20 percent defined-contribution plan in which all employees participate. The plan is integrated, and the plan contribution is allocated by giving all employees 7 percent of compensation *in excess of $10,000* (the integration level) and then dividing the remaining contribution on a pro-rata basis.

Note that while 20 percent of total compensation has been contributed to the plan, those making more than the integration level receive more than 20 percent of their compensation. Without integration, each employee would have received exactly 20 percent of compensation.

> By all means, recognize that plan integration is not designed to "rip off" low-income employees. Rather, integration merely allocates pension contributions disproportionately, recognizing that lower-income employees are receiving a substantially higher percentage of their retirement benefits from Social Security than are the higher-income employees.

Table 4.8 Allocation of Plan Contribution in an Integrated Defined-Contribution Pension Plan

Employee	Step 1: Determine plan contribution				Step 2: Make first allocation			Step 3: Make second allocation		Step 4: Compute total allocation
	Salary −	Integration level =	Excess income	Percentage of excess	First Allocation (1)	Remaining to be allocated	Percentage of compensation	Second Allocation (2)	1 + 2	Percentage of compensation
Doctor	$ 80,000 −	$10,000 =	$70,000 ×	7% =	$4,900	$18,560 ×	$\frac{80}{118}$ =	$12,583.05	$17,483.05	21.85%
Nurse A	12,000 −	10,000 =	2,000 ×	7% =	140	18,560 ×	$\frac{12}{118}$ =	1,887.46	2,027.46	16.90%
Nurse B	10,000 −	10,000 =	0 ×	7% =	0	18,560 ×	$\frac{10}{118}$ =	1,572.88	1,572.88	15.73%
Nurse C	10,000 −	10,000 =	0 ×	7% =	0	18,560 ×	$\frac{6}{118}$ =	943.73	943.73	15.73%
Receptionist	6,000 −	10,000 =	0 ×	7% =	0	18,560 ×	$\frac{6}{118}$ =	943.73	943.73	15.73%
				Total of first allocations	$5,040[a]			$18,560.00[a]	$23,600.00	

Total income of participants $118,000

Defined contribution × 20%

23,600[a]

Total plan contribution $18,560.

[a]$23,600 − $5,040 = $18,560.

Integration of Defined-Benefit Plans There are many formulas by which defined-benefit plans may be integrated, but by far the easiest to see is a type of integration known as *direct offset*. The term means that the plan is integrated by subtracting directly from the defined pension benefit the anticipated retirement annuity from Social Security. The annual contribution is then computed as in any defined-benefit plan.

The impact of this type of integration is dramatic: All employees receiving their entire defined benefit from Social Security receive no allocation of the plan contribution. Table 4.9 takes another look at the employees we originally considered in Table 4.6. Compare the results of the two tables to see the effect of the offset integration.

Again, the purpose of the integration is not to discriminate against the low-income employee, but rather to remove the discrimination against the high-income employee that is inherent in the Social Security pension benefit.

Table 4.9. Computation of Required Annual Contributions for Two Employees: Offset Integrated Defined-Benefit Pension Plan

	Employee A	Employee B
Employee compensation	$50,000	$10,000
Defined benefit (50% of compensation) ⎫ a	25,000	5,000
Social Security annuity ⎭	5,000	4,200
Required annuity from plan	$20,000	$ 800
Years until retirement	10 years	40 years
Length of retirement annuity	15 years	15 years
Required accumulation at retirement (The present value of the retirement annuity)	$PV = \$20{,}000_{15} \times 9.712^{b}$ $PV = \$194{,}240$	$PV = \$800_{15} \times 9.712^{b}$ $PV = \$7{,}769$
Required annual contribution (The annuity that will accumulate the required plan value at age 65)	$\$194{,}240 = PMT_{10} \times 13.181^{c}$ $PMT_{10} = \$14{,}736.36$	$\$7{,}769.00 = PMT_{40} \times 154.762^{c}$ $PMT_{40} = \$50.20$
Percent of total contribution allocated to participant's account	99.7%	0.3%

[a]This integration takes place at this point by offsetting the pension benefit with the Social Security annuity.
[b] Interest factor from Appendix A.4.
[c] Interest factor from Appendix A.3.

Integration of Keogh Plans While the 1974 Pension Reform Act enables integration of a Keogh plan, the regulations defining how this integration is to be accomplished have not been issued to date.

Access to Funds in the Retirement Trust

It is the strong feeling of the authors that the only purpose for constructing a retirement plan is to provide a source of income in retirement years. For that reason we seldom advocate attempting to gain access to a retirement fund assets under any circumstances in preretirement years. Such a course of action only increases the probability that the plan will not meet its desired objectives. This disclaimer notwithstanding, you should be aware of the provisions of the law in this area.

Don't use your funds early

Keogh Plans For a Keogh plan, the entire question of access to plan assets is academic, since it is essentially forbidden. The law defines retirement age (for purposes of becoming an annuitant in the plan) as age 59½. This means that even if a participant in the plan retires prior to that age, that person is not entitled to receive a retirement annuity from the plan until age 59½. The one possible viable exception to this rule allows preretirement withdrawal of an annuity from the plan in the event of total disability.

The only other manner in which individuals may gain access to funds in their account is to terminate participation in the plan and withdraw their asset accumulation. Unless the accumulations are very small, the consequence of such a course of action is disastrous. If this type of termination is effected, the entire value of an employee's account is taxed at once as current income, plus an additional penalty tax.

Terminating a Keogh plan has severe tax effects

Pension and Profit-sharing Plans The circumstances under which a participant in pension and profit-sharing plans may gain access to plan assets are somewhat more loosely defined than the mandatory requirements of the Keogh plan. The trust instrument, for example, could allow a participant to receive an annuity in the event of total disability, and could define retirement age at any age decided upon by the employer. That is, the retirement age for corporate employees could be defined as age 40, instead of age 59½, the minimum age under the Keogh, or as age 65, the normal expected retirement age.

Another means of allowing plan participants to have access to accumulations in the plan is by careful use of an employee-borrowing agreement. Under such an agreement, written into the trust, plan participants may be accorded the privilege of borrowing from the plan.

Access to funds through borrowing agreements

Such loans must be considered from two points of view: the view of the trustee of the plan, and the view of the plan participants who may choose to borrow. The trustee's viewpoint will be considered in Chapter 5, which deals with investment of plan assets. Plan participants should consider the impact of such a loan carefully in making the decision whether or not to borrow. While such loans seem to provide an easy access to cash, the borrower should remember that the financial security of the family may be seriously impaired by such a practice. If a pension plan is being used to reduce the need for life insurance, as will be advocated in Chapter 7, that objective can be seriously hampered by the participant borrowing a large portion of the plan accumulation. Since the benefit which the family would receive from the trust is reduced by the amount of an outstanding loan, it would be dangerous to assume that the accumulation in the trust has replaced any of the need for life insurance.

Coordinate borrowing with your life insurance program

There are instances when amounts accumulated in a plan are substantially greater than will be needed to fund a comfortable retirement. In these cases, borrowing of this excess amount may be warranted. It is a good idea, however, to establish in your own mind a minimum-funding standard: the amount, at a point in time, that is required to meet your own future needs or the needs of your family in event of your death. Under no circumstances should your borrowing dip into that amount. If you follow that guideline, it will be difficult to jeopardize your future financial security or your family's.

Who Will Be Trustee of Your Plan?

Selection of a trustee is important

The plan you ultimately adopt will create a trust to hold the plan assets, and thus requires a trustee to administer the affairs of the trust and manage trust assets. Selection of this trustee is among the most important decisions relative to the plan.

Institutions as trustee: Keogh plan

Keogh Plans If you elect the Keogh alternative, you must appoint an institutional trustee such as a bank trust department, insurance company, mutual fund, or savings and loan association. Each of these institutions has preapproved or *prototype* plans, which have general approval of the IRS and which will be adopted by you, thus avoiding the legal costs associated with constructing a plan.

Two traps you should avoid

While this affords a cost saving, you must recognize that the institution you select has a vested interest in obtaining your account. Many such trusts contain provisions that may render them unacceptable to you. A common feature in many such profit-sharing plans requires mandatory contributions for your employees, but voluntary contributions for yourself. Such a requirement in essence makes the plan a pension plan for common-law employees, and a profit-sharing plan for yourself. To avoid such a trap, you should have your legal counsel analyze carefully any plan you may consider adopting.

The most viable trustees for Keogh

The other trap, which will be more difficult to avoid, is the fact that the company whose prototype trust you adopt will sell you their product. Chapter 5 raises serious questions about the suitability of funding a plan with either life insurance or mutual funds. That leaves bank trust departments and savings and loan associations as perhaps the most viable Keogh alternatives.

What a commercial bank charges

A commercial bank will charge you from ½ to 2 percent (depending on the bank) of asset value annually to manage your investment fund. The bank may extend you the privilege of exercising investment discretion, but usually prefers that you elect one of several pooled investment funds—stocks, bonds, or a combination—that they offer. While the fee sounds low, ½ percent of *asset value* may amount to 10 or 15 percent of the *income* earned on those assets—and that is a lot. You must also recognize that the fee does not usually cover the cost of plan administration, tax returns, IRS and Labor Department filings, vesting and participation schedules, and so on. This additional work must be done by your accountant or outside plan administrator—at extra cost, of course.

The savings and loan association generally does not charge a fee for investment management. Their returns range between 5 percent for passbook savings and 7 percent for savings certificates.

A savings and loan association

Corporate Plans The same institutions that offer you prototype Keogh plans generally make available prototype pension and profit-sharing plans. A good word of advice is . . . don't use these prototypes! With Keogh you had no choice. With corporate plans you do. Look for the best (which may mean expensive) tax counsel you can find and retain this attorney to draw a plan to fit your specific needs. Only by drawing your own plan, with professional help, can you be assured that your needs relative to defined-benefit versus defined-contribution plans, pension versus profit-sharing plans, integration of benefits, and trusteeship, all will be properly considered.

To get the best corporate plan, retain counsel

After the trust is drawn, you can still name an institutional trustee, but you can also name yourself, or a committee of the employees of the corporation. Read carefully in Chapter 10 about the responsibilities of trustees before you decide. And assess your own personality. If there is any chance you will do something either foolish or illegal while you are trustee (the list of such things is in Chapter 10), don't name yourself. By using some combination of plan administrator-actuary and investment adviser, however, you should be able to reduce costs and improve investment performance over what an institution will do for you and at the same time stay out of trouble.

You can be a trustee yourself

Summary

After comparison of all the pros and cons, the tough decision still remains. Which type of plan are you going to select?

Several years ago, passage of the Pension Reform Act had many convinced that the Keogh plan, with its increased contribution limits, was the cheapest and best way for most professionals to go. This was particularly true if contributions in excess of $7,500 were not anticipated.

After experience with the new law, however, the tables seem to be turning. Inflexibility of the prototype Keogh trusts, the opportunity to use defined-benefit and integration formulas, and more restrictive vesting schedules—all lean in favor of the corporate plans.

Overall flexibility favors corporate plans

The opportunity to put away substantially greater amounts, coupled with the ability to get access to those funds by employee borrowing agreements, make the corporate plans almost hands-down winners.

BIBLIOGRAPHY

Pension Reform Act of 1974: Law and Explanation. Chicago: Commerce Clearing House, 1974.

While the law itself is of little interest to lay people, the explanation of the law is clear, concise, and easily understood.

Randle, Paul A. "Your Retirement Plan and the Magic of Time." *Dental Economics,* May 1977, pp. 61–64.

An article demonstrating the importance of starting a retirement plan as early as possible.

CHAPTER 5

The Pros and Cons of Professional Incorporation: Play by the Rules and Win Big

After reading this chapter, you will understand:

- The differences between a regular business corporation and a professional corporation.
- The circumstances that make professional incorporation profitable.
- How to keep your corporation out of trouble.
- The fringe benefits that help reduce the cost of corporate practice.

Many years ago the U.S. Supreme Court, in a landmark decision, held that a corporation is almost an artificial person, and has many of the same rights as an individual. It may own property, earn income, must pay taxes on that income, may sue or be sued—just as an individual may so do. Furthermore, a corporation is given two additional rights that give it significant advantages over other types of business entities.

The first is that an individual businessman may die, or sell his interest in his business, either of which will cause his proprietorship or partnership to be dissolved in the eyes of the law. But, if an individual stockholder in a corporation dies, or sells his shares in the corporation, the corporation lives on perpetually. This perpetual existence is essential in large business since it would be impossible to gather all owners together to reorganize the company every time another owner died or sold his interest in the company. This would be required, however, were it not for the perpetual life of the corporate form.

Two important privileges of a corporation

A professional corporation can have perpetual life like a regular business corporation, but only if there is more than one professional in the corporation. In a one-person corporate practice, death would dissolve the corporation since only the professional—not the heirs—may own stock in a professional corporation.

The second privilege granted to corporations is a *corporate veil* drawn between the corporation and the owners (stockholders) of the corporation. This term means an incorporated business may incur liabilities for which its stockholders are not personally responsible. This contrasts to a proprietorship or partnership, in which the individual business owner is personally responsible for any action or liability of the business. This right is also an essential ingredient for most large businesses since it would be impossible for them to raise large amounts of capital if every potential shareholder faced personal responsibility for every action of the business.

There is no corporate veil for the professional

It would be ideal from the professional's viewpoint if the corporate veil that shields the stockholder from corporate liability existed in a professional corporation. A corporate engineering firm could then handily forget about professional liability or errors-and-omissions insurance since the corporate veil would protect the principals of the corporation from potential liability. It is important to stress, however, that this limitation of liability *does not extend to professional corporations.*

> The state laws that allow professional incorporation specifically mandate that a professional practicing in a corporate setting shall be personally liable for his or her actions. The professional may not hide behind the corporate veil.

Professionals can incorporate, under special rules

For many years most states prohibited professionals—such as physicians, dentists, veterinarians, the engineering professions, lawyers, and certified public accountants—from incorporating, primarily because of society's view that such professionals should be personally liable for their professional actions. Unfortunately, this prohibition also precluded the use of attractive corporate fringe-benefit programs that were available to other high-income individuals plying their trades in the corporate form. After many legal battles, professionals have been granted the right to incorporate, but only under a special set of rules that restrict ownership of such corporations to professionals, and allow the corporate veil to be pierced in questions of professional liability.

The Purpose of Professional Incorporation

Unlike other business corporations, which may be incorporated for many different reasons, a professional practice requires incorporation only if employee fringe-benefit programs—especially a pension or profit-sharing plan—can be profitably used in the corporation. We hasten to point out that other businesses, incorporated for any other reasons, can also take advantage of retirement programs, and the other employee-benefit programs discussed in this chapter; their use is not limited to professional corporations. But again we stress that there is only one reason for professionals to incorporate, and that is to create valuable—to them—fringe-benefit programs.

Benefit programs: the reason for incorporation

Given the legal restrictions on professional corporations, it may seem axiomatic that their only use is to enable creation of benefit programs. In spite of this, the authors see many professional practices that are incorporated without a retirement plan or other benefit programs in existence. The frequent plaint of professionals in these practices is, "I really can't see any advantage to professional incorporation—my income is no higher than it was before I incorporated." If there are no benefit plans in these corporations, it would be a miracle if the income had increased. In fact, net income should have gone down because of the higher cost of corporate practice.

Even where benefit plans are in existence, the oft-voiced objection to corporate practice is its higher cost—higher legal fees, higher accounting costs, higher consulting fees, along with the nuisance factor of having to meet all the requirements of acting like a corporation. What such objectors frequently fail to take into consideration are the great tax savings associated with pension or profit-sharing plan contributions. If the marginal tax bracket of the professionals in the corporation is 50 percent, every dollar contributed to a pension or profit-sharing plan cuts the tax bill of the individuals involved by fifty cents. Or, stating it another way, if a contribution is made to a pension plan, the Internal Revenue Service contributes half the dollar, with the individual involved contributing the other half.

Tax savings can offset high costs

Even in such cases it is conceivable, although not likely, that the costs of corporate practice could exceed the benefits. One step anyone contemplating incorporation should take is to make a careful study of the costs as well as the benefits of incorporation in order to determine that the latter exceeds the former by a substantial margin.

Yet costs must not exceed benefits

The Requirements of Operating a Professional Corporation

If you intend to incorporate, the most important thing to remember is that your corporation is a legal entity separate and distinct from yourself. This new artificial entity is created as the result of you, through your legal counsel, filing articles of incorporation with the secretary of state of the state in which you practice. The state, in turn, issues a charter that creates the corporation. While this is a relatively simple step, the legal fees to accomplish it may range from $500 to $2,000.

Filing articles of incorporation

As part of the legal process your attorney should furnish you with the following: articles of incorporation; a corporate charter; a corporate seal; a set of corporate bylaws (the rules by which the corporation will be run); a minute book, including minutes of the organizational meeting; instructions on how to conduct corporate meetings, draw resolutions, and so on; new tax numbers for the corporation; and finally, a face-to-face conference in which you receive a detailed briefing of

What you need from your attorney

what has been done for you. When you walk out of the meeting you should know how to operate your corporation, retirement plan, medical-reimbursement plan, wage-continuation plan, and group life insurance plan. The articles of incorporation themselves are only so much legal boilerplate, largely the product of a magnetic-card typewriter. If you pay to be incorporated, then, make certain the services include those listed, not just the boiler plate.

At all times you must remember that you and the corporation are completely different entities. It is mandatory that clear distinction be made between the acts of the corporation and the acts of you as an owner of the corporation.

Remember: you are not the corporation

> The iron-clad rule is: If you incorporate your practice or business, act like a corporation.

Selecting a Name The articles of incorporation which your legal counsel files with your secretary of state must include a name for the new entity being created. The corporation could bear your own name, followed by a corporate designation. John Doe, D.D.S., A Professional Corporation; Richard Roe, M.D., P.C.; Smith and Jones, C.P.A.s Inc.; Ann Anderson, Professional Engineer, Ltd.—all may be acceptable appelations, depending on the state you live in. Some states do allow the use of pseudonyms, such as Gotham City Veterinary Clinic, Inc.; The Orthopedic and Fracture Clinic, P.C.; or Architectural Associates, A Professional Corporation.

Selecting the name itself is the easy part of the exercise; from that point on matters become more complex. Since a separate legal entity exists, it is now of utmost importance that the entire professional practice be conducted through the new entity. This means that it will be necessary to open new bank accounts for the professional corporation; obtain new tax numbers from the Internal Revenue Service and your state tax agency; print new letterheads, business forms, and billing forms showing the new name; change telephone listings, and even change the name plaque on the office door.

> The critical point, though these seem like small matters, is to provide proof to the Internal Revenue Service and other state and federal authorities that there is a clear distinction between yourself as a professional and the professional corporation for which you work.

The kind of mistake you don't want the Internal Revenue Service to find is the one made by a professional in a large midwest city who had been incorporated for over two years: That doctor made all the changes recommended above, except he continued to stamp all checks received in the practice *For Deposit Only to the Account of John Doe,* instead of *For Deposit Only to the Account of John Doe, P.C.* When the IRS discovered the mistake, it held that no corporation existed in fact, and treated all corporate income as if it belonged to the doctor involved. The most costly consequence of this mistake was disqualification of the corporate pension plan by the IRS. This resulted in reincluding all plan contributions in the doctor's personal income. Don't let this happen to you.

A costly mistake you can avoid

Formalities of Corporate Practice Because the corporation is a separate legal entity, law and regulation require that corporate business affairs be handled in a necessarily formal—almost stodgy—manner.

First, the stockholders of the corporation must meet annually in order to elect the board of directors of the corporation. If you are the only stockholder, this is an easy task. If you are engaged in some type of group practice, there should be a formal meeting of the professional stockholders in order to elect the board.

Hold an annual stockholders' meeting

Second, the board of directors of the corporation must, in a formal meeting, elect the officers of the corporation. The exact number of officers involved depends on the state law, as well as the actual needs of the corporation. Some states require that there be more than one officer, even if the corporation is a one-person practice. Depending on state law, it might be possible for you to name yourself both the president and secretary-treasurer of the corporation. In other states it may be necessary that you name a second professional, or perhaps your spouse, to fill one of the offices.

Elect officers

For a large group practice, it may be desirable to have one or more vice-presidents in addition to the president, secretary, and treasurer. In all cases, a secretary will be required, and there is some merit in considering your attorney or accountant to fill this role in order to ensure the scrupulous record keeping that is of utmost importance in maintaining the formalities of corporate practice.

Keep scrupulous records

Third, while the board of directors may delegate day-to-day responsibilities for operating the corporation to the corporate officers, it is still necessary that the board ratify, *by formal resolution,* the major actions of the officers. Generally, most states do not require a resolution of the board to pay day-to-day expenses, to make regular purchases of supplies, or to authorize other routine transactions. The board should, however, resolve to enter into all contracts of employment, borrowing or leasing contracts, decisions to hire or fire, decisions to adopt a pension or profit-sharing plan, decisions relative to contributions to those plans, and all other major transactions.

Ratify major actions by formal resolution

The secretary of the corporation is charged with the responsibility for maintaining a book of minutes detailing the resolutions that, in turn, reflect the actions of the board. In the case of a one-person professional corporation, where you are the only member of the board, it sounds a bit absurd to hold a formal meeting with yourself to ratify the kind of actions described. Indeed it might be a bit absurd. It is, nevertheless, essential that you do more than just think about these actions. If you, as the sole director, decide to do something, record that action as a formal resolution in the minutes of a board-of-directors meeting. Only with that record will it be possible to prove that the actions taken by the corporation were indeed corporate actions and not the actions of you as an individual.

Record your own actions as sole director

> It is probably impossible to state strongly enough how important the minute book is. It is the first thing any federal or state tax auditor will ask to see. In many cases such a request is a *gotcha*, since many professional corporations either fail entirely to keep the book, or plan to reconstruct a set of minutes at the end of the year from checkbook records.

Since corporate actions must be resolved in advance, the IRS fails to sympathize with year-end dummying up and is apt to disallow the missing actions of the corporation as being unauthorized. Even worse, it could disallow the corporation completely. This is a result better avoided.

Employment Contracts Since everyone working for the corporation, including yourself, is a corporate employee, it is important that each employee have a contract of employment. This employment contract may be quite different for the professional in the corporation than for auxiliary employees, but there should be a formal contract in both cases. The contract should spell out compensation, contributions that will be made to pension or profit-sharing plans, wage-continuation agreements, medical-reimbursement agreements, agreements to furnish life insurance, and all other fringe benefits. Again, the primary purpose of the contract is to show the IRS and other authorities that a separate legal entity does exist and that it has contracted for the services of its employees.

Have a formal contract with all employees

Another great value of the employee contract is that it forces you to set a contractual salary for yourself, and to pay that salary. In the case of a one-person professional corporation, the source of the corporate income is, of course, your income. It is, nevertheless, important that this be paid from the corporation to yourself as a uniform salary and that it not fluctuate wildly from month to month. Failure to pay a salary in the proper manner could very easily cause the IRS to rule that the corporation exists in form only. Proof of the contention would be wildly fluctuating income—evidence that you took income if and when you wanted it, just as a sole proprietor does.

Pay yourself a set salary

The Need for Corporate Income Case law seems to be crystal clear in holding that the primary purpose for incorporation is to earn profits. For this reason, it is important that your professional corporation show a profit after payment of all expenses, including your own salary. Just how large this profit must be is open for debate, but it is frequently conceded to be in the area of 10 to 15 percent of corporate assets. In other words, the law says the assets invested in the corporation must earn some rate of return; otherwise, there is no justification for the corporation to exist.

Show a profit: a must

> Since retention of any income in the corporation is subject to double taxation, it is immediately apparent that you do not want to leave any more income in the corporation than is absolutely essential to satisfy the law.

Double taxation means that the income will be taxed once at the corporate level and again at the individual level when the retained earnings of the corporation are distributed as a dividend.

Be aware of double taxation

One of the ways to keep the income of the corporation as low as possible is to keep the invested capital of the corporation at the lowest possible level. For this reason it is generally not desirable to allow the corporation to own the office building, medical or dental equipment, or even the office furnishings. If money is invested in these assets, then it is essential that the corporation show a return on the assets in order to justify the existence of the corporation. This means that the principal asset owned by the corporation will be the accounts receivable generated by the practice, plus the few miscellaneous assets that any practice will acquire.

Avoid ownership of buildings and equipment

The small amount of income that is retained in the corporation may be distributed periodically to shareholders of the corporation as a dividend. Remember, this distribution is subject to a second round of taxation. But most tax attorneys and accountants feel the double taxation on a small amount of income is a minor price to pay for establishing evidence that the corporation does exist to earn a profit, and that the profit is periodically distributed to stockholders of the corporation.

Distribute dividends: an advantage

Ownership of Corporate Assets The question that now arises is this: If the corporation does not own the business assets, who does? The answer is simple. You do. The most desirable arrangement is normally for the professional or professionals in a corporation to own the business assets and lease them to the corporation. Where there are several physicians or dentists in a corporation, the most viable option is for a partnership of the doctors to own the assets; the partnership then leases the assets to the corporation.

Own the business assets and lease them

Understand how to depreciate assets

The lease payments will, of course, be income to the individuals involved and could be subject to taxation at rates higher than the 50 percent maximum rate at which salary income is taxed. For the initial period of any asset life, however, the lease income is completely offset by the depreciation expense generated by the asset, since accelerated depreciation may be used. As the depreciation decreases in later years, one viable option is for you as the owner of an asset to make a gift of that asset to your children or to a trust of which your children are beneficiaries. The corporation may then continue to lease the assets from the trust, flowing income from the corporation directly to your children. The lease expense continues to be a business expense to the corporation. And since your children are in a low (or zero) income tax bracket, the lease income is essentially a tax-free distribution to them.

Keep lease-back transactions at arms length

In order to avoid problems with the IRS, it is important that such arrangements be "arm's-length transactions." This means it would be essential to name a trustee other than yourself to administer the transferred assets. This could be your bank, your accountant, or some other fiduciary. While there is a small cost associated with setting up and administering such a trust, the tax savings should be substantially greater than cost.

We hope you will understand that we have described, in several short paragraphs, strategies that are immensely complex and subject to change as the IRS code and its regulations are modified.

Rely on the best tax counsel

> In this area—perhaps more than any other—we urge you to rely on close support by the best tax counsel you can obtain. Remember, the entire purpose of the strategies outlined is to save you thousands of dollars. It does not pay, therefore, to be "penny wise and pound foolish." Get the help you need to make the strategy work, and don't begrudge the cost—it will save you big bucks.

Administration of the Pension Plan While technically not part of day-to-day corporate affairs, one of the most important management functions that must be performed is administration of the corporate pension and profit-sharing plan. Since the sole objective of incorporation was establishment of that plan, it would be unfortunate to have the plan disqualified because of failure to meet a requirement of the law, or because of unintentional oversight of some small detail.

Do not administer your pension plan yourself

Because of the extremely technical legal, accounting, and actuarial requirements of the law, it is important that you not attempt administration of the pension plan yourself. Depending on the qualifications of your legal and accounting advisers, one or both of them may have to be involved.

Your attorney, too, from time to time will be involved in amending the plan to meet requirements imposed by changes in the law or regulations. Your accountant will also have to be involved in maintaining the financial records of the plan and computation of investment performance. Either one or the other will have to assume the responsibility of filing forms and reports required by the IRS or Labor Department on an annual basis, as well as other special reports as they are required. In addition, if you have selected a defined-benefit plan, an actuary will have to be retained periodically in order to determine whether the minimum-funding standards of the plan are being met.

Because of the complexities of the Pension Reform Act of 1974, a number of firms specializing in plan administration are springing up around the country. For a relatively low cost, such firms fill one or more of the functions we've described. Since these firms do not usually practice law, they will frequently work in conjunction with your legal counsel to maintain the legal aspects of the plan. In addition, however, they maintain all plan records, file tax returns, determine investment performance, maintain vesting and participation schedules, and perform the periodic actuarial studies. Because they specialize, their cost is frequently lower than what would be incurred by retaining an attorney, accountant, and actuary to fulfill three separate roles.

Firms that specialize in plan administration

The Fringe Benefits that Come with Incorporation

While the primary purpose for incorporation remains, once and for all, to establish a pension or profit-sharing plan, there are additional fringe benefits that may also be extended to employees of the corporation. These are of such a minor nature that they would never justify incorporation of themselves but frequently can be used profitably once the corporation is formed.

Group Life Insurance Under the current tax code, the Internal Revenue Service allows the corporation to provide group term life insurance to each of its employees in an amount up to $50,000. There are several key words in the description of this fringe benefit. One of them is *group*. The Internal Revenue code is explicit in stating that insurance provided through this fringe benefit must be of a group type. This means that it must be extended to each of the employees of a corporation, without discrimination, and on a group basis. Thus, no evidence of insurability may be required—a regulation that can cause problems as we shall see.

In their eagerness to sell life insurance, many agents conveniently fail to recall this fact and consequently sell insurance products that are clearly outside the scope of the law. Others require a dual set of applications from each employee, one application requiring a physical examination and the other not. After evidence of insurability is established, the medical application is discarded. Still another tactic is to require, as a condition of providing the group coverage, purchase of an

Problems you should understand about group life insurance

accompanying insurance policy that requires a medical examination. By these means the insurance company can determine in advance which employees are insurable and which are not. Any of these tactics is clearly outside the scope of the law and will invalidate the group insurance program if discovered by the IRS.

Since the program is a group fringe benefit, all employees, as we have said, must participate—though not necessarily to the extent you do. To avoid discrimination, however, the extent of their participation should be proportional to yours. For example, if $50,000 in coverage is twice your annual salary of $25,000, an employee earning $12,000 should be given two times $12,000, or $24,000, in insurance protection. Note that providing this benefit for your employees can easily offset the savings you achieve through your own small benefit.

Do not use cash-surrender-value products

Another key word in the description of the coverage that may be provided is *term*. The only premium the IRS allows as a tax-deductible expense is for term insurance protection. Because the commission structure on term products is so low, however, many agents purposely sell cash-surrender-value products in group insurance programs. In such cases, the IRS requires that all premiums in excess of the allowable term rate be taxed as income to the employee. Because of this treatment, the very act of giving this fringe benefit to the employee frequently costs the person more in taxes than insurance protection is worth. For this reason, it is never advisable to use cash-surrender-value products in a group term life insurance program.

Group term insurance offers little benefit to you

In the final analysis, the value of the benefit that can be provided by a group term insurance program is very small and the cost relatively high. Because the $50,000 maximum coverage is such a minor part of your own insurance requirement and because the cost of $50,000 in term coverage is so small, your personal benefit is relatively insignificant. Thus, since the costs of this type of program frequently outweigh the benefits, our advice is to be sure you analyze the figures carefully after your silver-tongued agent leaves.

An employee-disability plan is not always advantageous

Wage-Continuation Plans Another fringe benefit that may be extended through the corporation is an *employee-disability* or *wage-continuation* plan. Such a plan could call for continuation of the salary of an employee in the event of a disabling illness or accident. Most professional corporations may not particularly want to extend this fringe benefit to employees other than the professionals; yet this may be required, to some extent, to avoid discrimination. This adds an element of cost to the program that, like the insurance program, is frequently great enough to offset the benefit.

Since the primary interest is in providing disability benefits to the professional in the corporation, another thorny question arises: The only source of income to the professional corporation is the professional; thus the corporation lacks the means to continue salary payments should the professional become disabled. For this reason, it is necessary that any wage-continuation plan in a professional corporation be funded through the purchase of disability income insurance.

The premiums on disability insurance, if used to fund a wage-continuation plan, constitute a legitimate tax-deductible expense to the corporation. Unfortunately, however, a disability benefit when paid to the professional is then considered taxable income. In contrast, if you purchase a disability income policy outside the corporation, with your own after-tax income, the disability income benefit is exempt from payment of income taxes.

This all boils down to the fact that if the disability income policy is purchased in the corporation, roughly twice as much coverage is required than if it is purchased outside. When this fact is coupled with the provision that similar coverage may be required for other employees in the corporation, there may be little or no savings associated with the use of a corporate wage-continuation plan. By all means analyze the numbers very carefully to make certain that the program is, in fact, justified.

Buy disability insurance outside the corporation

Medical Reimbursement Plans One of the very real benefits of corporate practice has recently been taken away from you. Until the Revenue Act of 1978, the IRS allowed classification of corporate employees into different groups and allowed different levels of reimbursement for medical expenses for each of the different employee classifications. It was possible, for example, for a corporation to reimburse all medical expenses, including eye glasses, prescription drugs, and dental work, for the executives of the corporation and their families and still agree to a lower level of reimbursement for other employees. Since you are the executive, this was obviously an important fringe benefit in professional corporations.

What the Revenue Act of 1978 does

Under the terms of the Revenue Act of 1978 such plans are still permitted, but discrimination is not allowed. Specifically, all benefits paid to one class of employee that are not accorded to another class of employee are fully taxable to the person receiving them. This still, of course, allows the corporation to furnish tax-free medical benefits, including a medical insurance plan, to all employees as long as it is done in a nondiscriminatory fashion.

As with other fringe-benefit programs, you should be careful to note that simply because the corporation agrees to reimburse medical expenses does not guarantee that the corporation will have sufficient resources to do so—a consideration especially important here, since the costs of a catastrophic illness or accident would be impossible for the corporation to bear. For this reason, it is generally advisable to fund a medical-reimbursement program with a major-medical insurance policy. The premium payments on this policy may also be considered part of the medical-reimbursement plan, a tax-deductible expense to the corporation, and a tax-free benefit to the employee.

How to fund a medical-reimbursement program

While there was no question about including a medical-reimbursement plan in a professional corporation prior to the Revenue Act of 1978, it is now necessary that you carefully weigh the benefits you receive against the cost of providing similar benefits for other employees of the corporation. The odds are you will elect to keep

What medical costs you will cover

benefit levels relatively low—say a medical insurance policy for all employees—and forego reimbursement for other types of medical costs.

Summary

The benefits of incorporation

This chapter makes it clear that there are costs as well as benefits in the professional corporation. The benefits are easily measured: Each time the corporation contributes one dollar to your retirement plan or reimburses you one dollar paid for medical expenses, your personal tax bill is reduced by as much as fifty cents. Stating the benefit another way, your participation in a pension or medical-reimbursement plan is subsidized, for up to 50 percent of its cost, by the federal government.

The cost of incorporation

Like all other benefits, those arising out of corporate fringe benefits can only be acquired at a cost. For a professional corporation these costs are easily identified: They include the initial cost of incorporation and construction of employee benefit plans, the annual administration of the corporation and the benefit plans, and the cost of employee participation in those plans. Each of these costs is reduced to as little as 50 percent of its pretax amount because of the tax-deductible nature of these expenses.

In addition to the monetary costs, there is a certain nuisance factor associated with operating a professional corporation. If detail is not your cup of tea, it is essential that these nuisance details be taken care of for you by your attorney, accountant, or pension fund administrator.

We say the benefits win

Are the costs exceeded by the benefits? We believe that even with relatively modest pension or profit-sharing contributions, the benefits should easily outweigh the costs—and the nuisance. In the final analysis, however, the decision to incorporate—or not—is up to you. Weigh the costs against the benefits. Consider all the pros and cons.

But you make the choice

Do not rely on rules of thumb or estimates; insist that your accountant or consultant prepare hard numbers so you can convince yourself of the merits of this important step.

BIBLIOGRAPHY

Gorlick, Allan. *Now That You've Incorporated*. Oradell, N.J.: Medical Economics Books, 1975.
A clear, well-written book on the requirements of corporate practice.

Randle, Paul A. "The Perils of P. C." *Dental Economics*, July 1976.
An article explaining the requirements of corporate practice and possible pitfalls to be avoided.

CHAPTER 6

All About Insurance: Insure for Surgery but Pay for Runny Noses

After you have read this chapter, you will be able to:

- Understand the basic concept of risk transfer, and how risk is transferred through the use of insurance.
- Decide when to transfer risk to an insurance carrier, or bear it yourself.
- Differentiate between the types of insurance products available.
- Understand how insurance premiums are computed.
- Analyze your life insurance needs by conceptualizing the basic elements.

Throughout the normal course of life there are many risks to which you are exposed. While many risks that you encounter daily are inconsequential from a financial standpoint, there are a few that have truly catastrophic consequences. The purpose of this chapter is to help you decide which of these risks you can realistically bear yourself, and which must be covered by insurance.

You must transfer some risks

What Is Insurance?

Ultimately, your insurance portfolio should depend on your ability and propensity to assume risk.

Insurance can be acquired to hedge against practically any type of risk. Some companies, notably Lloyds of London, specialize in underwriting insurance for many uncommon, even bizarre, risks. The more common risks, to which we are all exposed, include auto collision and auto liability; property loss from theft or fire; medical, personal, or professional liability; loss of income from disability; and loss of life. As you read about these types of insurance, remember that the same principles apply to any other insurable risk.

The common risks

Insurance is a mechanism whereby you can transfer some, or all, of the financial risk of a calamity from yourself to an insuring party. The insurance company, as compensation for assuming the risk, must levy a charge in the form of a premium. If you wish to assume a portion of the risk yourself, the premium will be reduced to reflect the transfer of less risk to the insurer. This is the basic concept of insurance.

The Insurance Principle. Suppose historical evidence reveals that in a typical population of 1,000 automobile owners, 14 of them will be involved in an accident over the next year with the resultant damage averaging $600 per wreck. Since none of us knows to whom the accidents will happen, we collectively decide to eliminate the risk of the potential $600 personal loss by sharing the cost equally among 1,000 friends. Since we know the total damage claims will equal

$$14 \text{ accidents} \times \$600 = \$8,400,$$

we must collect a premium of $8.40 from each of the 1,000 participants to cover the losses. Claims will be made against this fund as accidents occur. If you happen to be the victim of such an accident, the $600 damage claim will be settled with no further cost to you. If, on the other hand, you happily avoid an accident, your $8.40 contribution will have been "lost," discounting the fact that it may have purchased some peace of mind.

Extending the example a bit, suppose we decide collectively to underwrite individually only a portion of the accident risk. That is, if any one of us is involved in an accident, we shall personally be responsible for the first $100 of damage and then call upon our insurance fund for the remainder. Since the claims will now average only $500, our total insurance fund must equal

Sharing risk lowers premiums

$$14 \times \$500 = \$7,000.$$

As a result, the annual accident insurance premium for each of us will decline to $7. This simple example serves to illustrate how the principle of insurance works and further, how premiums can be reduced by personally assuming a portion of the risk.

The Costs of Insurance. In actuality, insurance premiums must include costs other than claims. These include brokerage fees, commissions, and overhead expenses of the insurance company. Further, the process of premium determination is made much more complicated because of different risk categories attributable to age, sex, economic status, education, location of residence, and so forth. The increasing cost of many types of insurance in recent years have been occasioned more by rising damage costs due to inflation than by increased claims frequency.

Nevertheless, the essential point remains that if you are willing to assume a portion of given risk yourself, you can significantly lower premiums. In the employment of an insurance strategy you should avoid both overinsuring and underinsuring. By overinsuring we mean insuring for small potential losses which could be covered out of income or savings; underinsuring means the purchase of policies with claim limits so low that one is unprotected against large losses.

Avoid overinsuring and underinsuring

Five Types of Insurance for Professionals and Entrepreneurs

To illustrate this concept of risk transfer and risk sharing let's look at the types of insurance policies typically owned by most professionals. By analyzing each of these briefly, we can help you to make better decisions about what kinds of insurance you yourself actually require.

Automobile Insurance. Everyone who owns an automobile has a policy of insurance on that car. This policy is really several—perhaps many—different types of coverage that are outlined on endorsements, which are in turn stapled together to make up the actual policy. Each of these endorsements is actually a miniature insurance policy in and of itself, covering a specific risk. The total cost of your policy will, to a large extent, reflect how many endorsements you opt to purchase.

Your costs are tied to endorsements

Most policies include at least two basic coverages: collision and public liability. Collision coverage insures you from your own recklessness. That is, if you are responsible for damaging or destroying your own car, the collision coverage insures against that risk. This is by far the most costly element of your auto policy, made all the more costly by the fact that we frequently carry far more coverage than necessary.

A large percentage of all claims on this coverage are for low-cost fender-bender accidents. Since most of us could bear the risk of a $300–400 loss ourselves, we could cut our premium appreciably by including a $50, $100, $500, or $1,000 deductible—depending on the degree of risk we feel we can accept—in our collision coverage.

You can cut high cost of collision coverage

Less frequently understood is the fact that your collision insurance premium does not decline in future years as your now new car grows older and less valuable. Perhaps the collision coverage is required when the cost of loss is high. Three years from now, however, when the car has depreciated significantly, it may be that collision coverage should be dropped entirely.

The second major coverage of most auto policies is public liability. Contrary to what most of us believe, this is a relatively inexpensive part of our policy. Its purpose is to protect us financially from liability incurred as a result of our carelessness. While the risk of such liability is relatively low, the cost could be catastrophically high. Unfortunately, we are often significantly underinsured in this area; a $100,000 damage award, after all, is more than most of us could comfortably bear. Because high-income professionals are sometimes the victims of high liability claims, wisdom dictates that you carry the

High liability coverage is essential

highest possible limits—at least $100,000—in this area. This type of liability is simply not a risk you can bear yourself.

The other endorsements of the typical auto policy you should analyze yourself in order to make a judgment as to their need. They include comprehensive (wind damage, vandalism, and such); uninsured motorist coverage (damage caused by someone without liability coverage to pay your claim); medical payments (duplicative if you have a medical policy); towing; and so on. You must decide when insurance costs may be cut by bearing some of these risks yourself.

Forms: classes of coverage on your property

Property Insurance. Like auto insurance, a property insurance policy is a collection of endorsements that specify the coverage you desire. Usually these policies, whether written on your home or office, are categorized into *forms*, or classes of coverage. A *Standard Form*, or class 1, fire policy insures against the fewest risks; while an *All Risks*, or class 5, policy insures against everything except war, nuclear radiation, earthquake, and flood—and the latter two perils can be insured against if you desire.

As risk classes broaden to include more and more risks, the premium must of course increase significantly. At the same time, the risks added to the policy have a significantly lower probability of ever occurring. Because a great deal of money can be spent to insure against perils that have only a remote chance of causing loss, it is important that you analyze with care exactly what you want to insure against and purchase coverage accordingly.

Professional liability coverage is essential

Liability coverages. While self-insurance might be perfectly appropriate in the area of automobile collision, it could have disastrous consequences in the areas of professional or personal liability. While the probability of claims being awarded in either area are relatively low, the size of the claim, if awarded, is likely to be financially catastrophic. Clearly, this is not the area in which it is wise to save insurance dollars.

Own an umbrella liability policy

In addition to standard liability coverage—professional liability, personal liability (which is generally written as part of a homeowner's policy), and office liability—most high-income professionals should own an umbrella liability policy. It is relatively inexpensive and takes over where your basic liability policy leaves off. If, for example, your professional liability policy provides $100,000 in protection, the umbrella policy would usually extend that protection to $1 million.

While it is irksome to be faced with premium payments for these types of coverages, today's adversary approach to the solution of personal problems makes it necessary.

Disability Income Insurance. Disability insurance provides an income if you are disabled because of sickness or accident. Several guidelines should be considered when thinking about the monthly income you will need from such protection:

Self-insure for a period of time. You almost certainly don't need protection from the first day of disability. The availability of savings, accounts receivable, and other assets will give you the ability to weather either a short-term disability or the first months of a permanent disability. Because a large number of disabilities are of a short-term nature, a waiting period of 180 days usually cuts the cost of a basic policy by about 50 percent.

Self-insure to cut costs

To the largest extent possible, you should reduce benefit levels to a reasonable estimate of needed income. Plan on tightening the family's belt in the event of disability. Much as you would like to, you simply cannot go on living according to your previous financial standard after disability occurs.

If you are totally disabled, you will be entitled to disability benefits other than those provided by insurance. These may include Social Security, workman's compensation, veterans benefits, income from investments, and disability withdrawals from your retirement plan. Your estimates of insurance coverage should be reduced by these amounts.

By all means, be realistic. While the loss of an arm could permanently disable you as far as a given profession is concerned, it does not prohibit you from retraining yourself for another profession, although we recognize the strong psychological investment professionals have in their occupations. Many professionals insist—at high cost—on being insured in their particular profession, yet people change careers and occupations all the time, and there's no reason you couldn't, too. A less restrictive definition of total disability would result in large savings in insurance expenditures.

Be realistic in your amount of coverage

Medical Insurance. Of all the areas where the concept of self-insurance has applicability, the area of insuring the cost of illness is the most ignored.

Several years ago the authors were retained by a large professional association to evaluate the group health insurance program of the association. A bitter battle with a state Blue Cross–Blue Shield company resulted because of the association's desire to include a $1,000-deductible option in addition to the basic Blue Cross–Blue Shield full-payment program. As Table 6.1 shows, the cost savings were material—more than 50 percent in most cases—and it was anticipated that virtually 100 percent of the members of the association, all high-income professionals, would select the deductible option.

Assume some of the risks of medical coverage

The battle was won, the option included; and then, 93 percent of the enrollees opted for the high-cost plan. Puzzling? No, unbelievable. Of all the groups in the world with the ability to bear $1,000 worth of risk to effect enormous savings in insurance costs, this was the group. You should examine your health insurance program to see if you have the same opportunity.

The main purpose of each of the preceding five sections is not to provide an exhaustive explanation of insurance, but to illustrate the risk-

Table 6.1 Medical Insurance Rates—Monthly Dues

Option I—full coverage					Option II—$1,000 deductible				
Age of member	Member only	Member and spouse	Family	Member and children	Age of member	Member only	Member and spouse	Family	Member and children
Under 30	10.88	28.29	42.48	25.08	Under 30	7.34	17.63	22.47	12.07
30–34	12.94	30.19	44.38	27.17	30–34	8.35	19.49	24.22	13.08
35–39	14.60	32.06	46.24	28.83	35–39	9.15	21.12	25.85	13.88
40–44	17.08	36.34	50.54	31.27	40–44	10.56	24.26	28.99	15.29
45–49	20.13	42.55	56.74	34.32	40–49	12.47	28.40	33.13	17.20
50–54	24.16	50.98	65.16	38.35	50–54	15.05	34.00	38.73	19.78
55–59	28.94	61.44	75.32	43.13	55–59	18.19	40.74	45.47	22.92
60–64 (not eligible for Medicare)	34.20	72.26	86.45	48.39	60–64 (not eligible for Medicare)	21.78	48.49	53.22	26.51

transfer process. We hope you can see when a risk should be transferred and when it could profitably be kept by yourself.

In general, our experience shows that people are frequently overinsured in all areas except for the loss of life. Because life insurance is so costly, many individuals frequently buy less coverage than is realistically needed. Since life insurance is so important to total financial planning, it is covered in greater detail in the following section and in Chapter 7, as well.

Life Insurance

Life insurance is a major financial responsibility

In no realm of financial planning does there seem to be more confusion than in the area of life insurance. One of your major financial responsibilities, however, is to provide adequate resources for the support of your dependents in the case of your death. As a result of that responsibility, you probably find yourself constantly approached by life insurance salespeople of all types, each selling a great variety of products. These salespeople seem to appear in greater abundance at specific times in your career, such as graduation from professional school, marriage, and the appearance of each family addition. We want to give you some fundamental tools whereby you may analyze your life insurance needs intelligently and thus come to an understanding of what type of life insurance products will best meet those needs.

The risk that you may die

Of the catastrophic risks you face, certainly one of great concern is the possibility that you may die. Aside from the mental and emotional strains of such an occurrence, you must consider carefully the economic consequences your loss of earning power brings to those who have depended upon you for income. Insurance, again, is simply a mechanism whereby the risk of this large, catastrophic loss is shared by many individuals.

Consider, for example, a life insurance company that writes insurance for a representative group of 100,000 30-year-old males. It can predict from the use of mortality and actuarial tables that exactly 200 (these numbers are purely hypothetical, used simply to illustrate the principle of life insurance) will die this year. Thus, if the company writes a one-year, $1,000 policy of life insurance for each of those 100,000 individuals, it must charge a premium of $2 for each $1,000 policy written. It will then have collected $200,000 in policy premiums that will be distributed in the form of $1,000 settlements to each of the 200 beneficiaries of those that die.

This $2 premium, of course, would be a pure premium in that it would not cover the costs of operating the company, sales commissions, and so on. In reality, life insurance premiums will be determined not only by the estimated needs for death-benefit settlements, but also by the expenses of running the company, and the provision for reserves.

How premiums are determined

A life insurance company has the advantage of reliable mortality and actuarial information, enabling accurate predictions of death rates. Thus it can construct premium structures to reflect anticipated death claims and overhead expense.

> A life insurance company can bear the risk of large death claims simply because it collects policy premiums not only from individuals who will die but also from many more individuals who will live.

Now let us examine the main types of life insurance. Although there are dozens of different types of life insurance policies on the market today, they are all variants of two distinct categories of insurance protection: first, policies that provide insurance coverage only and are commonly called *term* policies; and second, policies that provide some form of saving or investment program in addition to insurance protection. These are called *whole-life,* or more correctly, *cash value* policies.

The two main types of life insurance

Cash Value Insurance. Let's examine the characteristics of cash value policies first. Suppose that you purchase a $10,000 insurance contract, which will be paid up at age 65. Throughout the life of that policy you will pay equal annual premiums. In the early years of the policy, a large portion of the premium is used to pay the sales commission of the selling agent. A much smaller portion is used to purchase insurance coverage. A still smaller portion of the premium will be deposited in your account as savings—or cash value. As you continue to make your equal annual payments, the cash value portion of the policies will increase while the insurance portion of the contract will decrease.

Cash value policies contain an investment

For example, as illustrated in Figure 6.1, suppose that you were to die at age 38. Your designated beneficiary would receive the $10,000

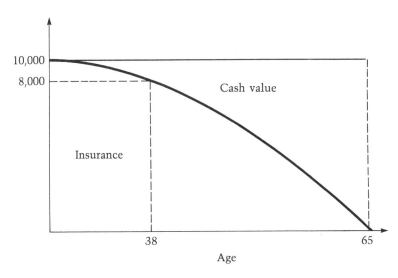

Figure 6.1 The changing mix of insurance and cash value for a whole-life policy.

face amount of the policy. Eight thousand dollars of that settlement (again, the figures are hypothetical) would be in the form of insurance proceeds, while the other $2,000 would come from the cash-value accumulations of the policy. Notice that at the maturity date of this policy, age 65 in this case, the total $10,000 face amount would be solely in the form of cash value. At this point no insurance is provided; the death benefits would come entirely from the accumulated cash value. Should you decide to discontinue this form of insurance, the company would refund the cash value that has accumulated over the years for which the policy was held.

It is clear, therefore, that whole-life insurance has two component parts: First, there is the insurance whereby you protect your family from the economic consequences of death. Second, there is the investment portion of the policy, to which you make contributions toward a savings plan in order that cash will be available in the event of death or the maturity of the policy.

There are many good points in favor of holding whole-life insurance policies. However, if you are to purchase life insurance rationally, you must always separate the insurance aspect from whatever investment features the policy may have. It is often difficult to separate these decisions when they are mixed together in such a thoroughly confusing fashion. Once you understand your choices, however, you can make a much more rational analysis by asking two questions: First, is the insurance coverage provided by the policy obtained at costs that are competitive with other forms of insurance? And second, does the performance of the invested cash value provide a rate of return equal to that which could be obtained by a personally managed investment portfolio?

Two questions to ask about cash value insurance

Term Insurance. The other broad category of insurance consists of those products that provide insurance coverage only. These policies are called term insurance. When you purchase a term insurance policy, you are buying only life insurance coverage; there is no investment portion to your policy and thus no cash value accumulations.

Term insurance does not accumulate cash value

There are several variants of the term insurance policy, however. Let us examine one. Suppose you desire to buy constant term insurance coverage equal to $10,000. If you anticipate holding this policy for a long period of time, theoretically the premium that you should pay should be recomputed and adjusted upward each year to reflect the higher probability of death as you get older. It is easy to see why the cost per $1,000 of insurance would be expected to rise throughout your lifetime. This phenomenon reflects the actuarial certainty that a larger percentage of older people die in any given year than younger people.

Insurance companies, however, find it clumsy to recompute premiums each year, primarily because a steadily increasing policy premium often makes the policy much more difficult to sell. Insurance companies will, therefore, often get around this difficulty by collecting equal annual premiums for several years, then adjusting the premium upward as the policy is renewed. These stairstep adjustments mean that you pay more than the pure premium in the first years of the period; while in the later years of the period, the actual premium will be less than the pure premium.

Figure 6.2 illustrates these premium relationships. The solid, increasing line represents the larger and larger premiums that would be required if they were to be recomputed each year to reflect the increasing possibility of your death. The broken line represents the actual premium that would be paid for, say, a 5-year renewable term policy. That is, every 5 years your policy premium would be increased to reflect the higher cost of coverage at an older age. Whereas in the first few years of each 5-year interval your actual premium exceeds the pure premium, in the later portion of each interval the reverse will be true. This kind of coverage is known as 5-year or 10-year, renewable term insurance.

Premiums increase with renewable term insurance

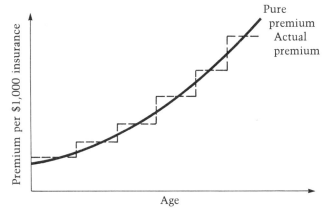

Figure 6.2 Comparison of pure premium versus actual premium: premium paid on a level term policy.

While this type of coverage meets the needs of pure insurance coverage, we must add that it is possible to purchase annual renewable term coverage, in which the premium is increased each year. On this type of policy the actual premium closely approximates the pure premium and, as such, provides a constant amount of insurance coverage at the lowest possible cost. Consequently, annual renewable-term coverage is a much more economical way to buy a constant amount of coverage than 5- or 10-year renewable term.

There is another variant of term coverage: It may be desirable to carry a large amount of life insurance at the beginning of your career and then decrease the insurance coverage as other assets are built up throughout your working life. This insurance coverage can be obtained from a decreasing term policy, which costs less than almost any other insurance alternative.

The advantage of decreasing term insurance

Table 6.2 illustrates the basic mechanics of decreasing term life insurance coverage. Recall again the example of a population of 100,000 American males from which it was expected that 200 would die during their thirtieth year. Thus, the pure premium would be $2 per $1,000 of insurance sold; and should you die that year, your death benefit would be equal to $1,000. However, as you get older, but maintain the $2 premium intact, the death benefit will continually decline—reflecting the fact that as each year passes, it can be predicted that a higher percentage of those 100,000 people will die. Thus, if the annual premium remains the same, the insurance company is required to split up the constant premium income among a larger number of beneficiaries. As a result, the death benefit provided continually declines. In our hypothetical example in Table 6.2, notice that the death benefit has declined to $571 after 4 years—again reflecting the greater probability of death occurring at age 33 as compared to age

You accept declining coverage

Table 6.2 Computation of Death Benefit from Decreasing Term Coverage

Death at age	Total number of insureds	Predicted deaths	Annual premium	Death benefit per 1,000 coverage	
30	100,000	200	$2.00	$\frac{\$200,000}{200}$	= $1,000
31	100,000	250	2.00	$\frac{200,000}{250}$	= 800
32	100,000	300	2.00	$\frac{200,000}{300}$	= 667
33	100,000	350	2.00	$\frac{200,000}{350}$	= 571
⋮	⋮	⋮	⋮	⋮	
65	100,000	10,000	2.00	$\frac{200.000}{10,000}$	= 20

30. Decreasing term insurance, therefore, provides you with the alternative of lower but constant premiums throughout the life of the policy at the expense of continually declining coverage.

What Are Your Insurance Needs?

One of the most useful applications of the present-value tools developed in Chapter 2 is in determining precisely how much insurance protection you require at any given point in your lifetime. Consider the following absurdly simple example:

You decide that in the event of your death your family would require $20,000 annually to cover their normal living expenses. Further, suppose this stream of income is required for only 10 years should you die today, and investment opportunities are available yielding 7 percent per year.

Future requirements determine present needs

Table 6.3 illustrates the simple calculations needed to determine your insurance requirement throughout each of the next 10 years. The left column lists the years for which income must be provided, and the middle column the income requirement of your family based upon your perceptions of their needs and goals. Recalling the present-value concepts of Chapter 2, you can see that the insurance necessary in any given year is simply an amount equal to the fund that will provide an annual annuity equal to the remaining income requirements. It is precisely this present value that is computed and listed in the right column of Table 6.3.

Continuing with the example, suppose that death occurred during year 1. Your family's annual income requirement for the next 10 years is $20,000. You know that if we have a lump sum equal to the present value of the required income stream, your heirs could invest that fund at 7 percent and subsequently make annual withdrawals from that fund to meet the family income needs. Such a fund would have to equal $140,480. That is, if the death benefit provided to your beneficiaries from your life insurance was equal to $140,480, they could make annual withdrawals in the amount of $20,000 per year for 10

Table 6.3 Determination of Life Insurance Requirement

Year of death	Income requirement	Insurance requirement
1	$20,000	$140,480
2	20,000	130,300
3	20,000	119,420
4	20,000	107,780
5	20,000	95,320
6	20,000	82,000
7	20,000	67,740
8	20,000	52,480
9	20,000	36,160
10	20,000	18,700

years. At the end of the tenth year, the initial fund of $140,480 would be depleted.

As you can see from the right column, your insurance requirement is continually decreasing. This is due, of course, to the fact that as each year goes by, there is one less year remaining for which an income flow must be provided. For example, if you were to die at the beginning of the seventh year, only $67,640 of insurance benefits would be necessary to provide for the remaining income flow required by your family. Finally, if your death should occur at the beginning of the tenth year, you need only provide income for one year and your insurance requirement has thus decreased to $18,700.

How your insurance requirements decrease

Perhaps the most common misconception in analyzing life insurance needs is the notion that you have only to add up the annual income requirement needed by your family in the event of your death. This analysis assumes that the death benefit received is simply buried in a tin can, or hidden in the mattress, instead of being invested at some rate of interest.

Remember: your death benefit is earning money

If you assume that the death benefit is invested in the trust department of a bank—thus yielding an annual return—then it is obvious, using present-value techniques, that merely adding up the annual income need would greatly overestimate the actual amount of insurance protection required.

As might be expected, real-life situations are much more complex than this simple example. The income stream may be needed for a period of 40 to 50 years instead of the 10 in the example. On the other hand, Social Security benefits received by the family will reduce the need for insurance protection. Also, your spouse's potential earnings will undoubtedly contribute to the income flow; or she or he may remarry in the event of your early death. Personal and family goals relating to children's careers will certainly have an impact upon the estimated income requirement as the years go by. Further, assets will be building in your estate in some other form such as retirement plans, pension plans, or other investment portfolios—all of which could provide income for the surviving family.

All these factors will considerably complicate the cash flows. Conceptually, however, the problem is precisely as our example illustrates. That is, the estimation of your insurance requirement entails estimating the annual income requirement of your family, then calculating the present value of that required income stream. Such a present-value figure represents the amount of assets that must be provided by insurance coverage.

Use our present-value techniques

A much more complicated and realistic example of life insurance analysis will be presented in the next chapter. It will illustrate, nevertheless, that in the majority of situations, life insurance requirements will decrease throughout a lifetime. This reflects the fact that the length of time for which an income stream must be provided is continually decreasing while there is a simultaneous build-up of assets in other forms. Thus, it is not uncommon to see an insurance requirement disappear entirely well before retirement age. This decreasing pattern of insurance need will greatly influence the type of insurance product you will ultimately purchase.

Your insurance requirements may even disappear

Summary

Use insurance only if the risks are too costly

It is important always to bear in mind the fundamental purpose of insurance. Insurance of any kind is merely a mechanism whereby the cost of catastrophic loss can be spread among many individuals. Those who suffer a catastrophic loss obtain a measure of economic security from the premiums paid by the many who do not experience the loss.

Insurance should be utilized only when it is necessary to provide a hedge against risks that are so large that we are not willing to assume them ourselves.

> Overinsurance—the provision of coverage for small, infrequent, or inconsequential losses—can be expensive. Your particular insurance package should depend ultimately on your willingness and ability to assume risk.

Finally, since life insurance is such a major component of your insurance portfolio, you should attend carefully each decision as to needs and how those needs are to be met. Fundamentally, however, your life insurance requirement is obtained by calculating the present value of the income stream that is to be provided by the insurance. This concept is so central to insurance planning that we will devote the next chapter entirely to the subject.

BIBLIOGRAPHY

A Family Guide to Property and Liability Insurance. New York: Insurance Information Institute, 1973.
    This booklet treats the essentials of both homeowners and automobile insurance.

Kelsey, R. Wilfred, and Daniels, Arthur C. *Handbook of Life Insurance.* New York: New York Institute of Life Insurance, 1966.

This is a nontechnical treatise on the major elements of life insurance, as well as the particulars of various insurance products.

Lang, Larry R., and Gillespie, Thomas H. *Strategy for Personal Finance.* New York: McGraw-Hill Book Co., 1977.

Chapters 13 through 16 provide a concise and nontechnical presentation of the insurance decision. Included is a discussion of risk management in general, as well as an excellent presentation of specific insurance types such as life, health, disability, property, and liability.

CHAPTER 7

Determining Your Life Insurance Needs: How to Have Enough Without Going Broke

After reading this chapter, you will understand:

- How to determine the optimum amount of life insurance you require.
- How to correlate your life insurance program with the asset accumulations in your pension plan in order to reduce drastically the amount of life insurance needed.
- The exact types of life insurance that will fill your needs at the lowest possible cost.

The amount of life insurance you need—even the type of insurance that should be used to satisfy that need—are subject to debate. Precisely what you want to accomplish with your insurance program is a matter of personal choice, not a hard and fast economic law that you must follow. What is scarcely debatable, however, is the fact that the need should be satisfied at the lowest possible economic cost to you. This is true irrespective of how much insurance you require or how you satisfy that requirement.

Satisfy your need at the lowest cost

There are several approaches that could be used in determining your life insurance needs, and they yield quite different results. Neither is right or wrong, and the purpose of the chapter is not to convert you to any one approach, but to show you how each approach attempts to use insurance to meet specific needs. In the final analysis, you must decide which needs must be met and construct your life insurance plan accordingly.

Estate Conservation with Life Insurance

A powerful argument frequently used by the life insurance industry is that you should have sufficient life insurance to pay the estate taxes that will be incurred at the time of your death. This, the argument

The industry wants your estate taxes paid

continues, will keep your hard-won estate intact for your family, rather than having it broken up to pay estate taxes. "Most importantly," the industry argues, "some type of cash-surrender-value policy fills this need most efficiently. No matter when you purchase the policy, the premiums stay level for your lifetime. And since you may need to keep the policy in force for many years until you die, you want to make certain that the premium amount is not increased to higher and higher levels as you get older."

The industry's argument is most persuasive. You have worked all your life to accumulate a large estate, and the last thing you want to do is to leave it to the Internal Revenue Service in the form of estate taxes when you die. Perhaps you should spend a few dollars now for life insurance to keep your estate intact for your family after your death. So your thinking might go. While the logic seems unassailable, there are several weaknesses in the argument that make this approach to determining life insurance needs not only costly but potentially dangerous.

Weaknesses in the estate approach

Weakness No. 1: The Policy Will Never Be Cancelled. Since the insurance is being purchased to pay for future estate taxes, you must assume that the insurance policy will stay in force until death. This means that what you receive at death is the face value of the policy—*not* face value plus the policy's cash-surrender value. It is important that you recognize this fact, since one of the arguments used in favor of cash value insurance is that your ultimate cost is reduced by return of the large accumulations in the cash-surrender value of the policy. Obviously, if you keep the policy in force until you die, you will never surrender it, and hence you will never get back the cash-surrender value.

You must surrender to get cash value

Let us state this principle explicitly: The death benefit of any cash value policy consists of (1) pure insurance coverage, which decreases annually; and (2) the savings portion of the policy (that is, the policy's cash-surrender value). The sum of 1 and 2 will always equal the face value, or death benefit, of the policy.

Your death benefit is always the face value

In other words, you are really purchasing a decreasing term insurance policy plus a "savings account." You may have the savings account any time you wish—either by borrowing against it or by surrendering the policy. But you can never have both the death benefit and the savings account. Table 7.1 illustrates this principle for an actual whole-life policy. You can see, in this example, precisely how the life insurance being purchased decreases annually as the savings portion of the policy increases.

> Once again, the message is that if you buy insurance coverage to pay estate taxes, your cost will never be reduced by a return of cash-surrender values.

Table 7.1 Amounts of Insurance, Cash-surrender Value, and Total Death
Benefit: $100,000 Whole-Life Policy Purchased at Age 42

Age	Insurance +	Cash-surrender value =	Total death benefit
42	$100,000	$ 0	$100,000
43	99,570	430	100,000
44	97,580	2,420	100,000
45	95,555	4,445	100,000
50	84,106	15,894	100,000
60	61,031	38,969	100,000
65	50,503	49,497	100,000
72	37,727	62,273	100,000

In order to compute the exact cost of this type of coverage, suppose Dr. Smith, age 42, buys a $100,000 whole-life policy to provide for
payment of estate taxes in the event of his death. The annual premium for the coverage would be approximately $2,538. This kind of
policy also pays dividends, as we discussed in Chapter 6, and the annual dividend could be used to reduce the premium payment. Remember though, dividends are not guaranteed. They may or may not
be paid, according to projections made by the company.

If our Dr. Smith, now 42, lives to his expected age of 72, and then
dies, Table 7.2 computes the present value of his annual premiums
(net of projected dividends). You will recall that present-value cost is
the measure of the total economic cost of the policy for as long as it is
needed—in this case, until Dr. Smith's expected date of death at age
72. The present-value cost of keeping the policy in force until that
time is $25,890.

If what Dr. Smith really wants to do is buy $100,000 in coverage
and keep it in force until he dies, a much less expensive approach is to
buy a $100,000 annual renewable term (ART) policy. As you will re-
member, the premium for this type of coverage starts out quite low,
and increases over time because of the increasing probability of death.
During the latter years of your life, when probability of death is increasingly high, the premium becomes very large—much larger than
the premium for the whole-life policy.

*The advantage of an
ART policy*

Your insurance agent, in fact, may attempt to convince you of the
merits of whole-life over ART by showing you a graph of the annual
premiums for the two kinds of policies. Table 7.2 makes the same
comparison. And as you can see, the insurance agent is right. There is
no question that ultimately the annual premium for ART coverage
will become significantly higher than the premium for the whole-life
coverage. In spite of this fact, the ART coverage is much less expensive when the costs are computed on a present-value basis, as Table
7.2 shows: only $17,676 as opposed to $25,890. Why? Because the high
premiums on the whole-life coverage are paid in the early years of the
policy, whereas just the opposite is true in the case of the ART product. A perfect illustration of the time value of money.

*An example of the
time value of money*

Table 7.2 Annual Premiums and Total Economic Cost for $100,000 Whole-Life and ART Policies Purchased at Age 42 and Held Until Death at Age 72 (negative numbers shown with minus sign)

		Whole-life policy					Annual renewable term policy			
Year	Age	Premium	− Estimated dividend	= Premium	× Present-value factor[a] at 7%	Present-value of = premium	Premium	× Present-value factor[a] at 7%	= Present-value of premium
1	42	−$2,924	$ 0	−$2,924	1.000	−$2,924	−$ 339	1.000	−$ 339
2	43	− 2,924	269	− 2,655	.935	− 2,482	− 368	.935	− 344
3	44	− 2,924	350	− 2,574	.873	− 2,247	− 403	.873	− 352
4	45	− 2,924	431	− 2,493	.816	− 2,034	− 444	.816	− 362
5	46	− 2,924	512	− 2,412	.763	− 1,840	− 491	.763	− 375
6	47	− 2,924	595	− 2,329	.713	− 1,661	− 541	.713	− 386
7	48	− 2,924	677	− 2,247	.666	− 1,497	− 594	.666	− 396
8	49	− 2,924	759	− 2,165	.623	− 1,349	− 649	.623	− 404
9	50	− 2,924	841	− 2,083	.582	− 1,212	− 704	.582	− 410
10	51	− 2,924	925	− 1,999	.544	− 1,087	− 764	.544	− 416
11	52	− 2,924	1,009	− 1,915	.508	− 973	− 1,043	.508	− 530
12	53	− 2,924	1,094	− 1,830	.475	− 869	− 1,137	.475	− 540
13	54	− 2,924	1,180	− 1,744	.444	− 774	− 1,239	.444	− 550
14	55	− 2,924	1,260	− 1,664	.415	− 691	− 1,350	.415	− 560
15	56	− 2,924	1,352	− 1,572	.388	− 610	− 1,481	.388	− 575
16	57	− 2,924	1,434	− 1,490	.362	− 539	− 1,624	.362	− 588
17	58	− 2,924	1,516	− 1,408	.339	− 477	− 1,780	.339	− 603
18	59	− 2,924	1,600	− 1,324	.317	− 420	− 1,949	.317	− 618
19	60	− 2,924	1,662	− 1,262	.296	− 374	− 2,134	.296	− 632
20	61	− 2,924	1,725	− 1,199	.277	− 332	− 2,334	.277	− 647
21	62	− 2,924	1,790	− 1,134	.258	− 293	− 2,551	.258	− 658
22	63	− 2,924	1,927	− 997	.242	− 241	− 2,787	.242	− 674
23	64	− 2,924	2,011	− 913	.226	− 206	− 3,044	.226	− 688
24	65	− 2,924	2,096	− 828	.211	− 175	− 3,325	.211	− 702
25	66	− 2,924	2,180	− 744	.197	− 147	− 3,634	.197	− 716
26	67	− 2,924	2,264	− 660	.184	− 121	− 3,974	.184	− 731
27	68	− 2,924	2,349	− 575	.172	− 99	− 4,348	.172	− 748
28	69	− 2,924	2,433	− 491	.161	− 79	− 4,751	.161	− 765
29	70	− 2,924	2,517	− 407	.150	− 61	− 5,179	.150	− 777
30	71	− 2,924	2,602	− 322	.141	− 45	− 5,625	.141	− 793
31	72	− 2,924	2,686	− 238	.131	− 31	− 6,085	.131	− 797
				Present value of premiums		$25,890			$17,676

[a]From Appendix A.2.

While the economic cost of the ART policy is significantly lower than the economic cost of the whole-life policy, one difficulty remains: Where do you get the money to pay the horrendously large premium payments on the ART policy in latter years? Table 7.3 shows that a savings account—or better yet, a pension plan—funded with the premium savings realized by buying the ART policy will allow sufficient monies to be withdrawn to make the large premium payments required on the ART policy in its latter years—and still leave you with a substantial nest egg.

Your own cash-surrender-value policy

Incidentally, you have now built your own cash-surrender-value policy—ART coverage plus a savings account. Only this time you get the death benefit *plus* the cash-surrender value if you die—an advantage you do not have with the whole-life policy.

Table 7.3 Effect of Funding a Savings Account or Pension Plan with the Savings Realized with ART Coverage (negative numbers shown with minus sign)

Year	Age	Net premium whole-life	ART premium	Difference (savings)	Accumulations at 5%	7%
1	42	−$2,924	−$ 339	$2,585	$ 2,585	$ 2,585
2	43	− 2,655	− 368	2,287	5,001	5,053
3	44	− 2,574	− 403	2,171	7,422	7,578
4	45	− 2,493	− 444	2,049	9,842	10,157
5	46	− 2,412	− 491	1,921	12,256	12,789
6	47	− 2,329	− 541	1,788	14,656	15,472
7	48	− 2,247	− 594	1,653	17,042	18,208
8	49	− 2,165	− 649	1,516	19,410	20,999
9	50	− 2,083	− 704	1,379	21,760	23,848
10	51	− 1,999	− 764	1,235	24,083	26,752
11	52	− 1,915	− 1,043	872	26,159	29,497
12	53	− 1,830	− 1,137	693	28,160	32,255
13	54	− 1,744	− 1,239	505	30,073	35,018
14	55	− 1,664	− 1,350	314	31,890	37,783
15	56	− 1,572	− 1,481	91	33,576	40,519
16	57	− 1,490	− 1,624	− 134	35,121	43,221
17	58	− 1,408	− 1,780	− 372	36,505	45,874
18	59	− 1,324	− 1,949	− 625	37,705	48,461
19	60	− 1,262	− 2,134	− 872	38,718	50,981
20	61	− 1,199	− 2,334	− 1,135	39,519	53,414
21	62	− 1,134	− 2,551	− 1,417	40,078	55,736
22	63	− 997	− 2,787	− 1,790	40,292	57,848
23	64	− 913	− 3,044	− 2,131	40,176	59,766
24	65	− 828	− 3,325	− 2,497	39,688	61,453
25	66	− 744	− 3,634	− 2,890	38,782	62,865
26	67	− 660	− 3,974	− 3,314	37,407	63,951
27	68	− 575	− 4,348	− 3,773	35,504	64,655
28	69	− 491	− 4,751	− 4,260	33,020	64,921
29	70	− 407	− 5,179	− 4,772	29,899	64,693
30	71	− 322	− 5,625	− 5,303	26,090	63,919
31	72	− 238	− 6,085	− 5,847	21,548	62,546

The insurance industry traditionally will argue that you lack the willpower to build such a savings account on your own.

> Remember, you are responsible for your own financial affairs and are not really dependent on the insurance industry to act as a schoolmaster for you.

The insurance industry will also say that the projected rates of return on your savings account are unrealistic because of income taxes that must be paid on earnings. However, you might note that 7 percent is a conservative estimate of possible return in a tax-deferred pension or profit-sharing plan; and 5 percent could easily be earned in tax-free municipal securities.

Another industry argument is that the term coverage will expire someday—perhaps just before the death benefit is required to pay estate taxes. All such arguments notwithstanding, ART coverage is just

You can pay the ART premiums

as permanent as the cash-value policy. It may be kept intact until age 100 if necessary—which should cover most contingencies adequately.

One final plea by your agent may show the advantage of being able to borrow the cash-surrender value of your whole-life policy. Any such argument defeats the very purpose originally used in selling the insurance: to keep the policy intact to pay estate taxes.

Policy loans reduce your death benefit

> Remember, any outstanding policy loans will be deducted from the death benefit of the policy. If in fact you need the face value of the policy to pay estate taxes, you should not borrow from it.

Simply stated, if the objective in buying insurance is to conserve one's estate, the job can be done least expensively with ART coverage.

Weakness No. 2: Do You Want to Prepay Death Taxes? Another major weakness in the estate-conservation approach to life insurance applies equally to both policies analyzed above. Either policy may be too costly since, when you buy life insurance to pay future estate tax, you are really prepaying your estate tax liability with the life insurance premiums.

Whole-life coverage prepays taxes

The only way you can win when playing this kind of game is if you buy the insurance policy today and die tomorrow—or in the near future. If that should happen, then you have truly transferred the cost of your estate tax liability to the insurance company. If not—if you live for 40 years before you die—then the insurance company is really bearing no risk. You are paying the entire cost, but you are paying to the insurance company instead of to the tax collector. Taxes are onerous enough as it is; there is little merit in prepaying them many years in advance. The longer you can defer the payment of the estate tax liability the better off you are.

Weakness No. 3: Is Your Estate Large Enough to Conserve? A third major weakness in this approach to determining life insurance needs is that it fails to consider whether your estate is sufficiently large or liquid to support your estate intact for heirs if the assets in that estate cannot replace your lost income.

What Dr. Smith (and perhaps you) is really concerned with is not conserving his estate, but protecting his family against the economic consequences of his untimely death. He wants to make certain his wife and children will have a continuing stream of income to meet their daily living costs, to provide education for his children, and to make possible all other objectives the family has been striving for.

Your estate may not require insurance

It really makes little difference where the money comes from to supply these needs. If Dr. Smith has no assets that in turn can supply this stream of income, it is essential that he buy life insurance protection. On the other hand, suppose that over the years he has accumulated a large block of assets in his retirement plan and elsewhere and that block of assets is sufficiently large to meet all the needs of his family, including death taxes. In this case, he quite obviously has no need for life insurance. He already owns enough assets to adequately meet the needs of his family.

Determining Your Life Insurance Requirement: The Income-Stream Approach

The income-stream approach to determining life insurance needs is almost the antithesis of the first method. Instead of attempting to keep the estate intact, the assumption is made, almost explicitly, that the estate will be depleted. Instead of worrying about the block of assets you are going to leave your heirs, your concern is to protect your family against the economic consequence of your untimely death. You want to make certain that your wife and children will have a continuing stream of income available to supply a monthly paycheck—just as if you were still on the scene.

If your concern is protection, not assets

Who decides upon the income needs of your family? You do. We've told you that. Only you are sufficiently familiar with their needs to make a realistic projection of their future financial requirements. Yes, we have mentioned this before, but we stress it again because you are continually besieged by salespeople who want you to buy their insurance policy for any one of a thousand reasons, none of which have anything to do with your real needs. Let's look at the points you should consider in estimating those income needs, using our Dr. Smith as the example.

Determining the Income Requirement. Suppose Dr. Smith, who knows he needs insurance, is trying to estimate how much he needs. He has furnished the following facts:

- Dr. Smith is 42 years of age; his wife is age 40.
- He has two children, a son age 12 and a daughter age 9, and anticipates no additional family members.
- The estimated income his family would need in the event of his death is $20,000 per year, adjusted to reflect a 4 percent annual inflation rate. This required income stream is forecast in column 4 of Table 7.4. The need will decrease when the last of his children leave home.
- Educational aspirations for his children include 4 years of college plus 3 years of dental school for his son, and 4 years of college for his daughter. He wishes to provide $2,000 per year to help defray these educational costs. Note that the income stream shown in column 4 increases during the years these children will be in college.
- In the event of Dr. Smith's death, his survivors will be entitled to Social Security benefits as estimated in column 5 of Table 7.4. This benefit is reduced as one of his children leaves home,

Facts you might furnish

Table 7.4 Estimated Income Needs and Sources

(1) Year	(2) Age	(3) Wife's age	(4) Required income	(5) Estimated Social Security benefit	(6) Wife's salary	(7) Income Deficit and (4 minus 5 and 6)
1	42	40	$20,000	$10,600	0	$ 9,400
2	43	41	20,800	10,600	0	10,200
3	44	42	21,632	10,600	0	11,032
4	45	43	22,497	10,600	0	11,897
5	46	44	23,397	10,600	0	12,797
6	47	45	24,333	10,600	0	13,733
7	48	46	27,306	10,600	0	16,706
8	49	47	28,319	10,600	0	17,719
9	50	48	29,371	10,600	0	18,771
10	51	49	32,466	10,600	0	21,866
11	52	50	33,605	10,600	0	23,005
12	53	51	34,789	7,200	0	27,589
13	54	52	34,021	7,200	0	26,821
14	55	53	24,016	7,200	0	16,816
15	56	54	24,977	0	0	24,977
16	57	55	25,976	0	0	25,976
17	58	56	27,015	0	0	27,015
18	59	57	28,095	0	0	28,095
19	60	58	29,219	0	0	29,219
20	61	59	30,388	0	0	30,388
21	62	60	31,603	0	0	31,603
22	63	61	32,868	0	0	32,868
23	64	62	34,182	3,600	0	30,582
24	65	63	35,550	3,600	0	31,950
25	66	64	36,972	3,600	0	33,372
26	67	65	38,450	3,600	0	34,850
27	68	66	39,988	3,600	0	36,388
28	69	67	41,488	3,600	0	37,988
29	70	68	43,251	3,600	0	39,651
30	71	69	44,982	3,600	0	41,382
31	72	70	46,781	3,600	0	43,181
32	73	71	48,652	3,600	0	45,052
33	74	72	50,598	3,600	0	46,998
34	75	73	52,622	3,600	0	49,022
35		74	42,098	3,600	0	38,498
36		75	43,782	3,600	0	40,182
37		76	45,533	3,600	0	41,933
38		77	47,354	3,600	0	43,754
39		78	49,248	3,600	0	45,648
40		79	51,218	3,600	0	47,618
41		80	53,267	3,600	0	49,667
42		81	55,398	3,600	0	51,798

drops to zero as the second leaves home, and is reinstated after Dr. Smith's widow reaches her own retirement age. While the benefits projected in Table 7.4 have been held constant at their current levels, the law provides that they will actually increase by a factor approximately equal to the cost of living. Holding the Social Security benefits constant adds a large margin of safety to the projections.

- To be on the safe side, Dr. Smith assumes that his wife would not remarry or be employed after his death. This adds another measure of conservatism to the estimates since, in all probability, it would not be her desire to spend the rest of her life doing needlework.
- The deficit between required income and income sources is shown in column 7 of Table 7.4. This deficit must be made up either from assets Dr. Smith owns, or from life insurance.

Determining the Insurance Need. Once the required stream of income has been estimated, the life insurance need may be computed using the following steps:

- Column 4 of Table 7.5 computes the liquid asset portfolio required to supply the income deficit shown in column 7 of Table 7.4. This asset requirement represents the present value, at 7 percent, of the required income annuity. Note that the requirement increases for the first few years (as the children are in college) and then drops rapidly thereafter. This reflects the fact that every year that passes prior to Dr. Smith's death shortens the required income stream by another year.

Assets required diminish

- From this asset requirement can be subtracted the value of Dr. Smith's tax-qualified pension plan, assumed to earn 7 percent per annum. He has $47,160 in the pension plan at the present time, and makes annual contributions of $6,500. The estimated accumulations in the plan are shown in column 5 of Table 7.5.

The tax-qualified pension plan

- Dr. Smith and his wife will also accumulate other assets, as shown in column 6 of Table 7.5. It is assumed, however, that these assets will provide little liquidity or income to his family in the event of his death, and therefore the projections made in column 7 of Table 7.5 assume that only 25 percent of other assets will be available to meet the income needs of his family.
- In spite of this assumed illiquidity, Dr. Smith's death tax liability must still be computed on the total value of his assets (pension plan excepted). The estimated death tax liability has been projected in column 8 of Table 7.5.
- Dr. Smith's insurance needs are shown in column 9 of Table 7.5. In year 1, he needs $247,454, which will meet the estimated income requirements of his family when combined with the modest retirement fund he will have at that point. Note that by year 10 of the program the need has declined to $224,920, but by the end of year 19 the need for life insurance has been completely eliminated. Note also that after a slow start the life insurance requirement declines annually—first, because every year Dr. Smith lives, the income stream his family needs is, of course, one year shorter; and second, because the rapidly increasing value in the pension fund portfolio further reduces the need for life insurance protection.

An exact way to determine insurance needs

Table 7.5 Estimation of Life Insurance Requirement

(1) Year	(2) Age	(3) Wife's age	(4) Asset requirement	(5) Pension plan accumulations	(6) Other assets	(7) Liquid value of other assets (25% of column 6)	(8) Estimated federal estate tax	(9) Estimated life insurance requirements (4 minus 5 and 7, plus 8)
1	42	40	$309,614	$ 47,160	$ 60,000	$ 15,000	$ 0	$247,454
2	43	41	321,229	56,961	64,200	16,050	0	248,218
3	44	42	332,801	67,448	68,694	17,174	0	248,179
4	45	43	344,292	78,670	73,503	18,376	0	247,246
5	46	44	366,363	90,677	78,648	19,662	0	256,024
6	47	45	378,316	103,524	84,153	21,038	0	253,754
7	48	46	390,103	117,271	90,044	22,511	0	250,321
8	49	47	399,535	131,980	96,347	24,087	0	243,468
9	50	48	408,543	147,718	103,091	25,773	0	235,052
10	51	49	417,718	164,559	110,308	27,577	0	224,920
11	52	50	422,854	182,578	118,029	29,507	0	210,769
12	53	51	427,838	201,858	126,291	31,573	0	194,407
13	54	52	428,267	222,488	135,131	33,783	0	171,996
14	55	53	429,547	244,562	144,591	36,148	0	148,837
15	56	54	441,622	268,182	154,712	38,678	0	134,762
16	57	55	445,810	293,455	165,542	41,385	0	110,970
17	58	56	449,222	320,496	177,130	44,282	0	84,444
18	59	57	451,762	349,431	189,529	47,382	0	54,949
19	60	58	453,323	380,391	202,796	50,699	0	22,233
20	61	59	453,792	413,519	216,992	54,248	0	0
21	62	60	453,042	448,965	232,181	58,045	0	0
22	63	61	450,939	486,893	248,434	62,108	0	0
23	64	62	447,336	527,475	265,824	66,456	0	0
24	65	63	445,927	514,608	284,432	71,108	0	0
25	66	64	442,956	500,841	304,342	76,086	0	0
26	67	65	438,255	486,110	325,646	81,411	0	0
27	68	66	431,643	470,348	348,441	87,110	0	0
28	69	67	422,923	453,482	372,832	93,208	0	0
29	70	68	411,880	435,436	398,930	99,733	0	0
30	71	69	398,285	416,127	426,855	106,714	0	0
31	72	70	381,886	395,466	456,735	114,184	6,896	0
32	73	71	362,415	373,358	488,707	122,177	16,420	0
33	74	72	339,578	349,704	522,916	130,729	23,301	0
34	75	73	313,061	324,393	559,520	139,880	28,895	0
35		74	282,522	297,310	598,687	149,672	34,934	0
36		75	261,105	268,332	640,595	160,149	41,453	0
37		76	236,388	237,326	685,437	171,359	48,491	0
38		77	208,067	204,149	733,417	183,354	56,089	0
39		78	175,814	168,649	784,756	196,189	64,291	0
40		79	139,278	130,665	839,689	209,922	73,146	0
41		80	98,076	90,021	898,467	224,617	82,706	0
42		81	51,798	46,533	961,360	240,340	93,026	0

The advantage of conservative assumptions

In many ways the insurance requirement computed in Table 7.5 seems absurdly high. In part, this is due to the conservative assumptions that have been made: Living costs skyrocket but are not offset by increases in Social Security benefits or earnings on assets. Mrs. Smith never returns to work. She is estimated to live for a substantial period beyond her normal mortality. And yet, these all add a margin of safety to the estimates. The question is, can Dr. Smith afford to buy the required coverage?

How to Fund the Insurance Need

> The life insurance requirement of most professionals—
> constructed in a way to meet all the obligations of the family
> including payment of estate taxes—is initially much higher
> than is generally realized. From that point, however, it de-
> creases rather rapidly and frequently disappears entirely
> within a few years.

This is the most significant aspect of Table 7.5. Because of this
fact, such a program can frequently be funded with decreasing term
life insurance at a substantial cost savings.

By cost savings, we mean the total dollars expended on the insurance program—not the cost per dollar of coverage. Decreasing term
coverage costs almost the same per dollar of coverage as an ART policy. But since you are paying only for what you need instead of for
unneeded level coverage, the total dollar outlay can be significantly
less than any other type of insurance.

*Compare decreasing
term coverage with
ART*

Given the life insurance estimate outlined in Table 7.5, we can
determine the optimum way to satisfy that life insurance need. Table
7.6 illustrates. To be conservative, it recommends acquisition of
$275,000 in annual renewable term coverage.

Table 7.6 Recommended Insurance Coverage with a $275,000 ART Policy

Year	Age	Insurance requirement	Recommended coverage	Annual premium	×	Present-value factor at 7%[a]	=	Present value of premium
1	42	$247,454	$275,000	$ 932		1.000		$ 932
2	43	248,218	275,000	1,012		.935		946
3	44	248,179	275,000	1,108		.873		967
4	45	247,246	275,000	1,221		.816		996
5	46	256,024	275,000	1,350		.763		1,030
6	47	253,754	275,000	1,488		.713		1,061
7	48	250,321	275,000	1,634		.666		1,088
8	49	243,468	275,000	1,785		.623		1,112
9	50	235,052	275,000	1,936		.582		1,127
10	51	224,920	275,000	2,101		.544		1,143
11	52	210,769	247,500	1,865		.508		947
12	53	194,407	220,000	1,865		.475		886
13	54	171,996	192,500	1,865		.444		828
14	55	148,837	165,000	1,865		.415		774
15	56	134,762	137,500	1,865		.388		724
16	57	110,970	110,000	1,865		.362		675
17	58	84,444	82,500	1,865		.339		632
18	59	54,949	55,000	1,865		.317		591
19	60	22,333	27,500	1,865		.296		552
20	61	0	0	Total present-value cost:				$17,011

[a]From Appendix A.2.

*The need for
overinsurance early on*

Why ART insurance when the insurance requirement is decreasing over time? This type of coverage is needed initially to get past the fairly constant insurance requirement for the first ten years of the analysis. If everything goes as projected, the premium on the ART coverage will be held constant after the tenth year, turning the policy into decreasing term protection. In the meantime, the ART coverage removes much of the risk of error from the estimation process since it can be held at a constant level for as long as future conditions might warrant. The exact cost of providing the required coverage is also shown in Table 7.6.

It is significant to note that by using this kind of coverage, Dr. Smith was able to buy (initially) almost three times as much coverage as he purchased with a much higher premium in Table 7.2. As an extra bonus, the total economic cost for this adequate amount of coverage is far less than the $100,000 in whole-life (and even the $100,000 in ART) purchased in Table 7.2.

*The cost of whole-life
coverage*

Providing the same amount of coverage with whole-life would be much more costly, as Table 7.7 shows. While future premiums will be substantially reduced by dividends, the initial premium is prohibitively costly. And while the present-value cost of the coverage is substantially reduced by return of the cash-surrender value (this time you *will* cancel the policy when the need expires), the initial premium outlay is so high as to be very difficult—if not impossible—to meet.

Table 7.7 Meeting the Required Insurance Coverage with a $260,000 Whole-Life Policy

Year	Age	Premium	–	Projected dividend	=	Estimated net premium	×	Present-value factor at 7%[a]	=	Present value of premium
1	42	$7,602		$ 0		$7,602		1.000		$ 7,602
2	43	7,602		699		6,903		.935		6,451
3	44	7,602		910		6,692		.873		5,842
4	45	7,602		1,121		6,481		.816		5,289
5	46	7,602		1,331		6,271		.763		4,785
6	47	7,602		1,547		6,055		.713		4,317
7	48	7,602		1,760		5,842		.666		3,891
8	49	7,602		1,973		5,629		.623		3,507
9	50	7,602		2,187		5,415		.582		3,152
10	51	7,602		2,405		5,197		.544		2,827
11	52	7,602		2,623		4,979		.508		2,529
12	53	7,602		2,844		4,758		.475		2,260
13	54	7,602		3,068		4,534		.444		2,013
14	55	7,602		3,292		4,310		.415		1,789
15	56	7,602		3,515		4,087		.388		1,586
16	57	7,602		3,728		3,874		.362		1,402
17	58	7,602		3,942		3,660		.339		1,241
18	59	7,602		4,160		3,442		.317		1,091
19	60	7,602		4,321		3,281		.296		971

Present value of premiums: −$62,545

Present value of cash-surrender value $107,299 × .296: + 31,760

− 30,785

[a] From Appendix A.2.

These computations clearly show one of the great disadvantages to whole-life insurance coverage versus term: In spite of the fact that the economic cost of the whole-life policy may be reduced by dividends and cash-surrender values, the initial cash outlay is so high that it prevents the average individual from buying sufficient life insurance coverage to meet his needs adequately. Most professionals with several children require significantly more coverage than what can be afforded, even when all available income is allocated to purchase of whole-life coverage. By allocating even fewer of those dollars to term coverage, however, he can greatly increase the amounts of coverage, realistically providing for the needs of his family.

Part of the reason the whole-life coverage is more costly is because the coverage is constant for the entire period, rather than decreasing to match more closely the actual requirement. No matter how you make the comparison, however, the least costly way to meet this insurance need is with a term (either ART or decreasing) product. This was true when you bought insurance to keep your estate intact, and it is true as well when you buy insurance using this second approach.

Term insurance: the least costly

Caveat. The insurance industry has an eloquent plea against the arguments just presented. It is that you lack the will power to fund your own investment program or pension plan as was illustrated in Table 7.5. As we have pointed out before, this is something you, not your insurance agent, should decide, but by all means be realistic in your intentions. You can see that while this type of program has the potential to save many thousands of dollars, it also has the potential to bring disaster upon your family.

But you must maintain your pension plan

> If, for any reason, contributions will not be made *faithfully* to the pension plan, it is certain you will die without sufficient assets to provide for your family. Do not let that happen.

Summary

Whether you buy insurance to pay estate taxes, or to meet the financial needs (including estate taxes) of surviving family members, is a decision that you must personally make. But no matter what the insurance need, and no matter how you make the comparison, in almost every case the insurance requirement can be met with term life coverage instead of whole-life insurance at significant cost savings.

Perhaps the most compelling reason for the use of term insurance is that unlike whole-life, it allows you to buy sufficient coverage to provide realistically for your family in event of your death. The high annual premiums associated with whole-life coverage make large insurance purchases almost prohibitively expensive—one reason most individuals are significantly underinsured.

Rates vary greatly for term insurance

As a final word of warning when you shop for term insurance, remember that premium rates on whole-life coverage are comparable from company to company but the same does not hold true for term coverage. It is entirely possible for premium rates between any two companies to vary as much as 100 percent. For this reason, you should shop carefully and compare prices judiciously to be absolutely certain that you are getting the term coverage you need at the lowest price possible.

How to find the company you need

The large mutual insurance companies—the companies that advertise in magazines and on television—will seldom be your lowest-cost term providers. In fact, you may never have heard of most of the companies writing term protection at the lowest rates. This is understandable, since the premiums (and hence commissions) on these products are so low that no one will ever knock on your door to sell you the coverage. There are, nevertheless, many fine companies that specialize in writing term insurance. They are sound, well managed, financially secure insurers—they just choose to do business in a different way. You can find such companies through an independent insurance broker. Also, *Consumer Reports* has published an excellent guide to insurance that identifies many of these companies. If you have doubts, check with your state insurance commissioner as to the financial soundness of a particular company.

BIBLIOGRAPHY

Best's Flitcraft Compend. Morristown, N.J.: A. M. Best Co.

This annual publication is a company-by-company comparison of the life insurance products (and their cost) of all life insurance companies doing business in the United States. It is generally available in the reference departments of public and university libraries.

Cohen, Jerome B., *Decade of Decision.* New York: New York Institute of Life Insurance, 1974.

This is an excellent source for assistance in determining life insurance needs, and the best products to fill those needs.

Consumer Reports, January–March 1974.

A three-part series of articles comparing the insurance policies of over 100 major insurance companies.

PART Three

Investing as a Professional: Low-Return to High Fliers, and How to Use Them

CHAPTER 8

The Conventional Investments:
If You Opt for Safety

After reading this chapter, you will understand:

- The different types of risk to which you are subjected as you invest.
- How corporate and government securities can fit into your investment game plan.
- Techniques that can be used in evaluating and selecting securities for your portfolio.

This chapter will not help you get rich quick. If you want to be a high flier, you must wait until you get to Chapter 9. Since most of the investments discussed in this chapter will be characterized as having considerably less risk than those discussed in Chapter 9, the prospect for high returns will be much diminished, as will the prospect for catastrophic losses.

> With conventional investments, your money is likely to be much safer, but you do not have the prospects of making a quick buck.

The Nature of Investment Securities

As an investor, you have essentially two alternatives: First, you can lend your money to some borrower for a prescribed rate of return, called interest. Or, second, you can use your money to purchase partial or complete ownership in some income-producing asset. You may receive that income on a year-by-year basis; or the income may come all at once at sometime in the future because the asset appreciates in

Investments: debt and equity

value; or you may get some combination of the two. The income on this kind of investment is never contractual, as is the interest you are entitled to as you lend to a borrower. While the range of potential investments is very broad, each can ultimately be characterized as either a lending investment or an ownership investment.

The Lending Investment. If you should opt for the lending type of investment, there are indeed several advantages. Such investments are characterized by a legal binding document, called an *indenture.* The provisions in the indenture specify precisely the contractual obligations of the borrower. As a lender of funds—the purchase of a bond being the most common form of lending—you will have a claim to periodic interest payments. The contract, in which you are a partner, will have a specified lifetime or maturity. Upon maturity your principal dollar amount will be returned to you upon demand.

Bonds provide a more certain cash flow

You can see the advantages of this kind of investment: First, the rate of return is specified and as a result, lending investments are called fixed-income securities. Second, the borrower is legally obligated to make your interest payments prior to distribution of funds for any other purpose, including taxes. As a result, if the business is profitable at all you are assured of receiving your interest return. Finally, should the borrower default or go out of business, you will have first claim on assets. That is, if the company is dissolved, you will receive all, or at least a portion, of your principal as the assets are liquidated. Thus, the risk of holding debt securities is normally much lower than the risk associated with an equity, or ownership, investment.

Lending investments are fixed-income securities

The Ownership Investment. Alternatively, there are several vehicles by which a person can purchase complete or partial ownership of an asset. Examples include:

- Partial ownership of a corporation by purchasing shares of its common stock.
- Buying mutual fund shares.
- Ownership of small business, such as a retail store or a trucking operation.
- Ownership of real estate or other forms of income property.
- Ownership of investment objects such as gold, silver, art objects.

Regardless of the particular kind of investment, your return is solely determined by the income-generating capacity of the asset. If the asset does well, you may share in large returns as its partial or complete owner. If it does poorly, however, your returns will be small or possibly negative. The major advantage of an ownership investment is clear. While you are not guaranteed a specific rate of return, neither is there an upper limit on the potential return. You have the possibility, therefore, of very large gains.

An equity investment may bring large returns

On the other hand, the danger always exists that the rate of return might be very small, zero—or even negative. If a large enough loss is incurred, the entire investment might be jeopardized. Ownership investments are thus characterized as having a larger risk because of the uncertain nature of the return.

The risk is greater

With these guidelines in mind, let us examine a few of the specific types of risk to which you will be exposed in both debt and equity investments.

Elements of Risk

Risk is defined as the variability in an investment's expected return. The greater that variability, the greater is the investment risk. Since bonds yield a return in the form of a contractual interest payment, the variability in that interest payment is almost always much less than the variability associated with the dividends from a share of common stock. As a result, fixed-income investments are normally characterized as having much less risk than ownership investments.

Risk: variability in expected returns

As compensation for accepting higher levels of risk, investors expect—in fact demand—higher rates of return.

> The higher level of risk associated with a given investment, the more an investor must be compensated in order to make him willing to make that investment. This risk-return relationship is fundamental to financial decisions and is illustrated in Figure 8.1.

Points along the risk-return line of Figure 8.1 are labeled to illustrate where typical conventional investments might fall. There is little, if any, risk on a United States Treasury obligation, for instance, and they have a low rate of return. Investments further out on the line will provide a higher rate of return, but only as compensation for exposing you to higher levels of risk.

Higher risks expect higher returns

As Figure 8.1 shows, part of the return from any investment is a pure rate of interest or, theoretically, compensation for a nearly riskless investment. This pure rate of interest is part of the return whether you invest in treasury bills, corporate bonds, common stocks, or a speculative real estate transaction. The rate fluctuates from time to time as conditions affecting the availability of money affect its "price"—that is, the interest rate demanded in the marketplace.

Pure rate of interest is part of your return

Table 8.1 shows how this riskless rate has fluctuated in recent years. You should also note that as the riskless rate has changed the rates demanded on risky securities have fluctuated by roughly corresponding amounts.

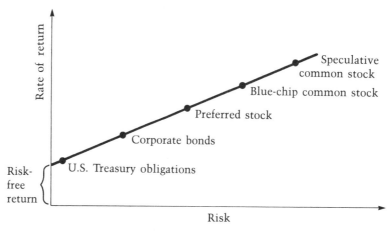

Figure 8.1 Investment risk-return trade-off.

If the yield on treasury bills represents the risk-free rate, Aaa bonds have earned a risk premium of between 2 and 3 percent over the past three years. The risk premium on Baa bonds has ranged between 3 and 5 percent through the same period. Since we sometimes tend to think of bond investment as something for widows and orphans—that is, without risk—the very size of these risk premiums should give you pause.

Check risks on offers of high returns

If you invest in a common stock that has the potential to earn 12 percent, you are being compensated 6 percent above the pure rate of interest for the riskiness of that security. Similarly, if someone offers you a potential 20 percent rate of return in a real estate transaction, you can only assume that the investment is significantly more risky than a U.S. Treasury bill.

No one is willing to pay a risk premium 14 percent above the pure return on your capital unless the investment is very risky. It may be a sobering thought to step back and ask yourself: "Where is the risk in this investment?"

Table 8.1 Selected Interest Rates, 1975–78[a]

Time		3-month treasury bills	Corporate bonds	
			Aaa	Baa
	1975	5.80%	8.83%	10.61%
	1976	4.98	8.43	9.75
	1977	5.27	8.02	8.97
January	1978	6.44	8.41	9.17
February	1978	6.45	8.47	9.20
March	1978	6.29	8.47	9.22
April	1978	6.34	8.56	9.32

[a]From *Federal Reserve Bulletin*, May 1978.

Each investor must decide the risk to which he is willing to be exposed. People who enjoy taking risk—and can afford it—can profitably invest in securities that fall far up the risk-return scale. On the other hand, conservative investors who are unwilling to accept high levels of risk should select investment at the low end of the scale.

Your entire investment portfolio need not be grouped about a single risk-return point. It may be that your retirement fund or pension plan should be invested in low-risk, low-yielding securities, because safety is the primary investment goal of those particular funds. Meanwhile, speculative funds could be invested simultaneously in vehicles far up the risk-return scale in the hopes of reaping large returns. Regardless of the investment, there are several types of risk to which you will be exposed, and a discussion of each follows.

You may vary the risks you take

Business Risk. Business risk results from fluctuations in the production and sales activity within any given firm or industry. Such fluctuations can result from any number of reasons. Shortages of raw materials, recessionary pressures on the entire economy, or a temporary slack in demand might occasion a significant decrease in production and sales. During such slack periods, firms will find their earnings seriously impaired, and thus the return (dividends) to ownership investors must be adversely affected. If the problem becomes serious enough, even interest payments to bondholders may be endangered. Thus, firms with high business risk will be those firms that are characterized by widely fluctuating sales; whereas firms with low business risk can be expected to maintain relatively stable sales patterns over time. The common stock of firms producing fad items, or firms whose sales are directly tied to overall economic activity, will have considerable business risk. Firms such as the public utilities, however, will have a much lower level of business risk because of the stability of earnings in that industry.

Business risk reflects fluctuation

Risk of Financial Collapse. There is always the risk that a firm, for any number of reasons, will simply go bankrupt. Bankruptcy can result from bad management practices as well as bad financial practices. The present difficulties of some of the large American cities indicate that the risk of financial collapse can occur in the public sector as well as in the world of private business. In evaluating investments, you should look carefully at the possibility of total financial collapse on the part of the issuing firm. Should such a collapse occur, the firm will likely default on all interest and possibly even the principal payments of a bond contract, and the probability is small that you would recover any percentage of your common stock investment.

What financial collapse can mean

Market Price Risk. The market price of a given investment may decline or increase because of changing investor preferences. Such unpredictable changes in preferences cause market price risk. In general, the more specialized an investment, or the more limited its resale market, the higher will be the market price risk. Such specialized in-

Market prices reflect change in investor preferences

vestment objects as coins, stamps, gold, wine, or art pieces can have considerable market risks simply because investment decisions are based upon whims, tastes, and emotions—and thus wide, unpredictable swings can occur in their market price.

Interest Rate Risk. Lending investments, such as a bond, are particularly vulnerable to interest rate risk. Suppose, for example, that you purchase a $1,000 bond for $1,000 and that it promises to yield an 8 percent annual rate of return. The interest flow on such a bond would be $80 a year until its maturity, say 5 years. Suppose further, however, that shortly after you purchase the bond, the market rate of interest on bonds of that type increases from 8 percent to 10 percent.

Volatile interest rates affect your investment

It would now be possible for someone to buy a $1,000 bond for $1,000 that would yield a $100 interest stream throughout the life of the bond. Suppose that you need to sell your bond prior to its maturity; so you offer it for sale to me. With a similar alternative yielding 10 percent, there is no way I will purchase your bond yielding 8 percent unless you discount the price of your bond to a point that it will yield me 10 percent.

You can see, then, that after spending $1,000 to purchase the bond, you can sell it shortly thereafter only by discounting its market price significantly below $1,000. This discounting is necessary because the general level of interest rates in the financial markets has risen. There is nothing the least bit theoretical about this concept, and in fact, you can use your knowledge of present value to determine the market price of the bond. The value of your bond will be exactly equal to the present value, at 10 percent, of the income flow provided by the interest payments, plus the present value of the $1,000 maturity payment. This value, computed in Table 8.2, is equal to $924.18 and represents the new market price of your bond. It is clear that you have suffered a loss of $75.72 on your purchase simply because the market rate of interest went from 8 percent to 10 percent.

What discounting means

> To summarize: When the general level of market interest rates rise, the price of outstanding bonds will fall. Conversely, when interest rates fall, the price of existing bonds will rise. This potential variability in bond values, occasioned by varying interest rates, is called interest rate risk.

Long-term bonds: a greater interest rate risk

Should a rise in the prevailing interest rates occur, interest rate risk creates two potential loss situations. First, there is the loss in the reduced market price, and second, there is the loss of interest income. If you decide to hold the investment until maturity you will avoid the loss from reduced market price, but you will have received a lower

Table 8.2 Computation of a Bond Price

Future interest payments = $80 per year for 5 years
Future principal repayment = $1,000, 5 years from now

$$\text{Present Value} = \$80_5 \times 3.791^a = \$303.28$$
$$+ \ 1000_5 \times .621^b = \ \underline{621.00}$$

Present Value — Total Value $= \underline{\$924.28}$

[a]From Appendix A.4, at 10%.
[b]From Appendix A.2, at 10%.

interest yield than you could have earned on a newer bond with the same risk. As you might expect, interest rate risk is greater on long-term bonds.

Government Securities

Now that we have examined different types of risk, you will be able to recognize them in the sampling of conventional investment vehicles we will discuss in this section.

U.S. Treasury Obligations. Without question, the safest financial instruments in the world are the debt instruments issued by the United States Treasury. Never has a treasury obligation suffered a default. They are backed by the full faith and credit of the United States Government, including its powers to tax and print money. Treasury investments, then, present a sound and secure investment alternative.

Treasury obligations are safe

Treasury obligations are categorized according to maturity. Short-term obligations, ranging in maturities from 30 to 180 days, are called treasury bills. Treasury bills are frequently auctioned by the government and the rate of return comes in the form of discounting from their redemption value at maturity. For example, suppose you purchase a $100,000 treasury bill for $97,012.86 that is to mature in 6 months. Such an investment would provide no interest flow throughout the life of the bill, but the discounted price would yield a 6 percent rate of return based on the maturity value of $100,000.

Treasury bills are short-term

Those securities of intermediate maturity, ranging from 1 to 5 years, are termed treasury notes. Long-term treasury obligations, ranging from 5 years to sometimes 30 and 40 years, are called treasury bonds. In contrast to treasury bills, the rate of return on a treasury bond investment is in the form of interest payments throughout the life of the bond. It is then redeemed at its face value upon maturity.

Treasury notes have a longer maturity

Long-term Treasury bonds pay interest

When safety and security is of primary importance to your investment strategy, treasury obligations provide an excellent investment medium. Further, there is always a large secondary market available in treasury securities; you can buy or sell treasury obligations at any point before their maturity. Their instantaneous marketability make treasury obligations an attractive investment medium for short-term idle funds.

The secondary market for treasury securities

*No income tax
liability is an
advantage*

State and Local Bonds. Most states and municipalities also issue long-term bonds, and many of these present excellent opportunities to invest in high-yield, low-risk securities. Further, state and local bonds have the added attractiveness of complete exemption from federal income tax liability on the interest earned. The interest earned may also be exempt from state taxation if the bond was issued in the same state where the investor resides. That is, state and local bonds issued by or in the state of Wisconsin are exempt not only from federal income taxation, but also from Wisconsin state income taxation as well.

As taxable income increases and the professional moves into higher tax brackets, the attractiveness of state and local bond investments increases. The relative investment attractiveness of similarly rated corporate bonds, as compared to state and local bonds, will be a function of the interest yield on the bonds as well as the marginal tax bracket of the investor. The following simple formula illustrates this relationship:

$$ym = yc\,(1 - t),$$

where

*Compare with
corporate bonds*

ym = yield on municipal bond,
yc = yield on corporate bond,
t = marginal tax bracket of the investor.

This equation can be used to calculate the rate of return needed on a municipal bond in order for it to be competitive with the higher yielding, but taxable, corporate bond. For example, suppose you have a corporate bond that promises to yield an 8 percent annual rate of return. If your marginal tax bracket is 35 percent, what is the annual yield on a state or local bond that would be equivalent to the proposed 8 percent corporate security? Substituting the appropriate values into the above equation, Table 8.3 shows that a municipal bond yielding 5.2 percent is equivalent, on an after-tax basis, to the corporate bond yielding 8 percent.

*Select your issuing
municipality with
care*

Because of the tax-exempt nature of municipal securities, these bonds become an attractive investment medium. However, the continuing financial trouble of New York City, which at one time almost resulted in its default on its bonded indebtedness, shows you that not all municipal bonds are free of default risk. You should analyze carefully, therefore, the issuing municipality and rely heavily on the rating agencies to assist in determining the investment quality of a particular municipal issue. We shall say more about these ratings since they can be extremely helpful to the investor.

Table 8.3 Computation of an Acceptable Municipal Bond Yield

Available yield on corporate bonds	= 8 percent
Your tax rate	= 35 percent
ym = 8 percent $(1 - .35)$	
= 5.2 percent	

Corporate Securities

Because of the sleepiness of the stock market in recent years, many investors have turned to all kinds of scuzzy alternatives to the more traditional investments. Much of our experience points to the fact that the turn should never have been made. The corporate securities—bonds, preferred stocks, common stocks—are still the principal investment medium in the United States and should be an important part of your portfolio. Consider their merits carefully as you read the following section.

Corporate Bonds. Corporate bonds provide another alternative for prudent and judicious investment. The risk associated with a particular corporate bond is largely a function of the financial integrity of the issuing corporation. The large, blue-chip companies provide investment alternatives that are nearly as risk free as U.S. Treasury securities. On the other hand, there is significant default risk associated with the bonds issued by smaller, struggling, unproven companies. To assist the investor in assessing the risk characteristics of particular security issues, investment agencies provide a complete analysis of, and assign an investment rating to, corporate bond issues.

Blue chips are almost risk free

Standard and Poor's and Moody's are the two largest of these rating agencies. Before ratings are assigned, professional analysts are employed to closely scrutinize all aspects of a corporation with outstanding indebtedness. Factors related to the demand for the corporate product, management policies and objectives, manufacturing technology, capital structure, past profitability, and all other factors that ultimately define the financial stability of the company, are carefully analyzed prior to the assignment of the rating. These ratings can be of great assistance to the investor in assessing the relative risks of corporate bonds.

Rely on investment ratings

Securities possessing the most sterling investment characteristics are given a Moody's Aaa rating. Rating categories then decline to Aa, A, Baa, and so on, as various investment characteristics deteriorate. Baa is normally the lowest rating carried by a bond that is still considered to be of investment grade. Similar ratings are assigned by Standard and Poor's. It is possible, however, to find securities that are rated Bbb, Bb, Ba, and lower. The investor should realize that investment in these securities is increasingly speculative as the rating drops and thus carries with it a significant degree of default risk.

Corporate bonds can be categorized into two broad groups: those that are secured, and those that are unsecured. A bond is said to be secured if there is a particular asset, a piece of property, or a claim to income, that is employed to pledge the payment of interest and principal of the bond issue. Mortgage bonds, for example, are secured by a lien on all or part of the property of the issuer. Should the issuer default, the mortgage bondholders would have first claim upon the proceeds from the sale of the property against which they hold the lien.

The two categories of corporate bonds

Collateral trust bonds and equipment trust certificates are additional examples of secured bonds. For the first type, the borrower

Secured bonds: assets are pledged

places the securities of other companies into a trust and then issues securities against the trust. With the second type, which are used extensively by railroads and airlines, title to the equipment is held by a trustee until the company has redeemed the bonds. Thus, the lenders can immediately take possession of the equipment and resell it if the borrower goes into bankruptcy.

Unsecured bonds are called debentures. Since debentures are not secured by a particular piece of property, they are covered only by the general credit of the borrowing corporation. Should the borrowing company default, debenture holders are simply general creditors of the corporation. As such, they will receive proceeds from bankruptcy prior to the equity holders, but their claim is subordinate to claims of the secured debt. Subordinated debentures are debt instruments of an even lower priority. Bonds that are unsecured of course, possess a higher degree of risk than do the secured bonds. As a result, they normally yield a higher rate of return to the investor. The particular provisions of a bond issue are set forth in a document called the indenture. Only upon an examination of the bond indenture will an investor find the particular attributes of any given issue, and thus it should be carefully studied before a bond is purchased.

Debentures are unsecured bonds

Study the bond indenture to judge risks

Preferred Stock. Preferred stock is a hybrid security, possessing some of the attributes of debt and some of the attributes of equity. It is like common stock in that it is included in the equity section of the balance sheet; payments to stockholders are called dividends; and dividends are not deductible by the corporation for tax purposes. Further, the payment of dividends is not legally required, and the issue has no fixed maturity.

Preferred stock: safer than some, riskier than others

However, preferred stock is also like debt in that the dividends have a fixed rate, and the holders are entitled to no more than the amount they paid into the firm in case of liquidation. Preferred dividends are always paid prior to any distribution to common stock shareholders; therefore, they are viewed as less risky than common stocks. On the other hand, firms do not have a legal obligation to pay preferred dividends as they do interest payments. As a result, preferred stock is considered somewhat more risky than bonds. Preferred stock, then, tends to fill a gap by providing an investment alternative between bonds and common stock.

What claims the common stockholder has

Common Stock. The residual owners of a firm are called common stockholders. As such, they have claim on the earnings of the firm, but only after all creditors have been paid. In case of bankruptcy and liquidation of the firm, the common stockholders are entitled to the net assets remaining *after* the claims of all other creditors have been satisfied. Common stockholders have voting rights that they exercise to elect the board of directors to act as their agents in running the firm.

Ultimately the financial returns to common stockholders depend upon the profits that generate from the firm's normal business operations. In fact, the ultimate value of the stock is determined by the level of earnings realized per share outstanding. Earnings per share, therefore, are of great interest to the potential common stock investor. Since there are a number of parameters—many of which are unpredictable—that greatly affect the earnings per share, investment in common stock is thought to be much more risky than investment in the other kinds of securities we have discussed.

Where the value of common stock lies

On the other hand, investments in the common stock issued by sound corporations, operating in fundamental and profitable markets, provide the promise of excellent long-term yields. Historically, stock market investments in the blue-chip companies, which have been held for a number of years, have often resulted in rates of returns close to 10 percent per year.

Long-term yields may be high

Mutual Funds. Mutual funds provide an indirect way of investing in the stock market. Instead of purchasing common stocks directly, investors entrust their money to a manager by purchasing shares of a mutual fund. The proceeds from the sale of mutual fund shares are then invested by the professional manager in the stock and bond markets. If the fund investments fare well, the mutual fund shares will perform equally well. Of course, a custodial fee must be paid to the advisor of the fund.

How mutual fund shares earn returns

Each person buying shares in the mutual fund has a pro-rata interest in each of the fund's investments. That is, a person who owns 1 percent of the fund's stock in turn owns 1 percent of all the stocks in the portfolio of the fund. If those stocks increase in value, the fund's net asset value will rise, and the fund shares will increase in value proportionately.

Mutual funds are required by law to state their investment objectives. Should you decide to purchase shares in a mutual fund, your first step is to select a fund that has objectives consistent with your own investment goals. The investment objectives of mutual funds can be broadly categorized into three areas: funds that stress income, funds that attempt to provide both income and growth, and funds that stress only growth.

Mutual funds must state objectives

Income funds typically hold a large share of their portfolio in bonds and preferred stocks. The portion of their portfolio that is comprised of common stocks is usually diversified across more than a hundred different companies. As such, these funds seek to minimize risk and conserve principal. Income funds are conservatively managed; safety of the fund and stability of income are the primary investment objectives.

Three kinds of mutual funds

The income-and-growth funds take a middle-of-the-road approach in selecting between returns and risks. As their name implies, these funds seek income from capital gains and dividends, but they do not invest in high-risk situations where principal may be lost.

They range from safety to high risk

Growth funds, some of which are also called "go go" funds, seek to maximize their returns by assuming very high risk. Of course, these funds may also seek income from dividends, but that is a secondary concern to their major objective of growth through capital gains.

In addition, there are many specialized types of mutual funds such as bond funds, preferred stock funds, and money market funds. These specialized funds provide a wide range of alternatives for the investor whose goals are consistent with large, professionally run, common stock portfolios.

The performance of mutual funds has, in recent years, been disappointing when compared with expectations—and in many cases, when compared with the popular market averages. Over the long haul, however, performance has been superior to investments in savings accounts, bonds, or other fixed-income securities.

Criteria for Investment Evaluation

We have touched briefly on only a few of the most common conventional investment alternatives. The particular alternative that appeals to you will be a function of your personal and family investment objectives. But, whatever the investment, it ought to be analyzed in light of a few specific criteria. If you make your decisions with these in mind, your investment decisions will be more intelligent and profitable. They are:

- Exposure to risk.
- Rate of return.
- Maturity.
- Flexibility.
- Tax features.
- General availability of the investment.

Use criteria to assess total risk exposure

Every investment entails various combinations of risk. That is, in every investment there will be some business risk, some risk of financial collapse, some market price risk, and some interest rate risk. The total risk exposure varies widely among different investments. You should attempt—at least qualitatively—to assess these risks in order to ensure that the proposed investment is suitable and consistent with your objectives.

Return should be consistent with riskiness

You should then determine if the expected annual rate of return is consistent with the riskiness of the particular investment. Remember that the return not only includes the investment's annual income, such as interest or dividends, but it also includes any loss or gain resulting from a change in the market price of the security.

For investments such as common stock the change in market price may be the major source of the return. For others, such as savings accounts, there is no change in the market price and thus the entire yield comes from the annual interest payments.

Investment maturities are normally grouped into three categories: short-term, which includes maturities of one year or less; intermediate term, maturities ranging from one to five years; and long-term, comprising maturities fives years and above. Normally, investments of longer maturities are viewed as somewhat more risky than those of shorter maturities, and thus should yield a higher annual rate of return. You should be careful to match the maturity of your investments with your projected income needs and goals and with the possible need for liquidity.

Investment flexibility refers to the ease with which an investment can be converted into cash. If an investment can be sold quickly, it is said to have a high degree of flexibility. Treasury bills are very flexible, while real estate investments are normally inflexible. Further, you should examine the possibility of price concessions, transactions cost, and penalties that might be incurred should the investment need to be liquidated quickly. The higher such costs are, the less flexible the investment will be.

Understand the degree of flexibility

Of no small concern are the tax features of a given investment. Some returns are taxable and some are not, depending on the nature of the investment. And even where returns are taxable, some portions of the returns may be taxed at different rates. Of course, the higher the investor's marginal tax rate, the more important tax considerations become.

Know the tax features of your investment

Finally, with respect to general availability, you must ask such questions as where can the investment be obtained, who sells or handles the investment, and how is the investment to be purchased? These procedural details will greatly influence the efficiency with which you can manage your investment portfolio when it includes these types of conventional investment alternatives.

Summary

The advantages associated with conventional investments—generally corporate and government securities—are clear and irrefutable. Such investments are easily identifiable; they are always available in whatever quantities desired; they can be purchased at very low cost (in terms of brokerage fees and commissions) compared to other types of investments; they have excellent liquidity; and portfolios may be constructed to structure risk according to the precise desires of the investor.

Your personal approach to the securities markets should vary according to your interest and the amount of time you have to devote to the subject. If your interest is great, nothing stands in the way of you becoming a knowledgeable expert, profitably managing your own securities portfolio.

If your time or interest do not permit personal involvement there are many investment advisors who specialize in managing individual portfolios. You should—through financial publications, friends, or even the grapevine—seek out such advisors. Talk to them. Compare their track records. Discuss investment philosophy. Ask about fees. Make your selection carefully.

Excellent books are available too

As a final word, recognize there have been volumes written on the types of investments discussed in this chapter—these few pages by no means exhaust the subject. Of all the topics covered in this book, none gives you a greater opportunity for additional reading. To the extent you are interested, therefore, we urge you to examine the books listed in the bibliography at the end of this chapter. We have described briefly the content and scope of each in order to help you select those of greatest interest to you.

BIBLIOGRAPHY

Engle, Louis. *How to Buy Stocks.* 5th ed. New York: Bantam Books, 1971.
A basic, easy-to-understand book that covers all aspects of common stock investments.

Malkiel, Barton G. *A Random Walk Down Wall Street.* New York: Norton, 1973.
A witty, enjoyable introduction to the stock market. It is extremely readable and gives sound advice on the pro's and con's of common stock investing.

Investment Companies. New York: Wiesenberger Financial Services.
This is an annual publication that reports detailed information on the performance for every available mutual fund.

Sauvain, Harry C. *Investment Management.* 4th ed. Englewood Cliffs, N.J.: Prentice-Hall, 1973.
This textbook has served for years as a basic source of sound and practical advice on investment management. It is easily read and understood, and contains a great deal of practical, down-to-earth advice. It is an excellent summary for the whole spectrum of investment alternatives.

Smith, Adam. *The Money Game.* New York: Random House, 1967.
Perhaps the most uncomfortably (at times) revealing look at investments and investors that has ever been written. While the book is great fun and the tone tongue-in-cheek, the truths are profound. Don't fail to read it.

Tax-Exempt Bonds and the Investor. New York: Securities Industry Association.

This booklet outlines simply the features of municipal bond investment alternatives. A copy may be obtained by writing to the association, 120 Broadway, New York 10005.

Understanding Preferred Stocks & Bonds. New York: New York Stock Exchange.

This booklet describes the nature and the provisions of these fixed-income securities. A copy may be obtained by writing to the New York Stock Exchange, 11 Wall Street, New York 10005.

CHAPTER 9

The High Fliers:
If You Thrive on Risk

After reading this chapter you will understand:

- The relationship between the riskiness of an investment and the return that the investment promises to earn.
- How to identify the high-risk investments.
- Analytical methods that will help you decide which high-risk investments you want to include in your portfolio.

When it comes to selecting an investment, more seems better than less: an investment promising a higher return frequently appears more desirable than an investment yielding a lower return. As a result, the investor often selects the high-return investment, only to be an amazed investor a few years later when the investment turns out to be eminently unprofitable.

More is not always better than less

The fact that the investment turned out badly does not mean that the promoter was a fraud or a crook (although we will not rule out that possibility); it simply means that the investment was a risky one. Because an investment is risky does not mean it should be avoided—indeed the contrary may be true. Many investors thrive on risk and will always opt for a more risky investment over a less risky one.

But many investors thrive on risk

Adam Smith pointed this out in his amazingly accurate profile of investors, *The Money Game* (New York: Random House, 1967). In that book, in an anecdotal sort of way, he showed that return is the farthest thing from the minds of many investors. For them, the most important thing is playing a game to which a high degree of risk is attached.

Go in with your eyes open

Assuming you are not a game player but are still willing to accept a high degree of risk for the possibility of a high potential reward, you should be absolutely certain that you have analyzed the investment thoroughly enough to understand the risks involved, and thus that you are going into the investment with your eyes wide open.

> Make certain that investment in high-risk ventures follows a careful analysis of hard numbers, not a rule of thumb, a feeling in the pit of your stomach, a hot tip, or the advice of someone who will make a profit by selling you the project.

A Further Look at Risk

Risk always involves variability

What is risk? While we looked at risk briefly in the last chapter, it deserves more detail here as we discuss highly risky investments. Frequently, when you hear the word risk, it has the connotation of something bad, or at the very least irresponsible—something to be avoided at all costs. It will be a good deal more useful, however, if you can think of risk in terms other than negative. Risk is really the chance, or probability, that the outcome of an investment will be other than what you expect it to be. This means the return could be either higher or lower than your expectation—not just lower.

Figure 9.1 depicts risk in this sense. If you are considering investing in a blue-chip common stock, or better yet, a portfolio of blue-chip common stocks, you could reasonably expect the rate of return, over the long haul, to be approximately 12 percent per annum. This 12 percent will not happen with perfect certainty; instead, there is some chance of earning more than 12 percent—perhaps a good deal more. There is also the probability, however, that you could earn a good deal less than 12 percent, and perhaps even sustain a loss on the portfolio. That variance from the expectation, shown in Figure 9.1, is the riskiness of an investment.

What you sacrifice to eliminate risk

Note that the riskiness of a high-quality corporate bond is substantially less than the common stock, but the potential return is also much less. You can completely eliminate the type of risk shown here by investing in a passbook savings account, but note what is being sacrificed in terms of potential return.

How much risk to assume is up to you

Just how much risk you want to assume is strictly up to you. Some investors are not willing to accept any risk, and hence must invest in projects that have relatively low rates of return; that is, projects that give them no compensation for risk. Other investors are willing to accept very high risks—even when there is only a small probability of earning a large return. Such investors may or may not understand the probability of earning a very low return, or sustaining a loss. Then again they may realize it and still be willing to take the risk. You decide what kind of investor you are—a risk taker or risk averter—but do not forget the relationship between risk and return.

Perhaps the most important thing to keep in mind when you evaluate high-risk investments is that you must expect and demand a very high rate of return to compensate you for the risks you are assuming. How high? Well, consider the return that could be earned in alternative investments.

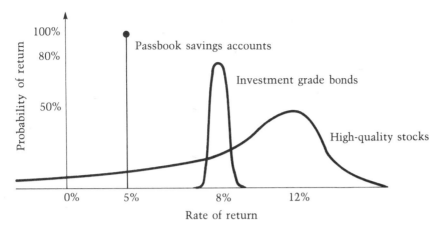

Figure 9.1 Depiction of investment risk.

What rate, for example, should you expect to earn in an extremely risky real estate venture? Undoubtedly the sales representative who is promoting the project would have you believe the returns will come with perfect certainty. Remember, however, that this cannot be the case or he would not be offering you a 25 percent return. What should you expect then? Certainly not 5 percent, since you can obtain 5 percent in a passbook savings account, with no risk. Not 6 percent, since you can invest in time certificates of deposit or government securities and earn that rate. While 9 percent may seem reasonable, you can invest in high-quality corporate bonds and earn 9 percent with only slightly more risk than you would be subject to in government securities. While 12 percent may seem adequate, you could probably select a portfolio of high-quality common stocks by throwing darts at a page of the *Wall Street Journal,* then lock the stocks up for an extended period of time and earn 12 percent on the portfolio.

Examine the alternatives

To earn still higher returns, you begin to enter the venture capital category. Be aware of this increased risk and, above all, demand a rate of return that you feel is reasonable compensation given the nature of your investment. Nevertheless, it would be absurd to accept anything less than 12 to 15 percent. Twenty or 25 percent may be a more realistic demand, and many intelligent investors expect a rate of return as high as 50 or 60 percent on venture capital investments. At such rates it is a certainty that almost all investments you analyze will be rejected as not filling the bill. That should not disappoint you, however, it should only serve to prove there are not many investments around that return the kind of yields salespeople sometimes promise.

How high the rates can go

Identification of High-Risk Investments

While it is impossible to identify all the characteristics of high-risk investments, most share a few elements in common. Promised high return is a sure-fire tip-off. Venture capital investments—that is, money to build a shopping center or start a new business—always fall into the high-risk category. Limited-partnership syndications, tax shel-

The tip-off is promised high return

ters, and oil or gas explorations are all very risky. They all deserve either a cold shoulder or, if you are willing to bear the risk, a very careful analysis before committing funds.

Venture Capital Projects. Investments that promise a high return are almost always a means of raising venture capital—that is, capital to start a new business, build a shopping center, buy an apartment house, buy equipment for lease to another business, or to finance some other new enterprise. The organizational form of the investment may be varied: It might be sale of stock in a new corporation. More frequently it will be a syndication, a group of investors who have banded together in a limited partnership. Less frequently it will be yourself, buying or building an apartment house, or starting a small business unassociated with your professional practice.

Venture capital funds new enterprises

In all such cases you owe it to yourself to analyze carefully the venture you are committing your money to. You understand your own profession well, but you probably know little about the business you are considering investing money in. What is the potential of the business? What is the quality of the management operating the venture? Is there really a market for the goods or service that will be sold? What would vacancies in an apartment building or shopping center do to the profitability of the asset? Are the payments you will receive from the investment guaranteed or merely blue-sky guesses?

Ask hard questions about the new venture

In all likelihood, you will not get very positive answers to any of those questions, which means you do not know enough about the investment to commit your money to it. If that is the case, be honest with yourself and consider less risky investments that will provide more certain—although lower—returns; you will probably end up with a far larger asset portfolio than you will achieve by taking fliers in high-risk, little-understood ventures.

Investments that Defer Income Until Later Periods. It is a commonly held belief—among investors and promoters of investments both— that it is advantageous for people in high-income brackets to defer investment returns until later years. By so doing returns can be taken as capital gains rather than as current income. You understand enough about the time value of money by now, however, to recognize the possible fallacy of this argument.

Apply the present-value concept

> Unless the potential capital gain is enormous, trading current income for capital gains may be the worst possible course of action you could select.

Table 9.1 shows two investments, one of which returns $10,000 per year (before taxes) for 30 years; the other $600,000 at the end of year 30. Assume the first is taxed at the highest marginal rate, 70 percent; and the second at a capital gains rate of only 25 percent. Further, assume you want to earn 15 percent in either project.

Table 9.1 The Value of Current Income Versus Capital Gains

Value of investment A		Value of investment B	
Annual income per year for 30 years	$10,000	Income from sale of asset	$600,000
Tax at 70%	$ 7,000	Tax at 25%	150,000
Net income	$ 3,000	Net income	$450,000
Present value $= \$3{,}000_{30} \times 6.566^{a}$ $= \$19{,}698$		Present value $= \$450{,}000_{30} \times .015^{b}$ $= \$6{,}750$	

[a]From Appendix A.4, at 15%.
[b]From Appendix A.2, at 15%.

As this striking example shows, investment B, although returning twice the income of A and being taxed at a much lower rate than A, is worth only a fraction of A. This is because dollars received at distant points in the future have little value today. Obviously, there are worse things in life than taxes.

As a general rule, in order for capital gains to be profitable, the value of the asset you are investing in must grow at a rate higher than your desired rate of return. This is true in spite of the fact that capital gains are taxed at one half your normal tax rate.

In order to profit from capital gains

Tax Shelters. Many of the high-risk investments that have been promoted in recent years have played down the income-earning potential of the asset in favor of promised reduction of federal and state income tax liability. Such a promise has great appeal to individuals in high income tax brackets, where one of the great pains of life is the large bill that must be paid to the tax collector each year. Furthermore, the schemes look almost foolproof.

Tax reductions seem attractive

Since the promoters are not promising income, it is unnecessary to make accurate projections of what the investment will earn. In fact, it may appear more desirable if it is possible to predict high expenses with almost perfect certainty.

Table 9.2 shows such an investment—in this case, an apartment house—that falls in the tax-shelter category. The cash flows projected by the offering circular proudly outline the fact that the operating expenses of the venture exceed the income in every year, giving the individual investor in this project a nice deduction against personal income. The objective of Table 9.2, which is an exact reproduction of an analysis performed in the offering circular, is the column on "Net Deductions," showing the tax reduction the investor will receive each year.

What the promoters present

As a matter of fact, the analysis is correct as far as it goes. The expenses can be predicted with relative certainty, and the fact that these expenses are incurred will reduce the income tax liability of the investor. Unfortunately, the analysis is somewhat incomplete since all it shows is the tax reduction that will result from the investment, not the cash flow the project will produce for the investor. Among the least important lines on an income statement is tax liability. The most important line is the number of dollars left over after all expenses connected with an investment, including income taxes, have been paid.

But the cash flow does not appear

Table 9.2 Analysis of Benefits for a Tax-sheltered Limited Partnership: The Way They Told It

	Tax analysis					
Year	Depreciation	Interest	Expenses of operations	Rental income	Net deductions	Taxes saved in 50% bracket
1	$3,669	$3,064	$5,244	$4,023	$7,954	$3,977
2	2,969	5,637	4,966	7,654	5,918	2,959
3	2,478	5,966	4,930	8,526	4,484	2,424
4	2,120	5,596	5,030	8,856	3,890	1,945
5	2,082	4,217	5,026	9,137	2,188	1,094

It may be useful, then, to complete the analysis started in Table 9.2 by computing the net cash flows this particular investment will earn for the investor. Table 9.3 sheds a slightly different light on the investment: Instead of returning an economic benefit of $3,977 in the first year, the net cash flow is actually negative. That is, the persons who bought this apartment house would have been better off had they never made the investment—in spite of the fact that their income tax liability decreased. The investment returns modest benefits from the

Net cash flows show the facts

Table 9.3 Analysis of Benefits for a Tax-sheltered Limited Partnership: The Way It Really Is

	Computation of annual net cash flows				
	Year 1	Year 2	Year 3	Year 4	Year 5
Rental income	$ 4,023	$ 7,654	$ 8,526	$ 8,856	$ 9,137
Less: Depreciation	−3,669	−2,969	−2,478	−2,120	−2,062
Interest	−3,064	−5,637	−5,966	−5,596	−4,217
Operating expenses	−5,244	−4,966	−4,930	−5,030	−5,026
Taxable income	$−7,954	$−5,918	$−4,848	$−3,890	$−2,168
Tax savings	3,977	2,959	2,424	1,945	1,084
Net income	−3,977	−2,959	−2,424	−1,945	−1,084
Plus: Depreciation	3,669	2,969	2,478	2,120	2,062
Net cash flow	$ − 308	10	$ 54	$ 175	$ 978

second year on, but nowhere near the large benefits shown in the promoter's analysis.

It is sometimes confusing to see your tax bill go down and then turn around and say that it is not beneficial. If so, pretend for a moment the first analysis is correct. If it is, you should go back to the promoters and plead that they raise the management fee they charge for administering the project. For every dollar they increase their fees, your tax liability will go down 50 cents. Likewise, it would be well for you to go to the bank and invite the banker to double the rate of interest on the loan financing the project. This will increase your interest expense and in turn cut your tax liability even more.

If your tax breaks alone are your criteria

If these steps appeal to you, an even more appealing argument should be to tell the promoters of the investment that they are ruining the whole thing by giving you the rental income. Why not invite them to keep the income, while you take only the expenses? This would further increase the tax benefit you get from the investment.

The arguments, of course, are all absurd. Payment of any cash expense cuts taxes, but leaves you with fewer dollars than you would have if you did not have the expense. Income is better than expense any day—even if it causes income tax liability to increase.

Income is always better than expense

The ultimate tax shelter is an investment so stupendously profitable that it increases your income tax bracket dramatically. While your tax liability will increase, you will also have more dollars after the payment of that tax liability.

Table 9.4 illustrates this principle, assuming that you are able to find an investment that (horror of horrors) yields a huge return, and is

Table 9.4 Your Total Income Picture with Two Types of Investments: A Tax Shelter versus an Income-earning Asset

	With a tax shelter			With a profitable investment		
	Business income +	Tax shelter income =	Total income	Business income +	Investment income =	Total income
Gross income	$100,000	$ 4,023	$104,023	$100,000	$ 4,023	$104,023
Cash operating expenses	−50,000	−8,309	−58,309	−50,000	0	−50,000
Depreciation expenses	0	−3,668	−3,669	0	0	0
Taxable income	$ 50,000	$−7,954	42,046	$ 50,000	$ 4,023	$ 54,023
Tax	−25,000	3,977	−21,023	−25,000	−2,816	−27,816
Net income	$ 25,000	−3,977	$ 21,023	$ 25,000	$ 1,207	$ 26,207
Plus depreciation	0	3,669	3,669	0	0	0
Net cash flow	$ 25,000	$ −308	$ 24,692	$ 25,000	$ 1,207	$ 26,207

taxed at a marginal tax rate of 50 percent. Note that while your tax bill has increased by $6,793 over what it was with the tax shelter, you also have more dollars on the bottom line. That is a real tax shelter.

It's worth paying the taxes

Much of the sales appeal of the tax shelter has, incidentally, been removed by passage of the tax reform act of 1976, and these changes will be outlined in detail in the last section of this chapter.

Evaluation of High-Risk Investments

Find the present value of the income stream

Unless you are willing to accept an investment as a blind speculation, you should be cautious to analyze the cash flows using the techniques shown in Chapter 2 and in the preceding section. This is easy in the case of some investments, because the returns can be predicted with a high degree of certainty. For example, suppose you are interested in buying a real estate contract that calls for 12 annual payments of $3,000 each, on which you want to earn 12 percent. You can determine the exact value of those benefits by finding the present value of the income stream. As the table shows, $18,582 is the maximum that could be paid for the asset and still earn 12 percent.

Table 9.5 Valuation of a Real Estate Contract

Annual income: $3,000 for 12 years
Desired return: 12%
Present value of benefits = $3,000_{12} \times 6.194^a = $18,582$

^{a}From Appendix A.4, at 12%.

Check the offering prospectus

Precisely the same techniques should be used in evaluating any other investment. The offering circulars of some investments will make this a relatively easy task by presenting carefully constructed estimates of cash flows. You will, of course, want to question the accuracy of the estimates, but at least you have a starting point. The offering material for other investments will contain no estimates of potential returns, but will assume (explicitly or impiicitly) that "this must be a good investment or we would not be offering it to you."

Question promises that may be blind speculation

Promoters of such investments frequently tell you that it is impossible to predict future returns. Instead they show you the success of projects they have promoted in the past and assure you that "equal or better performance should be achieved on this one." These kinds of promises rank as blind speculation, and you have to question seriously the desirability of committing yourself to such projects.

A Format for Analysis and Evaluation of Cash Flows. In order to value an asset, it is necessary first to construct series of cash flow estimates showing the potential future returns of the asset. The format that should be used is outlined in Chapter 3, as well as in the preceding section. At all times, remember that you want to know the value of the total asset, not the value of your equity position in the asset. If you can purchase the asset at the value you determine as viable, the returns provided by the asset will be sufficient to pay the interest on debt used to finance the investment, plus pay you your desired return on equity.

A somewhat simplified example shows how these cash flows should be constructed and valued. Suppose you have the opportunity to buy a fourplex apartment that has the following characteristics.

Follow this example of an income property appraisal

- The seller is asking $80,000 for the apartment; $10,000 of the cost is attributable to land.
- The annual rentals will be $12,000 per year.
- Operating expenses (exclusive of depreciation) are estimated to be 20 percent of the annual rental income, or $2,400.
- The asset will be depreciated on a 25-year life—for purposes of simplicity, on a straight-line basis. After subtracting the value of the land, this will give depreciation of $70,000 ÷ 25, or $2,800 per year.
- Even though the asset is depreciated for tax purposes, you estimate it will actually increase in value at the rate of 6 percent per annum. You anticipate holding the apartment building for 5 years; thus, your estimated future sales price is $107,000.
- The project will be financed with an 80 percent loan (20 percent down payment) at an interest rate of 9 percent.
- Your tax bracket is 50 percent for regular income and 25 percent for capital gains.
- The annual cash flows for the investment are shown in Tables 9.6 and 9.7.

You can see the annual cash flows

Table 9.6 Analysis of Cash Flows for Apartment Building

	Year				
Cash flows	1	2	3	4	5
Rental income	$12,000	$12,000	$12,000	$12,000	$12,000
Expenses	−2,400	−2,400	−2,400	−2,400	−2,400
Depreciation	−2,800	−2,800	−2,800	−2,800	−2,800
Taxable income	$ 6,800	$ 6,800	$ 6,800	$ 6,800	$ 6,800
Tax (50%)	−3,400	−3,400	−3,400	−3,400	−3,400
Net income	$ 3,400	$ 3,400	$ 3,400	$ 3,400	$ 3,400
Plus depreciation	2,800	2,800	2,800	2,800	2,800
Net cash flow	$ 6,200	$ 6,200	$ 6,200	$ 6,200	$ 6,200

Note that interest expense was not included in the cash flows computed in Tables 9.6 and 9.7. This is because the interest rate at which cash flows are valued should include the costs of all capital used in financing the apartment building. Thus, discounting the cash

Table 9.7 Additional Fifth Year Cash Flows: Apartment Building

Sale of building	$107,000
Depreciated value ($80,000 less depreciation)	−66,000
Gain on sale	$ 41,000
Tax (25%)	−10,250
Net income	30,750
Plus nontaxed portion of the sale (basis)	66,000
Net cash flow	$ 96,750

flows will automatically deduct the interest expense on the loan. Deduction of interest in the cash flow analysis would, therefore, result in double counting of that expense.

Finding the appropriate discount rate

Formulation of a Discount Rate. The appropriate discount rate is the cost of the money borrowed to finance the project, plus your desired return on equity (you could call that the cost of equity capital). Since the apartment building will be financed with an 80 percent loan at 9 percent, the after-tax cost of debt capital to you will be the cost of the interest, less the tax saving of the interest expense.

In your tax bracket, that is

$$\text{cost of debt} = 9\% - (9\% \times 50\%)$$
$$= 9\% (1 - 50\%)$$
$$= 4.5\%$$

The return you want on equity capital is up to you, but should be a function of the riskiness of the investment. As we have suggested, it ought to be higher than 10 or 15 percent, since these returns can be earned in more conventional investments with substantially less risk. Assuming 20 percent would be an adequate return, the overall discount rate can be computed as shown below:

Table 9.8 Computation of an Appropriate Discount Rate

Source of capital	Percent of capital used	×	Necessary return (%)	=	"Weighted" return (%)
Debt	80	×	4.5	=	3.6
Equity	20	×	20.0	=	4.0
			Total required return	=	7.6, or 8

Leverage increases risk

Note that the required return has been substantially lowered because of the great amount of leverage provided by the borrowed funds. Remember, this leverage greatly increases the risk of an otherwise risky investment. You may want to increase the required rate even further to help compensate for this double dose of risk. Many knowledgeable investors demand equity returns as high as 50 or 60 percent to help offset the effects of the extremely high risk involved in ventures of this type.

Valuation of the Investment. With the cash flows computed in tables 9.6 and 9.7, and the discount rate computed in Table 9.8, you can now value the investment to determine its economic viability by finding the present values of each of the cash flows at the required rate, as shown below:

Table 9.9 Valuation of the Project at 8 Percent

Present value of annual cash flow	$ 6,200$_5$ × 3.993[a] = $24,757
Present value of sale of building	$96,750$_5$ × .681[b] = $\underline{65,887}$
Value of investment	$\underline{\underline{\$90,644}}$

[a]From Appendix A.4, at 8%.
[b]From Appendix A.2, at 8%.

The last step in the analytical process is, of course, to compare the value with the seller's asking price. In this case, the value exceeds the asking price of $80,000, and thus your required return will be exceeded if all your estimates are correct—if everything turns out as expected. Those are big ifs—remember, there is no such thing as a risk-free investment.

Compare value with asking price

A Look at the Real World

Unfortunately, solving textbook examples is a slightly different problem from analyzing the prospectuses or offering circulars that are presented to you. Frequently it takes a trained analyst many hours to ferret out useful information from the mass of useless data presented in such documents; data must be reconstructed or recast in such a way as to make it usable. Still more frequently, there is no usable data at all, making a realistic analysis of the project completely impossible.

As a matter of practical fact, whether you have analyzable data or not is relatively unimportant, since most investments of the type discussed in this chapter are unprofitable. The authors have analyzed hundreds of limited-partnership investments and ranked them according to potential profitability. Table 9.10 shows the investments analyzed in that study, a total of 454 projects. In 307 prospectuses, or 68 percent of the projects studied, the promoters made estimates, ranging between 7 and 63 percent, of rates of return. In no case were the rates of return adjusted for time. That is, the estimates failed to take into consideration the present-value analysis we have been talking about in

A judgment about venture capital investments

Promoters may not adjust rates for time

this book; they relied instead on a simple percentage change in asset value. You know by now that if an asset doubles in value in 10 years, it has not earned a rate of return of 100 percent—or even 10 percent per annum. The prospectuses failed, in every case, to recognize that elementary fact.

Table 9.10 Limited-Partnership Offerings Included in the Study

Type of enterprise	Number examined	Number at 7%	Profitable at 10%
Cattle feeding or livestock breeding and herd development	21	1	0
Oil drilling or natural resource development	68	3	0
Miscellaneous, including motion pictures	83	7	0
Raw land speculation	56	28	0
Recreation (hotels, motels, condominiums, etc.)	62	12	0
Apartment complexes	85	28	1
Shopping centers, malls, and other commercial development	52	11	0
Farming, ranching (including orchards and forestry)	27	0	0
Totals	454	90	1

Limited partnership offerings analyzed

In order to assess more accurately the economic desirability of the investments examined in Table 9.10, the cash flow forecasts made in the prospectuses were subjected to present-value analysis using the same format outlined in the previous section. The discount rate in every case was 7 percent—the return that could have been earned on U.S. Treasury bills during the period of this study—and a rate considerably lower than should be demanded on such venture capital investments.

Except for obvious errors (such as showing a tax reduction resulting from payment of a cash expense as an economic benefit), the financial data contained in the prospectuses were assumed to be accurate; they were used in turn to construct the cash flows used in the present-value analyses of the projects. Since these data were prepared by the promoters of the investments they could safely be assumed to represent optimistic projections of performance, in no way biased against the venture.

Investments with no value above purchase price

The results of the present-value analyses are summarized in Table 9.10. As you can see, at a 7 percent rate, only 90 of the 454 investments, or 19.8 percent of those studied, had a value in excess of the purchase price. At 10 percent, only one of the projects was viable. Clearly, there were several messages hidden in this study that have a direct bearing on the unsophisticated investor. First, investments of this type are so difficult to analyze that it is almost impossible for anyone but the most highly trained analyst to decipher them. For the uninitiated to make a realistic estimate of value is virtually an impossible task. In fact, the best lesson we might learn is the prudence of acquiring a thorough, unbiased, professional financial analysis of any proposed investment before we commit our funds.

What you can learn

Second, the vast majority of these investments are unprofitable: only 20 percent would have been viable investments at 7 percent, and only one investment would have been viable at 10 percent. This means that finding the good investment is almost like searching for a diamond in a dung hill. Certainly a distasteful task, and perhaps a hopeless search.

Third, to rely on the profitability estimates made by the promoters is asking for certain disaster. If you want to make risky investments, that is up to you. But you should obtain and analyze the data required to invest intelligently.

Tax Shelters and the Tax Reform Act of 1976

On October 4, 1976, the President signed the Tax Reform Act of 1976. One of the primary objectives of this act was to eliminate loopholes in the tax law that significantly cut the tax liability of high-income individuals. It is interesting to read the notes of the Congressional Committee as changes in the law were discussed. Obviously the committee fully understood that most of the tax shelters have no economic viability. While such shelters result in a reduction of income tax liability to the owner, they give him no economic return and hence both the owner and the government have been losing because of them. In a real sense the changes in the law do you a favor by making it more difficult for you to get involved in these investments.

Some traditional tax loopholes eliminated

But the law has done you a favor

Since this is not a textbook on taxation, we cannot detail all the changes in the law, but the following sections outline briefly how tax shelters will be treated in the future.

Prepaid Interest. Prior to 1976, it was possible to prepay interest on a loan, taking the interest expense as a legitimate tax deduction. While this was a perfectly legal maneuver, it was never very smart. If you must pay interest, the worst way to pay it is in advance—that merely increases the effective rate of interest on the loan. The present law puts interest on an accrual basis, meaning that interest can only be paid as the expense is incurred, rather than in advance.

Prepaid interest is not allowed

Investment Interest. Formerly it was possible to deduct an unlimited amount of interest on a loan used to finance an investment. Under the present law the amount of such interest is limited to $10,000 plus the net investment income.

Total interest deduction limited

Points. Points, or the discount on a loan, are still deductible, but only on a loan for your principal residence. Points on a business loan or a loan used to finance an investment are no longer immediately deduct-

How points must be amortized

ible. Under the present law they must be capitalized and amortized (or written off) over the life of the investment.

Partnership Deductions. The limited partnership has been a principal vehicle for tax shelters, but the law has now placed significant restrictions on deduction of partnership expenses, except those in real estate.

Deductions limited to capital at risk

Deductions are limited to capital at risk. This means, for example, that depreciation can be taken on an asset only to the extent that you own the asset. If the asset is financed 90 percent with debt, and the lender has no recourse to you personally, you may not deduct depreciation, or any other expense, for the portion of the asset financed with debt.

Organizational and selling expenses may not be deducted in the initial period, as has been the case, but must be capitalized and amortized over at least a 60-month period of time. This prevents the immediate deduction of these costs, formerly touted as a major benefit of purchase.

Retroactive allocations prohibited

Retroactive allocations are now prohibited. An example of a retroactive allocation would be allocating losses incurred by the owner of an apartment building to a new partner. This is now prohibited—the loss must remain with the old partner. Special allocations of expenses have also been prohibited, and expenses must now be divided in the same ratio as income. Under the former law it was possible for one partner (in a low-income tax bracket) to take all of the income of a venture, allocating all of the depreciation expense to a second partner (in a high income tax bracket). This too is now prohibited.

Farm Deductions. Farms, ranches, orchards, poultry operations, and cattle feeding ventures have been favorite tax shelters. This was primarily because of high expenses; they were incurred on the front end and could be passed through to high-income partners. For example, all the feed required to bring a herd of yearling steers to maturity could be purchased on the front end and expensed at that time.

Farm deductions must be on an accrual method

The present law has taken a special look at farm deductions with the result that all costs of seed, feed, fertilizer, and so on, must be deducted in the year of use—that is, on an accrual method—instead of at the time the commodities are purchased. All poultry costs must be capitalized and amortized over the life of the poultry, rather than being expensed in the year of purchase. All costs associated with developing orchards, groves, forests, and vineyards, must be capitalized and depreciated rather than being expensed in the year of purchase.

Special Real Estate Rules. While real estate came out of the reform act unscathed as far as the capital-at-risk rule is concerned, Congress did impose two significant changes on real estate investment. First, a 100 percent recapture of all depreciation in excess of straight-line is now required on residential property. The fact that excess depreciation was not recaptured created a significant advantage for investment in

Two major changes for real estate investments

residential real property; this advantage has been eliminated by the new law.

Second, construction interest and taxes must be capitalized and amortized over time, rather than deducted in the year of construction. This significant change reduces the economic viability of any real property investment.

Hobby Losses. Many investments that have traditionally been used as tax shelters, while in fact being a hobby for the owner, have come under the scrutiny of the present law. Examples of these kinds of investments are cattle breeding, a family farm, horse or dog breeding, a private aircraft being leased to others, and so on. The law now requires that such "businesses" must be profitable in two out of five years if deductions are to be taken in the other years. This, too, is a significant change: It renders many playthings more expensive than they have been heretofore.

Hobbies have to be profitable now

Summary

Whenever you invest, you should examine an investment not only for its potential return, but also for its risks. High risk investments can be great fun, and maybe even eminently profitable; but before you jump in, be sure you are aware of the dangers to your financial resources and peace of mind.

CHAPTER 10

Investments in a Pension Plan: The Time for Prudence

Reading this chapter will help you understand:

- The large accumulation of assets that can be achieved in the pension plan portfolio with low-risk investments.
- The legal requirement that investments must be prudent.
- The many fiduciary responsibilities that the law imposes on the trustee of your pension plan.

For the individual who is able to construct either a Keogh or corporate retirement plan, the opportunity exists to build a portfolio worth many hundreds of thousands—perhaps millions—of dollars. These are heady sums; but if you are involved in the management of such portfolios, you should never lose sight of the basic facts.

> While most of the accumulation in the retirement plan may belong to you, contributions have also been made for employees, and there is a sacred trust to make certain those monies are available for all employees of the corporation at the time employment is terminated, or at retirement.

The responsibility for accumulated funds

Under the law this responsibility has had strong legal teeth applied to it. The only reason for these legal measures is to stress the primary purpose of retirement plans—retirement. As Chapter 5 points out, although there may be ancillary benefits to these plans, the principal objective must remain, now and forever, to provide a retirement benefit for corporate employees. Managing retirement fund assets to achieve any other objective will only get you into trouble.

Never lose sight of the pension plan objective

147

Investment Objectives for the Retirement Plan

It may help to start scared

If you spend much time thinking about the demands that may be made on a pension plan investment portfolio, you may get just a little bit scared—and that is a good way to be. Retirement may be a long way off; yet when it occurs (not just for you, but for any employee who participates in the plan), there must be sufficient value in the portfolio to pay the retirement annuity the employee has been looking forward to for 30 or 40 years. Besides the value in the plan, there must also be sufficient liquidity to meet payout demands. That may not appear to be a large problem, but if pension plan assets happen to be depressed, the cost of selling those securities at a loss, in order to make required payouts, is extremely high.

Why you must maintain liquidity

Of course, liquidity may not seem a serious problem if the first retirement from the corporation is 20 years in the future. On the other hand, retirement is not the only event that creates the need for liquidity. The termination of an employee with a vested interest in the plan may create an immediate need for liquidity. If all plan assets have been invested in 30-year bonds in anticipation of those far distant retirements, and if bond prices happen to be down at the time of termination, securities must be liquidated at a loss in order to meet the demands of the departing employee.

One of the most important benefits of your pension plan is to provide your family with an immediate source of funds in the event of your death. As your pension account grows each year, it gradually replaces the need for life insurance, as was shown in Chapter 7. If death occurs in a year when the securities markets happen to be seriously depressed, however, your family could be left in grave financial straits.

Fund your plan conservatively

All these potential difficulties underscore the necessity of funding the small pension plan in a conservative manner. The objectives should provide not only for asset growth, but also for sufficient liquidity to meet the needs of departing or retiring employees, or to meet the financial needs of your family in the event of your death.

What Kinds of Investments Should You Consider? For any tax-qualified retirement plan, some investments must be categorically dismissed. Even mentioning them seens unnecessary; yet from time to time such investments pop up in pension plan portfolios. Their presence indicates a serious breach of fiduciary responsibility on someone's part.

You do not want tax-free securities

Examples of such investments include tax-exempt municipal bonds, any of the so-called tax shelters, and investment in most depreciable assets. The reasons for excluding the first two categories should be immediately apparent. Since plan income is already tax deferred, all of the financial advantage to tax-free municipal securities and tax-sheltered investments is eliminated. And since a major portion of the economic benefit from depreciable property comes from depreciation tax savings, this economic benefit is completely lost too in the tax-qualified retirement plan.

Depending on the size of the plan and its needs for liquidity, certain other investments should be looked upon with a very jaundiced eye. All of the investments with potentially high returns also have such a high degree of risk associated with them that most are unacceptable in a small retirement plan. Investments in this category include growth-type common stocks; second mortgages; commodities or options in commodities; and options, warrants, or rights in corporate securities.

Nor are high-risk investments right

The list is by no means exhaustive, but you should see the picture. Selection of this type of investment might, if you hit it lucky, prove to be a wise decision. Because of the high probability of low return, or even loss, however, such investments frequently prove to be extremely poor choices for a retirement plan portfolio. In this portfolio there is no substitute for conservatism.

In large measure, then, what remains is listed corporate securities—common stocks, preferred stocks, and bonds—the securities that generally should be used to fund the portfolio.

Common Stocks. Of the three, common stocks frequently appear to be the most desirable alternative because of their potential to earn a higher rate of return than the other two. To a large extent this is true: a carefully selected portfolio of high-quality, blue-chip common stocks held for the long run could reasonably expect to earn a rate of return somewhere between 11 and 15 percent. The long-term aspect, however, must be stressed. This means that the portfolio manager, rather than "trying to beat the market" by trading from time to time, merely locks the securities up instead in a safety deposit box to avoid the temptation to trade. This is not to intimate that the securities should be forgotten: The manager might become aware of economic information or circumstances in which the company finds itself that would require a sale of the securities. But trading on a periodic basis to take advantage of price fluctuations of a stock would probably serve only as a damper on performance.

Common stock is for the long run

While the long-run performance on this portfolio may be between 11 and 15 percent, you should recognize that values will fluctuate greatly over time. If only the long run is important, these fluctuations are not troublesome. On the other hand, recognize that liquidity demands made on the portfolio by departing or retiring employees, or as a result of your own death, could come at a time when liquidity could be achieved only by selling securities at a large loss. If this is the case, funding the retirement plan portfolio even with this somewhat conservative investment could be a dangerous course of action.

How common stock might prove dangerous

Fixed Income Securities. An alternative to common stocks, which is extremely desirable today, is investment in fixed income securities—that is, preferred stocks and corporate or government bonds. While such investments might seem like an investment medium for widows and orphans, those may in fact be precisely the individuals for whom you are concerned. As Figure 10.1 shows, it is possible to invest in corporate, fixed income securities with attractive

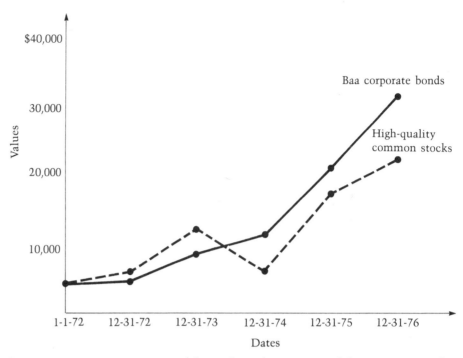

Figure 10.1 Comparative portfolio values for two portfolios, 1972–76. (Annual contribution to each portfolio = $4,500.)

Attractive yields, reduced fluctuation

yields, and significantly reduce—although not completely eliminate—the fluctuations to which common stocks are subject.

The portfolios shown in Figure 10.1 are two actual portfolios, one funded largely with common stock, the other funded largely with corporate bonds. In constructing Figure 10.1, it was assumed $4,500 per year was contributed to each portfolio. The graphs of performance speak for themselves. While the stock portfolio will undoubtedly outperform the bonds over the long run, it has not thus far. And should the assets have been required in 1974, the depressed price of the portfolio would have made liquidity very expensive.

Bonds and preferred stocks, of course, fluctuate in value too, but their fluctuation is almost solely a function of fluctuation in interest rates. As a result, the fluctuations will be significantly less intense than those to which the stock market is subject. For corporate bonds, even these minor fluctuations may be of minor concern, since the fixed maturity date (on which the corporate bonds will be redeemed by the corporation) always provides an exit from the bond at full value. Such an exit from preferred stocks does not exist, and a long-term trend of rising interest rates will permanently depress the price of preferred stocks. This requires that whoever manages your portfolio must be aware of interest rate changes so that investment in preferred stocks can be liquidated before prices become seriously depressed.

Always an exit from corporate bonds

But watch interest rates with preferred stock

Liquidity Needs of the Plan. Conservative and prudent management of the small pension or profit-sharing portfolio dictate that the first consideration be for liquidity. Return should not be completely sacrificed, but there should be sufficient liquidity to meet the needs of immediately departing employees, deaths, or retirement annuity payments. For this reason, it is frequently wise to place the first investments in relatively short-term certificates of deposit, and perhaps even passbook savings accounts. These yield a modest return—5 to 7 percent—and yet provide instant liquidity with little, if any, loss in value.

Some short-term securities are needed

From that point, a prudent course of action would be to begin to acquire a portfolio of high-quality preferred stocks and corporate bonds—certainly nothing below investment grade. Frequently, the temptation is to take advantage of the high yields and long maturities available on newly issued bonds. Remember, however, the risk of being locked into investments of 25 or 30 years, or more, and perhaps running into a serious liquidity problem. Although you may not want to avoid long maturities completely, it is well to build a continuing source of liquidity into the portfolio by staggering maturities. That is, you should buy bonds that mature every several years so that you have a constant turnover in the portfolio, thus providing liquidity to meet the kinds of needs we have talked about.

Staggering maturities is sound strategy

Inflation and Plan Assets. Unfortunately, inflation seems to be an inescapable fact of financial life, and its debilitating effect on the values of fixed-income investments is discouraging.

> It is almost a maxim today that any investment must grow in value at a rate more rapid than inflation in order to maintain purchasing power.

The result is purchase of many investments that are far too risky for any pension plan. Such high-risk investments subject the important asset accumulations in your retirement plan to both the risks of the marketplace *and* inflation. The authors have analyzed well over 1,000 retirement plan portfolios, of which only 42 percent are worth more than the sum of all contributions. If that is stated in too technical a manner, try it another way: 58 percent of all plans examined have lost money over the years. That is a tragic consequence of the laudable objective of trying to beat inflation.

The dangers of trying to beat inflation

Certainly the traditional hedge against inflation—the stock market—would have been the worst place to be invested during the past ten years. On the other hand, the traditional whipping boy of inflation—fixed income securities—proved to be the best hedge during this same period. What this ironic twist best proves, perhaps, is the lack of a sure-fire method of solving this serious problem.

Perhaps the best long-run hedge against erosion of purchasing power is the sheer accumulation of dollars. Whether your pension plan is a defined-benefit plan or not, it is a good idea to set a year-by-year

Accumulating dollars is the best hedge

minimum-funding standard, or target portfolio size, which takes into consideration erosion of purchasing power. As long as these target accumulations are being achieved, you know the plan has sufficient assets to meet retirement needs, or the needs of your family should you die. Once this minimum-funding standard is met, and there are still monies to be invested, you may wish to take a more aggressive stance and consider riskier investments. But build the minimum-funding standard—your financial security—first.

Have a minimum-funding standard

> Whatever you do, do not tinker with the futures of your employees, yourself, or your family by investing completely in investments that promise high return but also subject you to high risk.

What About Life Insurance in the Plan? Frequently pension plans are funded with whole-life insurance, which has the advantage that a portion of the premium can be paid, by the corporation, with pretax dollars. On the other hand, the earnings on a life insurance policy already accrue tax free, although at a very low rate. Since the pension plan earnings are already tax deferred, it is seldom desirable to fund the pension plan with a life insurance policy whose earnings are generally not taxed.

Funding by life insurance is seldom desirable

As you have already seen in Chapter 7, the cost of term life insurance is so low compared to whole-life that you are generally better off buying whatever insurance is needed outside the pension plan, and taking advantage of the tax deferred treatment of income to fund your pension plan with higher yielding assets.

You Must Be a "Prudent Man"

While no one is certain precisely what a prudent man (or woman) looks like—or even how he acts—the law, in stern tones, notes that the trustee of a pension plan must be prudent. To be precise, the law says the trustee, and the investment manager of a retirement plan, "... must carry out his duties with the care, skill, prudence, and diligence which a prudent man, acting in a like capacity, would use under conditions prevailing at the time."

Precisely what these requirements mean will undoubtedly be decided by the courts in future years. As trustee of your plan, however, make absolutely certain that the court cases cited in the future do not contain your name. That is a type of notoriety you do not need. To avoid this eventuality, it is important that you do nothing that might be construed as being imprudent (and hence illegal), or simply foolish, in terms of affecting the principal objectives of the plan. Liquidity, which we have stressed so heavily, must be in the plan. Should terminating employees not be able to get access to their vested interest because a second mortgage cannot be liquidated, or even as a result of investment losses in listed corporate securities, a lack of prudence might be easily shown.

Good reasons to be "prudent"

Failure to adequately diversify a portfolio—that is, to invest in many different securities instead of concentrating in one—could result in losses, and is specifically defined as an act of imprudence. Diversification is not achieved just by buying different securities, but rather by buying securities that are statistically unrelated to one another so that a single economic event could not cause all of the securities to perform poorly, or fail. Thus, lack of diversification could result from concentration of portfolio assets in a single high-risk investment—or even investment in assets that all have similar risk characteristics.

Failure to diversify is an act of imprudence

A not uncommon investment in a small retirement plan is the employee loan, made under the terms of an employee borrowing agreement, which we described in Chapter 4. Prudence dictates that such loans should be evaluated as carefully and secured as adequately as any other lender would expect them to be. Failure to evaluate the risk, demand adequate collateral, or set up a strictly enforced, contractual repayment schedule could easily be shown to constitute imprudence. In addition to the question of prudence, the question of legality arises. A prudent man does not break the law, of course, so be certain that your trust contains an employee borrowing agreement before you consider making loans to employees. Under no circumstances should a loan be made to the corporation—even indirectly—as this is defined as a prohibited transaction.

Employee loans: Be prudent with fund monies

Prohibited Transactions

In addition to the requirement for prudence, the law outlines in great detail a number of transactions that are illegal per se. These transactions are illegal if they occur between the plan and what the law calls a *party in interest* in the plan.

The penalties for prohibited transactions are extremely serious —made so to reflect the attitude of the Internal Revenue Service and the Labor Department toward abuses of pension plans. The current penalty is an excise tax of 5 percent (of the amount of the prohibited transaction), inflicted on the party in interest responsible for the violation. Failure to correct the problem after notification results in an excise tax of 100 percent of the amount of the prohibited transaction.

Violations bring heavy penalties

Ironically, the nature of most prohibited transactions is such that the transaction cannot be reversed without engaging in another prohibited transaction. If that sounds like double trouble, it is and only serves to underline the fact that prohibited transactions are better avoided.

Who Is a Party in Interest? The law is explicit in defining precisely who constitute parties in interest. They include each of the following:

- Employers of plan participants—that is, the corporation itself.
- Persons rendering service to the plan; these include investment advisors, accountants, administrators, actuaries, and fiduciaries of any nature.
- Employees of the plan itself (not the corporation) are considered parties in interest.
- Unions, or corporate employees who are officers of unions, are also considered parties in interest.

It should be noted that these latter two restrictions rarely apply to the small plan because there are no employees or because the labor force of most small, closely held corporations is generally not unionized.

Do not skirt the intent of the law

On occasion there is a temptation to skirt the intent of the law by engaging in a prohibited transaction via a circuitous route. An example would be making an employee loan to yourself and then using the proceeds to make a loan to your corporation, or even to buy equipment for lease to the corporation. The law makes it abundantly clear that involvement of a third party does not make the transaction legal. Specifically, the law defines all "... relatives, agents, and joint venturers" of the above as also parties in interest. If the definitions are not sufficiently clear that you can understand precisely who is a party in interest, use a rule of thumb: *It is anyone who has anything to do with the plan.* If you will follow that rule, you will stay out of trouble.

Third parties can be parties in interest

What Is Prohibited?

> The law explicitly defines transactions that are prohibited. Common sense would normally dictate that such transactions are better avoided, but sometimes common sense pales in the face of what appears to be a neat way to make a quick buck. There is only one word of advice that applies to those situations—don't.

Avoid illegal property transactions

The most common type of prohibited transaction involves sale, exchange, or lease of property between the plan and a party in interest. Among other things, this prohibition means that it is against the law for your corporate pension plan to buy or sell any asset from or to the corporation, to lease an asset to the corporation, to buy any asset that you have had in your personal portfolio, and so on—you begin to get the drift. This prohibition is perhaps violated the most since the temptation is so great to use that large pool of assets in the plan to do something productive for your business or for you personally. Since it is against the law, avoid the temptation.

In addition to buying, selling, or leasing property, any loan or extension of credit between a plan and a party in interest is prohibited. The most frequent violation in this area is a loan from the plan to the professional corporation, or vice versa. Both are prohibited, as are all other loans between the plan and any other party in interest.

Most loans are prohibited

It is important to note that this restriction does not prohibit loans to employees. The law specifically allows employees of the pension plan to borrow, *if the pension trust provides for employee loans, and if the trustee deems such loans to be prudent investments.* It would not, therefore, be prohibited for a plan to make a loan to you individually as an employee of a corporation. On the other hand, it might be very easy for you to turn such a loan into a prohibited transaction. A good borderline case, better not tested in court, would be a loan from the plan to yourself; you in turn lend the sum to the corporation to purchase an asset for use in the corporate business. That circuitous transaction could be deemed illegal.

Loans to employees are legal

A loan to yourself could be illegal

Transactions less likely to occur in small plans include the furnishing of any goods or services or facilities between the plan and a party in interest, or transfer of plan assets to any party in interest. The former is not likely to take place; the latter is clearly an illegal conversion of plan assets to your personal benefit and common sense should be prohibition enough against such an action.

As a general rule, any acquisition of employer securities is prohibited. While there are some exceptions to this prohibition, it would almost always hold in the case of the small, closely held corporation whose common stock is unlisted. It would always be true for the professional corporation. (The notable exception is that stock in a large, publicly held corporation could be acquired by a retirement plan within rather strict limits—an exception not germane to our discussion.)

Employer securities may not be acquired

Fiduciary Responsibilities

You may question why this chapter includes a section on fiduciary responsibilities, since most of us can scarcely pronounce the word, let alone understand what it means. A fiduciary, however, is defined as someone in a position of trust—for our purposes, with respect to the plan. Almost anyone who does anything or renders any advice with respect to a retirement plan is a fiduciary for that plan. This could include yourself if your legal counsel deems it in your best interests to be trustee of your corporate plan—a frequent occurrence. Since you may very well end up being a fiduciary, then, it is important to know what your responsibilities are.

Who and what a fiduciary is

General Responsibilities. First, the law states that all "fiduciaries must act solely in the interests of plan participants and beneficiaries,

Fiduciaries must act in a plan's best interests

and all actions must be solely to provide benefits for the participants, and defray expenses of the plan." In brief, this means that fiduciaries are acting for the plan and in its best interests—never for themselves. For example, it would not be wise, if you were trustee of the plan, to refuse employees indiscriminately the right to borrow under the employee borrowing agreement while granting such loans to yourself. At the same time, it is your responsibility as trustee to make certain that all such loans are prudent, and are granted after the same kind of scrutiny that a bank or other lender would apply.

They must conform with the plan trust

All plan fiduciaries also have the responsibility to conform with the plan trust, as well as other controlling documents. The trust carefully defines all legal actions of the trustee, and doing anything not authorized by the trust is an illegal action that constitutes a breach of faith on the part of the trustee. If, for example, the trust requires a committee of employees to review plan investment decisions, it would be foolish for you to make those decisions on your own—an act clearly outside the scope of your power as trustee.

Employers may not use plan assets

All fiduciaries have the responsibility to make certain that plan assets never be allowed to accrue to the benefit of any party in interest, including the employer. That is clear. No asset—cash, securities, real property, or any other asset owned by the pension plan—may be used by the corporate employer. At all times there are two separate and distinct legal entities: the corporation, and the retirement plan of the corporation—and the assets of the two must never be mixed.

Fiduciaries must use "reasonable care"

Not only are fiduciaries responsible for their own actions, but the law imposes an additional requirement on them to be watchguards over their brethren. All fiduciaries are expected to use "reasonable care" to prevent other trustees from committing a breach of fiduciary responsibility. This means that each fiduciary—trustee, investment advisor, or accountant—has the responsibility to keep a watch on the other fiduciaries involved in the plan to make certain they do not do something illegal. Knowledge of an illegal act, if no action is taken to correct it, could constitute an illegal act in itself.

Prohibited Transactions of Fiduciaries. As if we have not made the whole area of prohibited transactions and fiduciary responsibility complex enough, the law defines several actions fiduciaries might take that are specifically prohibited. Since you may be a fiduciary for your own plan, it is partially your responsibility to make certain they do not happen.

Make no asset transfers to a personal account

It is against the law for any fiduciary to deal with plan assets for a personal account. This means your trustee—you personally, or an institution—must not transact any asset transfers from the plan to a personal account.

No fiduciary may receive consideration for a personal account from any party transacting business with the plan. This is a prohibition easily violated in today's world, but it is important that it not take place. An example would be an investment advisor to your plan taking a kickback (or any other financial favor) from a securities broker to whom plan business had been directed.

No fiduciary may act in any transaction, in any capacity, with any party whose interests are adverse to the interests of the plan. The intent of this restriction is to make certain that any fiduciary of your plan is representing its best interests and not those of anyone with opposite interests. It would be difficult for your investment advisors to explain, for example, how they can represent your plan in negotiating the sale of a plan asset to someone else whom they also represent. For whom are they striking the best bargain?

Summary

At the beginning of this chapter, we said you might become just a bit scared as you proceeded with your reading. But such fear is not all bad—as we also said—since it will, we hope, discourage you from making imprudent transactions with your pension plan. By all means, however, do not let fear prevent you from constructing a plan—that can be among the wisest actions you ever engage in. Still, it is not a do-it-yourself project, so be certain it is done right. Seek the best legal counsel you can find, pay the fee willingly, and follow advice to the letter. Then invest plan assets conservatively and prudently. We can almost guarantee that at the end of your life you will have greater asset accumulations than could be achieved following any other course of action.

Our advice is to seek the best advice

CHAPTER 11

How to Finance Your Investments: Choosing the Best Way to Build Your Portfolio

After you have finished reading this chapter, you will understand:

- The concept of financial leverage and how it affects return on equity.
- The relative advantages and drawbacks of debt financing versus equity financing.
- That you must clearly separate the investment or acquisition decision from the financing decision.
- How to analyze lease arrangements to determine their implicit interest cost.

Now that you have learned the methods of analyzing the profitability of investment alternatives, you need to learn how to finance those investments. It is not accidental that we discuss separately how an asset is financed, for it is essential that the financing decision should be made quite independently of the investment decision.

Contrary to what many believe, the method by which an investment is financed has nothing to do with the profitability of the investment. If an asset yields 10 percent, that is its return—period—whether the asset is financed with debt, or with equity, or with any combination of the two. What *is* affected by financing is the rate of return on equity—the return on your personal commitment of funds to the investment. It can be more, or less, than the earnings on the total asset, depending on how the asset is financed.

The sections that follow make this distinction clearly, and will help you decide the best way to finance an asset.

How financing is separate from profitability

Debt Financing: Financial Leverage

Assuming financial leverage means borrowing

Whenever a firm, or an individual, borrows money to finance the purchase of an asset, the firm is said to have assumed financial leverage. A firm that has a high percentage of its assets financed with borrowed money is said to be in a highly leveraged position.

The Advantages of Leverage

> If it is possible to borrow money at a rate of interest lower than the rate of return earned by the asset, it is advantageous for the investor to finance it with borrowed money.

How it can be advantageous to borrow

Suppose, for example, you have the opportunity to buy an asset priced at $20,000, on which you expect to earn a rate of return of 10 percent. You are contemplating two alternative methods of financing that $20,000 investment: drawing the entire $20,000 from your savings account; or, withdrawing $10,000 from savings and borrowing the remaining $10,000 at 8 percent interest from your local bank. If your tax rate is 40 percent, what rate of return will you realize on equity—that is, on the money you have provided toward purchase of the investment?

What leverage gain means

Notice from Table 11.1 that the rate of return on equity is improved under the 50 percent-50 percent financing alternative. That is, the identical investment yields a higher rate of return per dollar of your equity if you finance half the asset with 8 percent debt. This leverage gain is due to you acquiring debt money at a lower rate of interest than the annual rate of return generated by the asset. As a result, the difference between the asset return and the cost of debt is a bonus to you.

Table 11.1 Effect of Leverage on Return on Equity

	100% Equity	50% Debt–50% Equity
Amount of investment	$20,000	$20,000
Return on investment	× 10%	× 10%
Dollar return	2,000	2,000
Interest expense	0	800
Taxable income	2,000	1,200
Taxes @ 40%	800	480
After-tax income	$ 1,200	$ 720
Return on equity	$\frac{1,200}{20,000} = 6\%$	$\frac{720}{10,000} = 7.2\%$

The Risks of Leverage. This simple example illustrates the great advantage that can result from the appropriate use of financial leverage. You must be careful, however, with your use of leverage, since it considerably increases the risk of a given investment. Suppose, for example, that your same $20,000 investment turns out to yield only 7 percent annually instead of the projected 10 percent. Such declines in expected earnings can be caused by all kinds of uncertainties and are thus not uncommon. Assuming the same 8 percent cost of debt, and 40 percent marginal tax rate, Table 11.2 illustrates the new computations of your return on equity.

But leverage can increase risk

Obviously, the rate of return on equity has now been eroded when leverage is used. *Leverage will always be detrimental if the cost of debt exceeds the return yielded by the asset.* In this case, the cost of debt remained at 8 percent, and thus the interest expense remained constant at $800. In the meantime, the rate of return on the total investment has declined to 7 percent; thus, only $600 of the before-tax income, and only $360 of after-tax income, was available for the equity portion of the asset. In simpler terms, this time the leverage hammered you.

Don't let cost of debt exceed returns

The central element of a financing decision is the realization that if you use borrowed funds, even small changes in the rate of return realized by the investment will result in relatively large changes in the return on your equity. Leverage is a two-edged sword, and any decrease in the rate of return on investment, particularly when it is below the interest rate of the debt, will result in a magnified decline in the rate of return to equity.

Why leverage is a two-edged sword

Since the riskiness of an investment is often measured in terms of variability of return on equity, the use of debt funds to finance an asset will always result in a considerably more risky investment, and this increased risk must be taken into account.

Since the cost of debt and your marginal tax rate are fairly certain bits of information, the decision about your leverage position rests primarily on an accurate estimate of the return generated by a potential investment. If you can be sure—or at least highly confident—that

How to judge your leverage position

Table 11.2 Computation of Return on Equity

	100% Equity	50% Debt–50% Equity
Amount of investment	$20,000	$20,000
Return on investment	× 7%	× 7%
Dollar return	1,400	1,400
Interest expense	0	800
Taxable income	1,400	600
Taxes @ 40%	560	240
After-tax income	$ 840	$ 360
Return on equity	$\frac{840}{20,000} = 4.2\%$	$\frac{360}{10,000} = 3.6\%$

the return on total investment will, in fact, exceed the cost of debt, then it is financially advantageous to finance the asset at least partially with debt funds. This will insure a relatively higher annual rate of return on the equity portion of the investment. If, on the other hand, there is much uncertainty surrounding the expected rate of return, then the more conservative strategy dictates financing the investment with a higher percentage of equity funds.

The truth-in-lending law is helpful

How to Finance Debt. Borrowing is perhaps the easiest of all financing alternatives to analyze. The truth-in-lending law requires that loan costs and effective interest rates on loans be clearly revealed to you by the lender. Even when they are not disclosed, it is an easy matter to employ the techniques developed in Chapter 2 to determine precisely the interest rates on any kind of loan.

Ways to borrow from a bank

A number of arrangements can be made with banks to acquire a loan. A secured loan can be obtained by placing the asset as security, and thus a lien on the asset will be held by the lender until the loan is fully amortized. Automobile loans are a common example of a secured loan arrangement.

To credit-worthy customers the bank will often establish a line of credit up to some predetermined maximum. This allows you to draw upon that line of credit easily and quickly without the necessity of loan security. A consistent record of repayment on a credit line will often occasion an increase in the maximum credit extended.

Bank cards: an expensive source of funds

Credit and bank cards provide an increasingly common source of debt funds. Bank cards such as Master Charge and VISA are handy in that money can be advanced quickly without the necessity of filling out long and detailed application forms. However, these sources of credit are extremely expensive compared to other alternatives. It is not unusual for interest rates on such borrowed money to be 18 percent per year, except in those few states that have usury laws restricting them to some lower rate. Thus, we recommend that any borrowing needs in excess of a couple of weeks be arranged with banks or other financial institutions.

> We feel safe in stating that almost without exception borrowing is the least costly of all financing alternatives. However, do not neglect the increased risk inherent in a leverage position: The decision to finance with debt funds should be made only after a careful assessment of the investment returns and the risks attendant thereto.

Equity Financing

Personal savings as a source of equity financing

As an alternative to debt, you may decide to finance an acquisition with some source of equity funds. The most obvious source of equity financing is your own personal savings. You should recognize immediately that this financing alternative has an implicit cost. Obviously, if you had left the funds invested in bonds, savings accounts, or some other interest-earning asset, you would have realized a rate of return that must now be foregone if those investments are liquidated.

The interest return sacrificed in order to finance the new investment, therefore, becomes an estimate of the cost of using your own money to finance the proposed acquisition. Precisely the same can be said for the equity money obtained from your associates. They invest only for the purposes of receiving a competitive rate of return. The implicit cost of equity financing could then be defined as the rate of return that must be realized in order to keep your associates happy and to ensure that they do not withdraw their money from the investment.

The implicit cost of equity financing

The important concept, however, is to recognize clearly that equity financing has a cost just as surely as debt financing or any of the other alternatives. In fact, in most cases, the cost of equity financing exceeds that of debt financing, although it does not expose you to the risk of a leverage position. Also, however, it does not allow the positive effects of return on equity that might be gained from the use of financial leverage.

Usually more costly than debt financing

Leasing

An increasingly common financing arrangement is leasing—a type of financing that does not appear on the balance sheet. Nevertheless, for your purposes, you should consider lease financing to be an alternate method of borrowing funds. That is, it is essentially debt financing.

Leasing—a kind of debt financing

There are three basic kinds of lease arrangements. One, called a sale and leaseback, requires that you sell real or personal property to a financial or leasing institution and simultaneously execute a contract to lease the property for a specified period. Such an arrangement is often employed to eliminate immediate cash flow deficiencies.

Three types of lease contracts: sale and leaseback

A second type, called a service or an operating lease, includes both the characteristics of debt financing and the inclusion of a contract to service the asset. This is often used for sophisticated office equipment—computers being the outstanding example. In many cases, the worth of the asset is not fully amortized over the period of the lease. That is, the payments over the term of the lease are not sufficient to cover interest plus the full original cost of the equipment.

Service or operating lease

The third type, called a financial lease, is essentially an installment loan contract in disguise. Such a lease does not generally include any service provisions and is not cancellable. Further, the lease payments over the term of the lease are sufficient to cover the interest plus full original cost of the equipment. Most equipment leases employed by professionals to acquire office equipment, automobiles, and medical or dental equipment are of the financial lease type.

Financial lease

These kinds of lease arrangements should be evaluated in much the same manner as debt financing. Just as surely as you must make an installment loan payment on a car, you must also make lease payments on leased assets.

Defaulting on lease payments is costly

> If you have any lease arrangements, check the contract: You will most likely find it difficult, if not impossible, for you to break. If it can be broken, it generally requires payment of a severe and very costly penalty.

In order to evaluate the cost of leasing we must again use the interest formulas from Chapter 2. For purposes of illustration, assume you need a $2,400 piece of office equipment. Of course, you have the option of borrowing the money to purchase the asset, but the sales representative has also offered you a lease arrangement that would cost you $107.16 per month for 2½ years. At the end of that time, for simplicity's sake, assume the piece of equipment will be fully depreciated and has no salvage value. Your task is to compute the implicit rate of interest on the lease arrangement to see if it is competitive with other financing alternatives.

Compute the implicit interest rate

Table 11.3 analyzes the rate of return (to the lessor—the cost to you) on the lease. While the monthly lease payment of $107.16 did not seem too imposing, the implicit interest rate of the lease agreement, 24 percent, is substantial. In fact, it is much higher than would have been required of you under a borrowing alternative.

When considering leasing an asset, you should always compute the implicit interest cost of such an obligation. In contrast to loan agreements, lease arrangements almost never provide information as to interest rate. This may change in the near future, however, since truth-in-leasing legislation is currently being considered at the federal level.

Residual value of an asset is crucial

A complicating factor in evaluating lease arrangements stems from the need to estimate the asset's residual value at the termination of the lease. Remember that at the end of the lease the asset belongs to

Table 11.3 Analysis of Leasing Cost

Cash price of asset = $2,400.00.
Monthly lease payment = $107.16
Maturity of lease = 30 months.

We know that

$$PV = PMT_{30} \times IF_4.$$

So

$$\$2,400_{30} = \$107.16 \times IF_4.$$

Or

$$IF = \frac{\$2,400}{\$107.16} = 22.396.$$

Referring to Appendix A.4, we find the interest factor of 22.396 associated with an interest rate of 2% per period for 30 periods. Since the period is one month, the annual interest rate is 2% × 12 = 24% per year.

the lessor. If the asset has a significant salvage value (it may even have appreciated in value), your implicit cost is significantly higher, since you must surrender the asset. With a $400 residual value included, the implicit cost of the lease in the preceding example increases from 24 percent to 31 percent per year. We have not shown the computation of the exact cost because it is a bit more difficult to compute than you probably want to tinker around with. Obviously, however, the higher the residual value, the higher the implicit cost of lease. In many lease contracts, called *net leases,* a residual value is guaranteed the lessor, increasing the implicit cost of leasing dramatically.

Net leases increase cost

While we did not show you the exact method of computing this implicit cost, there is a simple method for estimating the true, or implicit, cost, based on the old grade school formula

$$I = P \times R \times N.$$

The rate is estimated merely by solving for R instead of I. If you like formulas, follow along, thus:

$$R = \frac{I}{P \times N}.$$

Formulas that estimate true cost

Since the amount of principal "borrowed" with the lease is reduced monthly, the average amount of principal over the entire lease should be used, and the rate can be estimated as

$$R = \frac{I}{\frac{(P_b + P_e)}{2} \times N},$$

where

R = approximate annual interest rate;
I = dollar amount of interest paid (total of all lease payments minus the cost of the asset);
P_b = beginning principal balance (or initial cash cost);
P_e = the sum of a monthly lease payment plus the residual value, if any;
N = number of years in the lease contract.

For the lease illustrated in Table 11.3, the approximate cost is

$$R = \frac{\$814.80}{\frac{(\$2,400 - \$107.16)}{2} \times 2.5} = \underline{\underline{28\%}}.$$

(Here $\$107.16 \times 30 - \$2,400 = \$814.80$.) While this approximation is a bit high, it is close enough to be a reasonably good estimate of the true cost.

For the more complicated case, with the residual value, we get the following estimated cost:

$$R = \frac{\$814.80}{\frac{(\$2,400 - \$507.16)}{2} \times 2.5} = \underline{\underline{34\%}}.$$

(Here $400 + $107.16 = $507.16.) In this case, the approximation is again slightly high, but close enough so that you know you can borrow from your bank at a much lower rate.

Borrowing usually costs less than leasing

In summary, when considering a lease contract, you should analyze the implicit interest cost of such a contract and then compare that cost to the interest cost of borrowing the funds and purchasing the asset outright. In the vast majority of cases, borrowing will be less costly than leasing.

Summary

It is important to stress the need to separate the acquisition, or investment, decision from the financing decision. The decision to acquire an asset is made by discounting the flows generated by that asset at the desired rate of return, and comparing the present value of these benefits to the cost of the investment. The appropriate discount rate is the desired rate of return on the total investment, not the return to equity, and is not affected by the method of financing.

Once the investment is analyzed and is deemed to be profitable, then financing alternatives must be considered. The financing decision will be selected based upon the alternative that yields the largest return to equity, as long as it is simultaneously consistent with your risk preferences. Return on equity may be increased above the return on investment by using borrowed money, but remember the effect that it has on the riskiness of the venture.

Be scrupulous in separating your areas of decision

Financing costs, interest costs, or tax savings resulting from those costs, have no bearing on the rate of return of an investment. Interest expense reduces your tax liability, but does not make you better off. You can make financially sound decisions concerning investment strategy and financing strategy only when the investment and financing decisions are scrupulously separated and analyzed carefully.

BIBLIOGRAPHY

Randle, Paul A. "Buying Equipment Is Really Cheaper Than Leasing It." *Physician's Management*, April 1976, pp. 51–61.

———. "How Much Does Leasing Really Cost?" *Dental Economics*, June 1975, pp. 49–50.

These two articles analyze the cost of leasing equipment versus buying the same equipment.

Schall, Lawrence D., and Haley, Charles W. *Introduction to Financial Management.* New York: McGraw-Hill Book Co., 1977.

The impact of financing decisions and particularly how they affect return to equity is found in Chapter 9 of this basic text.

Weston, J. Fred, and Brigham, Eugene F. *Managerial Finance.* 6th ed. Hinsdale, Ill.: Dryden Press, 1978.

Chapter 18 of this comprehensive work contains an excellent discussion of the effects of financial structure and the use of leverage on the investment decision.

PART Four

Constructing Your Estate and Coping with Inflation

Estate Planning:
A Strategy You Can Master

After reading this chapter, you will understand:

- The impact federal and state death taxes will have on your estate.
- How to minimize these taxes through proper ownership of property and through use of correct estate-planning tools.
- How to help your family avoid many of the pitfalls that deplete the value of assets left to them.

When Benjamin Franklin said, "Nothing is certain but death and taxes," he failed to realize one of the difficult facts of financial life in this day and age.

> Today, federal and state governments have made certain that death *and* taxes are exquisitely intertwined with one another. For this reason, perhaps no area of personal financial planning requires more careful forethought and consideration than does the area of estate planning.

Serious mistakes in your estate plan could have the effect of significantly eroding the value of your estate and jeopardizing the future financial security of loved ones. Unlike other areas of a personal financial plan, those concerned frequently do not recognize mistakes or omissions in an estate plan until late in life, or even after someone's death, at which point of course it is either very difficult or impossible to make necessary corrections. Similarly, many tax-saving maneuvers must be initiated early to achieve maximum advantage. The key word is *planning*, and that requires some work on your part as well as assistance from the most competent legal and tax professionals available to you.

Above all, your estate must be planned

Gathering Required Information

The most important thing for you to keep in mind as you plan your estate is taking care of the needs of yourself and your loved ones. These are highly personal problems, and the estate plans that were drawn for your partner, or your brother-in-law, or Joe Blow, in no way relate to the problems you and your family face. Make certain that your estate plan is drawn for you and is not the product of an IBM Magnetic Card Typewriter.

It must be planned for you especially

Accordingly, make it easy for your attorney and accountant to help you by presenting them with a carefully constructed list of facts and objectives.

Identify Yourself Your attorney will need, for yourself and your spouse, your names, dates of birth, social security numbers, addresses (both your present residence and your permanent home), and your telephone numbers.

Personal information must be accurate

It is most important that your counsel understands your present marital status, whether you are now or ever have been separated or divorced, the names of prior spouses, and exact details of divorce agreements ending previous marriages.

Who Are Your Family Members? In addition to the personal information outlined above, your counsel will require the names, marital status, birth dates, and addresses of each of your children from present or previous marriages. Similar information will be required for parents of both you and your spouse, and brothers and sisters of each of you.

Who Will Handle Your Estate? It is important to have your legal counsel understand precisely whom you wish to handle your affairs after death, to shepherd your estate through the transition period, and to make certain that all your heirs are dealt with fairly. This executor, as the person is called, could be a family member, your legal counsel or accountant, or an institution such as a bank or trust company.

An executor should be named

Since your attorney may recommend the use of trust instruments as estate-planning devices, it is important that you identify which bank or trust company you would use if the need arises.

Who Will Take Care of Your Children? One of the most important matters you must attend to in an estate plan is to name a guardian for minor children should that be necessary. Since it might be a bit of a shock for someone to be notified of their appointment after your death, this is something that should be discussed with potential guardians before the final choice is made. The logical choice might seem to be your own or your spouse's parents, but after careful thought the logic of that choice dims. While they were undoubtedly good parents for you, their age frequently renders their selection impractical. Better possibilities are usually a brother, or sister, or a close friend.

And a guardian for minor children

Who Gets What? You can greatly ease your attorney's job by tentatively outlining how you wish your assets distributed after (or before) your death. Generally your first consideration should be to a surviving spouse and dependent children, with ultimate disposition of the assets to come after their needs have been met—perhaps many years from now.

Divide assets as you choose—but specify

Ultimate disposition may be according to any formula you choose and does not have to be on a per capita basis. The tendency is to think that fairness requires an equal distribution to each surviving child. As a matter of fact, true fairness should take into account the social and economic conditions of each of the children, and might therefore dictate one child receiving a far larger inheritance than another because of a peculiar need.

Generally there are specific assets that you want a particular person to receive. Your attorney should know what these are. This is especially true of personal property that has sentimental, although not necessarily monetary, value.

Specify personal property too

> In the absence of specific bequests, personal property frequently ends up in the grab bag, with family members fighting over distribution of it. Do not hesitate to leave your favorite shotgun to a particular son, or a diamond dinner ring with great sentimental value to a particular daughter. You may hesitate for fear of hurting feelings, but in the absence of such a bequest, feelings are apt to run even higher.

In addition to the lineal heirs normally considered, you may wish to supply your legal counsel with a list of favorite charities if there is any possibility of making a bequest to them.

Are There Any Special Instructions? If you have any special desires with respect to funeral or burial, tell your attorney about them. If you want it all simple, specify that you want to be buried in a pine box. If, on the other hand, you want to go out in a blaze of glory, make certain that you are buried in the finest rosewood casket with a New Orleans jazz band providing the funeral dirge. You can also specify cremation, donation of eyes or the body organs, or any other disposition that you wish to make of your remains.

And specify your own funeral arrangements

What Do You Own? The most important information your attorney will require changes constantly and therefore requires periodic updates of the entire estate plan. This information, which you should furnish to your counsel, is contained in a detailed balance sheet, or list, of all your assets and liabilities. You should include the name of each asset, the exact form in which title is held (that is, joint tenancy,

Furnish lists of assets and liabilities

tenancy in common, tenancy by entirety, and so on), its date of acquisition, its value on the date of acquisition, and an estimate of its fair market value today. On the liability side of the ledger, you should list all liabilities by name, amount of the original liability, the present balance owing, the date on which the liability will be discharged, and the asset, if any, that secures the liability.

To the extent possible, you should identify which assets were brought into the marriage by the respective spouses and which assets were acquired during the marriage with marital funds.

Let your attorney check your insurance policies

Your life insurance policies are important assets; and they, as well as all other insurance policies you and your spouse own, can tell your attorney important things about your estate. For example, the ownership of a life insurance policy has great bearing on whose estate the death benefit will be included in. And, while it may be clear that an automobile or fur coat is owned by your wife, the fact that the asset is insured under a fire insurance policy owned completely by you may serve to convince the Internal Revenue Service that you were the owner of the asset. By furnishing all insurance policies to your attorney, you can secure helpful recommendations concerning change of ownership in such policies to avoid difficulties after death.

Federal Estate Taxation

Federal taxes will be the principal charge

While the costs associated with probate and state death tax both erode the value of your estate, the principal charge against a deceased's estate comes in the form of federal estate taxes. Because of the number of states, it is difficult to make general comments about state inheritance taxes, much less to present information pertaining to each of the 50 states. State taxes, however, are essentially the same as the federal estate tax, although most have considerably lower rates and slightly different deduction and exemption features.

The gross value of your estate

The federal government requires that the federal estate tax return, Form 706, be filed within nine months of the date of death if there is federal estate tax liability. The taxable value of one's estate is generally considerably different from the gross value of the estate, and is computed according to the format set out in Table 12.1.

Your gross estate includes all assets owned by you, or you and your spouse jointly: cash, real estate, stocks and bonds, personal property, municipal securities, federal securities, the death benefit of life insurance policies *owned by you*, property transferred to others in which you maintain incidence of ownership, all gifts made to others within three years of your date of death, and all taxes paid on those gifts.

From this gross estate is subtracted expenses of your last illness and funeral expenses paid from the proceeds of the estate, all expenses associated with administration and probate of your estate, liabilities of the estate, and declines in asset value which occur during administration of the estate.

Table 12.1 Computation of Taxable Estate

Gross estate
   1. Cash
   2. Real estate
   3. Stocks and bonds
   4. Personal property
   5. Tax-exempt state and municipal securities
   6. Federal securities
   7. Jointly owned property
   8. Life insurance if the deceased owned the policy
   9. Transferred property on which ownership rights were retained by the deceased
   10. Gifts made within three years of death, and taxes on those gifts

Subtotal, gross estate

Category I deductions
   1. Funeral expenses paid out of the proceeds of the estate
   2. Expenses incurred in marshalling the assets of the estate, paying the debts of the estate, and distribution of the estate to beneficiaries
   3. Expenses incurred in the administration of assets not subject to probate
   4. Liabilities of the estate
   5. Losses to the estate incurred during administration

Subtotal, category I deductions

Gross estate
−category I deductions

= Adjusted gross estate

−Marital deduction

Category II deductions
   Contributions to charitable, educational, literary, religious, or scientific organizations

−Category II deductions

= Taxable estate

This computation results in the adjusted gross estate, from which may be subtracted the marital deduction—one half the value of the estate or $250,000, whichever is greater—if it passes to the spouse, and contributions to charitable, educational, or other nonprofit organizations. The remaining figure, subject to federal estate tax, is known as the taxable estate.

How to compute your taxable estate

The one-time unified tax credit

Like the federal income tax, the federal estate tax is a progressive tax, which increases as the size of the taxable estate increases—and that might strike you as being more regressive than progressive. But, wait, you get a break. From the tax to which the estate is subject there is a direct tax credit (tax reduction) of $30,000 for the year 1977, increasing annually until 1981, when the permanent credit will become $47,000. This is a unified credit, which means it may be used to offset either gift taxes incurred prior to death, or if unused, to offset the death tax. Table 12.2 shows the federal estate tax rates and the tax credits as they apply annually through 1981.

Table 12.2 Federal Estate and Gift Tax Rates

If taxable estate is		Tax is		
A	B	C[a]	+	D[a]
equal to or more than . . .	but less than . . .	tax on amount in column A. . .		rate of tax on difference between taxable estate and column A . . .
$ 0	$ 10,000	$ 0		18%
19,000	20,000	1,800		20
20,000	40,000	3,800		22
40,000	60,000	8,200		24
60,000	80,000	13,000		26
80,000	100,000	18,200		28
100,000	150,000	23,800		30
150,000	250,000	38,800		32
250,000	500,000	70,800		34
500,000	750,000	155,800		37
750,000	1,000,000	248,300		39
1,000,000	1,250,000	345,800		41
1,250,000	1,500,000	448,300		43
1,500,000	2,000,000	555,800		45
2,000,000	2,500,000	780,800		49
2,500,000	3,000,000	1,025,800		53
3,000,000	3,500,000	1,290,800		57

[a]From the tax computed in columns C and D, the estate may deduct (if previously unused against gift taxes) $38,000 if death occurs in 1979, $42,500 if death occurs in 1980, or $47,000 if death occurs in 1981 or later.

The Effect of Sole Ownership Confused? Probably, and perhaps a bit discouraged to boot. A better understanding may not clear up the discouragement, but will at least ease the confusion. Let's develop an example and follow it through several estate-planning options.

An example of estate taxes: sole ownership

Example 1. Assume that our Dr. Smith dies testate (having a will), leaving a gross estate *in his own name* of $600,000, and is survived by his widow. Dr. Smith's will provides for the full marital deduction. The executor of his estate must pay the expenses that qualify as Category I deductions. After funeral expenses ($10,000), administration expenses ($17,000), and liabilities owed by the estate ($43,000) are deducted, Dr. Smith's adjusted gross estate is $530,000. Since Dr. Smith lived in a state that does not have community property laws,

Mrs. Smith is entitled to a tax-free amount equal to 50 percent of her husband's adjusted gross estate (50 percent × $530,000 = $265,000) or $250,000, whichever is greater. This is the marital deduction. Dr. Smith also directed through his will that his church should receive a bequest of $50,000 from the nonmarital share. Smith's estate tax is computed in Table 12.3.

Table 12.3 Computation of Dr. Smith's Estate Tax, Sole Ownership

Smith's gross estate		$600,000
Less: funeral	$ 10,000	
administration costs	17,000	
liabilities	43,000	
		(70,000)
Adjusted gross estate		$530,000
Less: marital deduction	$265,000	
church donation	50,000	
		(315,000)
Taxable estate		$215,000
Preliminary tax (see Table 12.2)		$ 59,600
Less unified tax credit		(30,000)
Net tax		$ 29,600

Table 12.4 Computation of Mrs. Smith's Net Inheritance

Smith's gross estate		$600,000
Less: funeral expenses	$10,000	
administration expenses	17,000	
liabilities	43,000	
gift to church	50,000	
estate tax	29,600	
		(149,600)
		$450,400

Mrs. Smith is left with $450,400, as computed in Table 12.4. The figure of $450,400 would, of course, be diminished by applicable state inheritance or estate taxes as well as probate costs. Of the $450,400, Mrs. Smith would receive outright (or under conditions that would allow her to receive it without restriction) the marital share of $265,000. The remaining $185,000 should be available to her on a restricted basis only in order to shelter the $185,000 from taxation in Mrs. Smith's estate at the time of her death. If the draftsman of Smith's will put the proper restrictions on Mrs. Smith's use and access to the $185,000, only that portion of the $265,000 remaining in Mrs. Smith's estate, along with any other property Mrs. Smith owned at death, would be taxed in her estate.

Assuming Mrs. Smith had no other estate and that the marital share had not increased or decreased at the time of her death, and

How the marital share is made available

assuming Category I expenses on Mrs. Smith's estate of $25,000, the tax on Mrs. Smith's estate would be computed as follows in Table 12.5. The combined federal tax on the Smith's estate would then be $29,600 (on his estate) + $37,600 (on her estate), or $67,200.

Table 12.5 Computation of Mrs. Smith's Estate Tax

Marital share from Dr. Smith's estate (constituting her adjusted gross estate)	$265,000
Less: category I deductions	(25,000)
Taxable estate	$240,000
Preliminary tax	$ 67,600
Less unified tax credit	(30,000)
Net tax	$ 37,600

How estate taxes can be reduced

Quite unknowingly, Smith and his wife have taken advantage of several estate-planning devices that substantially reduce their taxes to a level far below what they might have been. These devices were first, making full use of the marital deduction; second, and most important, allowing only the marital share to pass directly to Mrs. Smith after Dr. Smith's death. Unfortunately many couples do not fare as well as Smith and his wife, as we shall see in the next section. (Nor would Smith have fared well had his wife died first. By owning all the property individually, he subjected the estate to great risk; we will also examine that problem.)

The Effect of Ownership Rights on Transfer and Taxation Except in community property states (at last count Arizona, California, Idaho, Louisiana, Nevada, New Mexico, Texas, and Washington) the tendency is often for married couples to own property as *joint tenants with full rights of survivorship.* Many married couples feel there is a distinct advantage to owning property in this manner so that upon death of one spouse, entire ownership of the property becomes vested in the surviving spouse. Frequently, in fact, individuals purposely own property as joint tenants because no will is required for a spouse to leave his or her interest in a jointly owned property to the surviving spouse. Many more couples give the matter no thought at all; they merely take title to property in the manner in which a $3.50-per-hour clerk in the real estate office filled out the deed. The result in either case is the same: frequently disastrous. A continuation of the previous example shows the disadvantage of owning property as joint tenants when the estate reaches taxable proportions.

Joint ownership of property may be a disadvantage

An example: joint tenancy

Example 2. Assume that our same Dr. Smith and his wife own the $600,000 estate in joint tenancy with full rights of survivorship. Mrs. Smith would not be obligated to pay her husband's creditors or

> There may be a distinct disadvantage to owning property as joint tenants in that the property may be subject to the federal estate tax once when the first spouse dies; and again a second time (without the benefit of a marital deduction) at the time of death of the surviving spouse.

Joint ownership of property may be a disadvantage

the charitable bequest he made, and no deduction would be allowed for the charitable contribution if made. Dr. Smith's estate, for federal tax purposes, would shape up as shown in Table 12.6.

Table 12.6 Computation of Dr. Smith's Estate Tax, Joint Tenancy

Smith's gross estate		$600,000
Less: funeral	$10,000	
administrative expenses	17,000	
liabilities	43,000	
		(70,000)
Adjusted gross estate		$530,000
Less marital deduction (greater of $250,000 or 50% of $530,000)		(265,000)
Taxable estate		$265,000
Preliminary tax		$ 75,900
Less unified tax credit		(30,000)
Net tax		$ 45,900

Mrs. Smith would now own outright the sum of $484,100 (less any applicable state inheritance or estate tax) computed as follows in Table 12.7. Assume that this $484,100 is Mrs. Smith's only estate and that she dies without increasing or diminishing its size. Assume further that the Category I deductions in Mrs. Smith's estate total $70,000, that she died leaving a will, and that she now makes the desired charitable bequest of $50,000 to her church. The federal tax on Mrs. Smith's estate would be as shown in Table 12.8. The combined federal tax on both estates would then be $45,900 (on his) + $79,594 (on hers), or $125,494 as distinguished from a combined tax of $67,200 in the first example, an increase of $58,294.

The big bite joint ownership can take

Table 12.7 Computation of Mrs. Smith's Net Inheritance

Estate passing to Mrs. Smith by survivorship	$600,000
Less: category I deductions	(70,000)
federal tax	(45,900)
Net to Mrs. Smith	$484,100

Table 12.8 Computation of Mrs. Smith's Estate Tax, Joint Tenancy

Mrs. Smith's adjusted gross estate	$484,100
Less: category I deductions	(70,000)
charitable bequest	(50,000)
Taxable estate	$364,100
Preliminary tax	109,594
Less unified tax credit	(30,000)
Net tax	$ 79,594

This illustration is somewhat distorted by reason of its failure to include state tax consequences and probate costs. But it illustrates in a graphic way the undesirable tax consequences of joint ownership.

An example: tenants in common

For individuals living in non-community-property states (where the ownership is automatically solved), a more viable approach to ownership of property may be for husband and wife to own property as *tenants in common,* instead of as joint tenants with rights of survivorship. Under the rules of common tenancy, an individual's share of interest in property will pass to his or her estate upon death, to be distributed according to the person's will if the person dies testate, or according to the applicable state law on intestate succession if the person dies without a will.

Example 3. Let's look at Dr. Smith once again. Suppose that Smith and his wife hold title to all of their property as tenants in common instead of as joint tenants with rights of survivorship. Further, suppose that in their wills, both Dr. and Mrs. Smith bequeathed their estates *in trust* in such a way as to give the other the economic benefit of their respective estates, without the surviving spouse formally taking ownership of the deceased partner's assets. Table 12.9 illustrates the total estate tax liability paid by both.

How this estate tax is kept low

As you can see, the total estate tax paid by the two is considerably less owning property as tenants in common than it was owning property as joint tenants with rights of survivorship. You should note, however, that we have not allowed the ownership of Smith's estate to pass to his wife, or vice versa, in the event of their respective deaths. It is this fact that kept the individual estates—and, therefore, the amounts of estate taxes—at the low levels in this example.

In this example, the surviving spouse could be entitled, under the terms of the trust receiving the deceased's estate, to all the income the trust produces plus, under certain circumstances, a portion of the assets. If the trust documents are properly drawn, the estate tax savings are still realized, and also Mrs. Smith retains a beneficial interest in her husband's estate. We will discuss trusts in more detail later in this chapter.

Sole ownership if the wife dies first

This example illustrates the tax advantage of common ownership over joint ownership. It may still seem that sole ownership, as illus-

Table 12.9 Determination of Total Estate Tax Liability, All Assets Owned as Tenants in Common

	Dr. Smith	Mrs. Smith
Gross estate	$300,000	$300,000
Less: funeral expense	(10,000)	(10,000)
administration expenses	(17,000)	(15,000)
liabilities	(43,000)	
Adjusted gross estate	$230,000	$275,000
Marital deduction	0[a]	0[a]
Less contribution to church	(50,000)	
Taxable estate	$180,000	$275,000
Preliminary tax	$ 48,400	$ 79,300
Less unified tax credit	30,000	30,000
Net tax	18,400	49,300
		$67,700

[a]The effect of the marital deduction is shown in this example by splitting the estate between the respective spouses to begin with.

trated in Example 1, is the most desirable of the alternatives we have looked at. While that is apparently true, go back and see what happens if Dr. Smith (who owns all of the property himself) is predeceased by his wife. Upon his death the tax will be frighteningly high, since Smith now lacks the marital deduction. Splitting property during one's lifetime, as was done in Example 3, avoids this scary prospect.

The advantage of splitting property

While common tenancy, then, may seem to be the least painful way out of a difficult problem, it presents its own serious problem. If Smith, as the breadwinner of the family, has earned all the funds to buy the assets owned by him and his wife, the splitting can only be accomplished by gift. And gifts may create an adverse gift tax problem. We will talk about gifts later in this chapter.

A possible disadvantage: the gift tax problem

> The gift problem underscores the need to plan a balanced estate early on—not late in life. By starting early with small nontaxable gifts, you can achieve a modicum of balance that can only be achieved at very high cost in later years.

Transferring Assets to Heirs

Having solved the estate tax problem, you now face the problem of making certain your assets are transferred to your heirs in the least costly, least painful manner possible. In this section we will look at devices that accomplish those ends.

Your will: what you want done

The Will and Will Substitutes A will is a legal document that directs the manner in which you desire to have your estate disposed of in the event of your death. Wills may be very simple or very complicated documents, depending on the requirements of the individual involved, but even the simplest must meet certain legal requirements if it is to be recognized as valid. The essential elements that should be included in a will are:

- The naming of an executor who will have the responsibility for administering the disposition of your estate,
- The distribution of your property to your heirs,
- The naming of a guardian for minor children, and
- The creation of *testamentary* trusts that may receive part of the property in your estate for the benefit of whomever you direct.

What probate means

After your death, but before your estate is distributed according to the terms of the will, certain legal steps are required. This process is known as probate. Depending on the complexity of the estate, the following steps may be included as part of the probate process:

The legal steps of probate

- A determination will be made to test the legality and authenticity of the will,
- The appropriate state court will direct the named executor to administer the settlement of the estate,
- The executor will assemble and maintain in safekeeping all deeds and other evidences of ownership to property that you had an interest in at the time of death,
- The executor must locate all liabilities that you had at the time of death,
- The executor is obligated to manage your financial interests during the period of time covered by the probate process,
- The executor will pay liabilities that were outstanding against you at the time of your death,
- The executor will pay all taxes due, including a final income tax return for you, income tax returns for your estate covering the period of time between your death and the distribution of your estate to your heirs, and estate and inheritance taxes based on the final value of your estate, and
- The executor's last obligation is the final distribution of the estate according to the directions contained in your will.

Probate is often a long, expensive, frustrating, and at times painful process for your heirs. Depending on the state you live in, the legal counsel for your executor will charge a fee of about 5 percent of the first $10,000 of an estate, ranging downward to perhaps 2 percent on assets exceeding $200,000.

Joint Tenancy Frequently, all or part of the probate process may be avoided by using other estate-planning devices in lieu of the last will and testament.

One method of avoiding probate for a portion of your estate is to use the joint tenancy form of ownership for property. As you will recall, all property held in joint tenancy at death automatically goes to the surviving joint owner, generally your spouse. The danger to this type of ownership has already been pointed out in that the total amount of estate tax paid may increase substantially because of the double taxation incurred at the time of death of the surviving spouse.

The danger of double taxation

Gifts A second way to avoid the probate for a portion of your estate is to make a gift of that portion of the estate prior to the time of death. Under previous federal law such transfers of property were taxable except that an individual had a single lifetime exemption of $30,000 in gifts, plus gift exemptions of $3,000 per year per donee. What this meant was that an individual could make gifts of up to $30,000 before any gift tax liability was incurred; and that in addition, this person could give up to $3,000 per year per donee (in excess of the $30,000 amount) without tax.

The Tax Reform Act of 1976 forever changed the tax treatment of gifts and makes the effective use of gifts as will substitutes much less desirable. Under this law, a $3,000 per year annual exclusion (per donee) remains, but the lifetime exemption of $30,000 has been eliminated. This means that any gift in excess of $3,000 in any year is now fully taxable. To make matters worse, the gift tax rate, formerly 75 percent of the estate tax rate, is now equal to the estate tax rate.

The recent tax reform act affects gifts

To replace the $30,000 lifetime tax-free gift exemption, the present law allows a $38,000 (in 1979, but increasing to $47,000 in 1981 and thereafter) lifetime unified tax credit. By unified, the law means the credit may be applied against either gift or estate tax liability. Assuming the entire lifetime credit was applied to gifts, it would allow tax-free transfers of about $175,625. This would use up the entire credit, however, requiring payment of all taxes due on your estate at the time of death.

The unified tax credit helps

The present law also makes all gifts (in excess of the $3,000 annual exclusions) cumulative, and thus the gift tax is always assessed at the highest marginal rates. To help you understand the impact of this rule, suppose our old friend Dr. Smith, as sole owner of $600,000 in assets and having been predeceased by his wife, decides to make annual gifts of $100,000 per year for each of 3 years to his only son. The gift tax due each year would be computed according to Table 12.10. As you can see, the tax rapidly increases because the cumulative gifts move into higher and higher tax brackets annually.

But all gifts are cumulative

An additional feature of the law makes it more difficult to reduce effectively the ultimate tax rate paid on the final estate by a gift program. The code requires that the final estate be "grossed up" by the amount of all gifts (in excess of $3,000 per year) made within 3 years

Gross estate must include gifts and taxes thereon

of the date of death. That is, all such gifts—and tax paid thereon—will be reincluded in the gross estate for purposes of computing the estate tax liability. Taxes paid on these gifts are deductible from the ultimate estate tax, but not from the taxable estate.

Table 12.10 Computation of Annual Gift Tax Liability

	1978	1979	1980
Gift	$100,000	$100,000	$100,000
Annual exclusion	3,000	3,000	3,000
Taxable gift	97,000	97,000	97,000
Cumulative gift	97,000	194,000	291,000
Preliminary tax (from Table 12.2)	22,960	52,880	84,740
Less: previous tax paid	0	0	(37,840)
unified credit	(22,960)[a]	(15,040)[b]	(4,500)[c]
Actual tax	0	37,840	42,400

[a]The unified credit is $34,000 for 1978; $38,000 for 1979; $42,500 for 1980; and $47,000 for all years after 1980.
[b]$38,000 − $22,960 = $15,040.
[c]$42,500 − $38,000 = $ 4,500.

Some advantage if you live awhile

If Smith died immediately after making the last gift in Table 12.10, all the gifts, plus taxes paid on them, would be reincluded in his gross estate, thus defeating the gift program. Should Smith live 10 years before dying, however, his total tax will be reduced somewhat as a result of the gift program, as Table 12.11 illustrates.

Table 12.11 Tax Effect If Smith Dies in 1988

	With gift program	Without gift program
Smith's original estate	$600,000	$600,000
Less: gifts to son	(300,000)	
taxes on gifts	(80,240)	
funeral expenses	(10,000)	(10,000)
liabilities	(43,000)	(43,000)
Adjusted gross estate	$149,760	$530,000
Less gift to church	(50,000)	(50,000)
Taxable estate	$ 99,760	$480,000
Tax (from Table 12.2)	$ 23,732	$149,000
Less remaining tax credit	(4,500)[a]	(47,000)
Tax	$19,232	$102,000
Previous gift taxes paid	80,240	0
Total taxes paid	$99,472	$102,000

[a]Smith, at the time of death, had $4,500 ($47,000 − $42,500) of unified tax credit remaining from the gift program.

Dr. Smith's gift program has now been moderately successful, in that he has reduced his total tax from $102,000 to $99,472—a very small advantage compared to the previous law, but an advantage nonetheless. The principal advantage to a gift program remains intact—and that is as a will substitute. The gift program still provides a certain way to avoid the problems and costs of probate, and thus is an effective will substitute.

The main advantage: a will substitute

Trusts Perhaps no area of estate planning is more subject to misunderstanding and confusion than is the area of trusts. Most confusing is determination of precisely what a trust does in terms first, of eliminating all or a portion of the estate from the probate process and second, of eliminating or reducing the amount of estate taxes incurred at the time of death. We hope the material that follows explains trusts in such a way that these two areas of confusion will be clarified and you will understand why trusts are effective will substitutes.

Trusts can be effective

First, you need to know a bit of legal terminology:

Trust. A trust is a contract dealing with the control and management of assets held by one person for the benefit of another person. Under the law, a trust is considered a separate legal entity—almost an artificial person—which may own property, earn income, and is subject to payment of income taxes.

You can understand the legal terms

Trustor. The trustor or grantor is the individual who entrusts, or places in trust, property with a trustee. The trustee is obligated to manage this property according to the instructions which he or she has received or receives from time to time—depending on the type of trust—from the trustor.

The trust and the trustor

Trustee. A trustee is an individual or institution that receives legal title to the property placed in trust, managing the property according to the terms of the trust agreement.

The trustee and the beneficiary

Beneficiary. The beneficiary of a trust is an individual who is entitled to receive the benefits of the property held in trust.

Essentially, a trust is an agreement that involves first, the trustor who transfers all or a portion of owned property to the trust; second, the trustee who receives legal title to that property and manages it according to the terms of the trust agreement; and third, the beneficiary who receives the benefit from the trust.

For our purposes, we will examine two types of trusts, intervivos and testamentary trusts, each of which can be used to achieve specific objectives.

Intervivos Trusts. An intervivos or *living* trust is so called because it is put into effect during the lifetime of the trustor. There are several ways which intervivos trusts may be used to either avoid the probate process, reduce federal estate tax liability, or both.

Intervivos is a living trust

One type of intervivos trust, called a *revocable* trust, allows the trustor effectively to control—for as long as he or she lives—the assets that he or she has placed in trust. The trustor may put assets into this trust at any time desired, and may likewise withdraw assets at any

The revocable trust is an example

time desired, thus giving rise to the term revocable. Because the trustor has full use of the assets that have been placed in trust, such a trust does not affect federal estate tax liability at the time of death. The full value of such assets would be included in the computation of federal estate tax liability.

Probate is avoided

> The advantage of a revocable trust is that at the time of death—since the assets are legally owned by the trust instead of by the individual—the probate process is avoided. This means that the assets owned by the trust may pass directly to the beneficiary of the trust, as the trustor had dictated, without passing through probate or being tied up by the probate process.

But management fees can add up

While probate fees and administration fees are thus avoided, if an institutional trustee has been named for this trust, a management fee of from ½ of 1 percent to 2 percent per annum of asset value will be charged for the management of the property in trust. One of the factors you should consider as decisive when you contemplate the use of this trust is whether or not the management fees paid over time will be less than the costs that would be incurred in the probate process.

Even in the absence of an institutional trustee during your lifetime, someone must manage the affairs of the trust, meeting all the legal requirements of that entity. Frequently, such trusts are established, assets transferred, and then totally disregarded. Your failure to recognize for years that a trust existed will probably disqualify the trust when the important test—your death—comes. So the advice is clear: if you form a revocable trust, make certain the legal requirements of trusteeship are met over the years. Otherwise, the exercise will likely go for nought.

Meet the legal requirements of trusteeship

The irrevocable trust: you have no control

Another type of intervivos trust is the *irrevocable* trust, so named because once the assets are placed in trust, the trustor relinquishes all control over them. This type of trust, too, has the advantages of eliminating the probate process and federal estate tax liability pertaining to the assets placed in trust. At the time assets are deeded to such a trust, however, such a transfer may constitute a taxable gift, and hence be subject to gift tax as outlined in the preceding section. Also, under certain circumstances, a gift made by creation of an irrevocable trust may not qualify for the annual gift exclusions mentioned in the previous section.

Assets may be a taxable gift

This trust is most effective for large estates

There are some serious disadvantages to the use of irrevocable trusts, not the least of which is the undesirability of an individual relinquishing control over all or a significant part of owned assets, leaving insufficient resources to last for the rest of the individual's life. An individual owning a large estate, however, could effectively reduce the size of the estate, thereby reducing future estate tax liability, by the judicious use of irrevocable trusts.

The Testamentary Trust. The testamentary trust is one that is created in the will of the trustor but is not activated, or does not come into effect, until his or her death. At that time the trust becomes the beneficiary (or one of the beneficiaries) of the individual's will. In turn, the beneficiaries of the trust could be the individual's spouse, children, charitable institutions, and so forth.

The testamentary trust is created in your will

> The most appealing feature of a testamentary trust is that an individual does not relinquish control of any assets during his or her lifetime. At the same time, it is assured that after death, the assets will will be managed according to the individual's desires and for the benefit of the heirs, as spelled out in the trust instrument.

Thus, the heirs are protected from unscrupulous individuals—or their own inability to manage the assets of the estate properly. This type of trust avoids neither the probate process nor federal estate tax liability, although properly drafted testamentary trusts can result in minimizing such liability on the death of the surviving spouse.

You do not give up control

Frequently the greatest advantage to the testamentary trust is to serve as a receptacle for the estate of a deceased spouse, to prevent assets from flowing into the estate of the surviving spouse. Thus, the trust can take advantage of the marital deduction, allow the surviving spouse to have all of the income from trust assets and even access to the trust assets if required, and still prevent a second taxation on death of the surviving spouse.

You can prevent double taxation

While there are many other ways in which trusts could be used either to minimize estate tax liability or to eliminate all or part of the probate process, these examples, particularly when coupled with the judicious use of wills and gifts, show how the effects of both probate and estate taxes can be reduced or eliminated. Table 12.12 summarizes graphically the various will substitutes discussed in this section, and shows their effect on both probate and the federal estate tax.

Estate-planning Problems Encountered with Life Insurance Life insurance salespeople sometimes claim insurance as a worthwhile investment, using the argument that the beneficiary of a life insurance policy does not pay income tax on death benefits received. We have already seen that life insurance is not an investment, and should never be considered as one. The agent's argument that insurance death benefits are not taxed as income is nonetheless true.

Remember: life insurance is not an investment

Death benefits, however, may be included as part of the deceased's estate, thus subjecting them to federal estate taxes. It is not unusual for an individual whose estate would not otherwise be taxed, because

Table 12.12 Effect of the Will and Will Substitutes on Probate and Federal Estate Taxes

Estate planning tool	Gift tax incurred?	Estate tax reduced?	Probate fees reduced?	Control of assets relinquished?
Joint tenancy in lieu of will	a	No	Yes	No
Will	No	No	No	No
Living trusts				
Revocable	No	No	Yes	No
Irrevocable	Yes	Yes	Yes	Yes
Testamentary trusts	No	No	No	No
Gifts	Yes	Yes	Yes	Yes

ªThere may be gift tax consequences that result from the creation of joint tenancies. These should be determined and evaluated before creating joint tenancies.

Death benefits may be taxed

of its small size, to have a fairly substantial taxable estate once the proceeds of insurance benefits are added to other assets. Since insurance is purchased to protect heirs or survivors against the risk of death, you should never allow such benefits to be subjected to estate taxation.

Three important insurance terms

As with trusts, it is helpful for you to understand some of the terminology of insurance in order to determine if insurance benefits will or will not be taxed in your estate:

The Insured. The insured is the individual whose life is insured by the policy of life insurance.

The Owner. The owner of a life insurance policy is the individual who holds the incidents of ownership. These include the right to designate the beneficiary, borrow against the cash value of the policy, and surrender or cancel the policy.

The Beneficiary. The beneficiary of a life insurance policy is the individual who will receive the proceeds of the life insurance policy in the event of the death of the insured.

Take care who owns the insurance

A mistake commonly made by individuals buying life insurance is to make the owner of the policy and the insured one and the same. For example, suppose our Dr. Smith buys a $100,000 policy of life insurance on himself, naming his wife as beneficiary. When Smith subsequently dies, the proceeds of the life insurance policy become part of his estate, and hence subject to the rules of estate taxation. While his wife is beneficiary of the life insurance policy, the death benefit she actually receives will be equal to $100,000 minus whatever estate taxes were paid on that amount. The mistake, of course, was for Smith to own the policy of life insurance on himself—a mistake he could have avoided.

How to avoid taxation of death benefits

For example, had Mrs. Smith purchased the policy of life insurance on her husband and paid the premiums thereon with her own money, then upon his death, the death benefit would have been paid directly to her—without being subjected to probate or estate taxes—

because she, not Dr. Smith, is the owner of the life insurance policy, as well as the beneficiary. The important thing to note here is that with this form of ownership the death benefits are paid to the beneficiaries of the policy fully without being first eroded by the payment of estate taxes.

There are many matters that should be taken into account in planning the ownership of life insurance policies—not the least of which is the stability of one's marriage. Generally, then, such ownership considerations should be only part of a carefully planned estate, along with other problems of asset ownership and use of wills, gifts, and trusts.

Something Old, Something New

You may have been thinking about getting around to planning your estate. Or, you may be smugly content in the knowledge that your estate plan was carefully drawn some time ago. In either case, the Tax Reform Act of 1976 made it a brand new ball game, and we recommend that you retain legal counsel to initiate or revise your estate plan.

The balance of this chapter is devoted to a side-by-side comparison of the changes in the law, so you can see how you have been affected by it. If you have an estate plan made before 1976, it will need an overhaul. If you have none, now is the time to see your attorney.

Tax changes you need to know about

Tax Rates. Present rates are significantly higher than the old ones—particularly for large estates. Estate and gift tax rates are now the same, reducing the desirability of gifts.

Exemptions. The $60,000 personal estate tax exemption and $30,000 lifetime gift exemption have been replaced by a uniform and unified lifetime tax credit—applicable against either gift or estate tax liability. This is equivalent to a personal exemption of roughly $175,625. The credit increases annually until it reaches a maximum of $47,000 in 1981.

Rates, exemptions, deductions

Marital Deduction. The marital deduction has been liberalized on several counts. It is now 50 percent of the marital estate, or $250,000, whichever is larger, instead of the previous 50 percent. Also, an unrestricted gift of $100,000 may be given a spouse, with no deduction for the second $100,000 given, and a 50 percent deduction for all gifts over $200,000—a change from the previous flat 50 percent deduction on marital gifts.

Orphan's Exclusion. The present law allows a tax-free transfer to minor orphaned children. The amount of the deduction is limited to $5,000 for each year each child is under age 21.

Exclusions, transfers, gifts

Generation-Skipping Transfers. The practice of skipping a round of taxation through use of a generation-skipping trust has been eliminated.

Gifts in Contemplation of Death. The old contemplation-of-death rule has been eliminated, and all gifts (except the $3,000 annual exclusion) made within 3 years of death, plus the taxes on the gifts are automatically reincluded in the estate.

Basis of Inherited Property. Perhaps some of the most significant changes in the 1976 law and the amendments to it of the Revenue Act of 1978 are in this area. Previously, the heir's basis (that is, the acquisition value of the property for tax purposes) was the fair market value of the property on the date of inheritance. That simple rule has been changed to rules complicated enough so that we suggest you consult a tax specialist when you need the details.

Tax basis, valuation, extensions

Valuation of Firms and Closely Held Businesses. Under the present law, such assets may be valued in their present use rather than highest-and-best use. This is designed to prevent breakup of such units in order to pay excessively high taxes.

Extensions. To avoid forced sales and "undue hardships," the present law allows extensions of 10 and over 15 years to pay estate taxes on farms and closely held businesses.

Exclusion of Retirement Benefits. Formerly, asset values in qualified corporate retirement plans were exempt from estate taxation before retirement, but not after. Under the present law the exemption is extended to postretirement values as well. In addition, values in Keogh or IRA plans, which formerly were always included in the gross estate, have been exempted.

Summary

Consult professional counsel

More than any other area of your financial life, the problems of estate planning require expert and continuing professional assistance. Because circumstances continually change, an estate plan is not a once-in-a-lifetime act, but a continuing process. The authors have seen thousands of dollars worth of legal work destroyed in a few minutes by an individual taking an action without considering the impact it would have on a carefully constructed estate plan.

> Retain the most competent legal counsel you can find early on in the estate-planning process. Have that person construct your plan and insist that you have a complete understanding not only of its objectives but how they are to be met: Make notes of all explanations. From that point be scrupulous in maintaining the objectives of the plan, consulting your counsel as often as necessary as circumstances change.

You may be reluctant to incur the costs of these periodic visits, but as this chapter points out, the savings to you or your heirs will far exceed the costs. You must preserve the integrity of your plan by consulting your legal counsel on every major financial transaction. What should be the form of ownership? From what funds should the asset be purchased? What impact would selling a particular asset have on a carefully balanced asset structure? Should some other asset be transferred from husband to wife—or vice versa—to compensate? These and other questions must be resolved prior to the transaction if the integrity of the estate plan is to be maintained intact.

And ask the important questions

BIBLIOGRAPHY

Randle, Paul A. "What Is Left of Your Estate Plan After the Tax Reform Act of 1976—Nothing."
   A 30-minute slide-tape autotutorial, available through the library of the American Association of Orthodontists.

Wolf, Harold A. *Personal Finance.* 4th ed. Boston: Allyn & Bacon, 1975.
   Chapter 12 contains an excellent discussion of the estate-planning process plus a glossary of estate-planning terminology.

CHAPTER 13

Inflation and Your Financial Plan

After reading this chapter, you will understand the effects of inflation on

- Management of your current financial affairs.
- Your life insurance needs.
- Retirement planning.
- Personal investment strategy.

In recent years each of us has become painfully aware of the economic realities of inflation. Each month our wives relate the horror stories of the grocery store; and while it's nice to know that junior is still alive, the letter from college sadly explains new and higher costs for everything. These nasty reminders of ever-increasing prices constantly reinforce our uneasy feeling that the cost of maintaining our current standard of living is becoming more difficult.

As a matter of fact, all our uneasy feelings are justified. Inflation *is* making it ever more difficult and costly to maintain our standard of living. Far more serious than the day-to-day effects of inflation, however, is the damage done to our long-range plans by the debilitating effects of long-run price increases. Largely because of this problem, we devote most of this chapter to a discussion of strategies that you might profitably employ in formulating your long-range plans.

Your long-range plans suffer most

Inflation and Your Short-Term Plans

Although the effects of inflation tend to be more profound on decisions of a long-run nature—such as pension or insurance planning—they also create some problems in the financial transactions you engage in from day to day.

Times of inflation require that you periodically review the adequacy of your various insurance policies. As prices and values rise, insurance policies must be reviewed or the coverage they provide becomes inadequate.

Review your insurance coverage

193

Consider, for example, your homeowners policy. If you have had occasion to relocate recently, or worse yet, to buy housing for the first time, you are well aware of the price explosion in housing. In recent years, market values have increased as rapidly as 20 percent per year in some locations. The point is, if you purchased an insurance policy on your home three or four years ago and promptly buried it in your files, it is almost certain to be inadequate today—perhaps providing as little as 25 to 50 percent of the coverage you actually require. Given the rate of inflation for the past decade—particularly in the area of residential housing—it is essential that you review your homeowners coverage *annually* to be sure that it is consistent with the increasing market value of your home.

Check homeowners, auto, medical, and disability

Precisely the same point needs to be made for several other types of insurance coverage. As claims on auto liability cases tend to increase, for instance, you should attend to the increase of those limits on your policy. Your expectations regarding the need for medical or disability coverage also require periodic review in light of changing costs and your changing needs. As years go by, given the inflationary environment, it is our judgment that you may in fact be unwittingly exposing yourself to more and more risk by simple failure to update your insurance coverage.

It is difficult to generalize about the effects of inflation in another area: your present individual life-style. Of course you are aware of its effect because of the well-publicized Consumer Price Index (CPI) released monthly by the Department of Commerce. You should realize, however, that you, as a professional, do not feel the effect of these price increases as severely as do other segments of the population.

Your advantage as a professional

For example, your mortgage payment, which is your cost of housing, remains constant over many years even though the CPI reflects a rapidly increasing cost for housing. At the same time you are able, to a great extent, to increase the price others pay for your services.

Statistics show that the average income of the self-employed professional has, over the years, risen at a rate significantly higher than the rate of inflation.

The built-in hedge

This built-in hedge against inflation makes it easier for you to adapt to the short-range effects of inflation than for other wage earners.

The bottom line is that while the effects of inflation on your day-to-day financial decisions is disconcerting, it can be accommodated with minor adjustments in insurance policies, shopping habits, and the price of your personal services. Its effects on your long-range plans are where you must exercise great caution.

Inflation and Your Long-Term Plans

You know that if you were to put $1.00 in a 6 percent savings account for one year you would end up with $1.06. If, during the same year, inflation occurred at a 6 percent annual rate, the prices of the goods and services you could purchase with that initial dollar would have also risen to $1.06. Thus, the real value of your savings account—that is, the purchasing power provided by your account—has just remained constant. It is clear, then, that to have a fund of money grow in real terms, it must be invested to yield a rate greater than the current rate of inflation. We saw in Chapter 2 the profound effects of compounding in the accumulation of an asset portfolio, particularly if the savings program begins early in life. Obviously, prolonged inflation has precisely the reverse effect on your store of assets. And like compound interest, the longer the time period over which inflation works, the more profound its effects.

Your investment yield must beat inflation

Suppose, for example, that you graduate from professional school at age 30, and initially earn $20,000 per year. You decide to implement a retirement plan to ensure that you can maintain at least the same level of real income that you now enjoy. Some quick calculations utilizing Appendix A.1, and assuming a 6 percent long-term inflation average, show that your retirement annuity at age 65 must be $153,722 just to maintain the purchasing power $20,000 gives you today. If, perchance, the inflation rate were to maintain a double digit level of 12 percent, you would require a retirement benefit of $1,056,000 per year to maintain the purchasing power of your current $20,000 income. We hasten to point out that we don't anticipate 12 percent annual inflation over a 35-year period of time. But whether the illustrations use 6 percent or 12 percent, you can see the debilitating, crippling effects of high, long-range inflation. Unless you compensate for these effects in your long-range plans, your hopes for the future can easily be devastated.

How inflation can hit a retirement plan

If inflation is here to stay, how do you account for it in your major financial decisions? You must face this question head on if your plans are going to reflect economic reality and be useful. Major financial decisions, such as life insurance needs or retirement fund development, are a function of cash flows over a considerable time horizon and thus absolutely require an explicit treatment for inflation to obtain the desired results.

Face inflation head on to save your future

Inflation and Life Insurance Needs. Your current life insurance planning may span a time horizon of close to fifty years. If those prove to be inflationary years, as most observers expect they will, your current life insurance purchases must reflect those expectations.

In factoring the problem of inflation into your forecast of insurance needs, your first task is one requiring both judgment and luck. You must make an estimate of your expectations regarding the level of inflation relevant to your long-range financial decisions. This is a dif-

Factor inflation into insurance forecasts

ficult task, fraught with uncertainty, but it is essential as a starting point. The future may prove your estimate incorrect, but you may be certain that even a grossly incorrect estimate of future inflation will result in a financial plan vastly superior to one you will get with no guess at all.

Estimating the rate of inflation

What should the size of your estimate be? A brief review of the historical record indicates that over the past 30 years inflation has averaged about 3.5 percent per year. However, over the past decade the annual inflation rate has averaged 6 percent. Evidence from available forecasts suggests that into the foreseeable future inflation is likely to be closer to the higher figure than the 3.5 percent average; and the authors frequently use 6 percent as their estimate of a long-range inflation rate in analyses they perform.

Modifying your program

Once you have established a rate you feel comfortable with, it can be incorporated explicitly into your insurance analysis by altering the magnitude of projected cash flows to reflect the estimated rate of inflation. This modification can be demonstrated in a simplified example. Remembering the essentials from chapters 6 and 7, suppose you design a life insurance program that will assure your beneficiary an income of $20,000 a year for 5 years from this date. Since your total insurance need is simply the present value of the remaining income requirement after each year, your annual insurance needs are summarized in Table 13.1. Under these conditions your present insurance need is $82,000, which if invested at 7 percent upon your immediate death would yield the required $20,000 annuity throughout the 5 years.

Table 13.1 An Analysis of Insurance Needs over 5 Years

Year	Income required	Insurance need[a]
1	$20,000	$82,004
2	20,000	67,744
3	20,000	52,486
4	20,000	36,160
5	20,000	18,692

[a]Assuming the insurance benefits are invested at 7%.

Suppose we complicate this simple example by assuming a 5 percent annual rate of inflation, still desiring to maintain the real income at its current $20,000 level. With inflation thus figured in, the annual insurance needs are presented in Table 13.2.

Maintaining real income

The effect of inflation is reflected in the ever-increasing stream of income required to maintain a *real* $20,000 annuity, which in turn dictates a higher level of insurance need each year to provide for this inflated income need. In fact, the insurance requirement has risen from $82,000 to more than $90,000 in anticipation of a 5 percent level of inflation—an illustration of a basic principle that can be easily applied to your own, more complicated situation.

Table 13.2 The Effect of Inflation on Income Requirement

Year	Income required to maintain $20,000 in purchasing power	Insurance need[a]
1	20,000	90,029
2	21,000	76,331
3	22,050	60,674
4	23,153	42,872
5	24,310	22,720

[a]Assuming the insurance benefits are invested at 7%.

In summary, the integrity of the results of these modifications to compensate for inflation depends, in large part, on the accuracy of your estimated inflation rate. If you are to err, we suggest it be on the high side. The error, then, will always be in the direction of overestimating insurance requirements—a result that will leave your family adequately protected.

It's better to overestimate

Inflation and Your Investment Strategy. Since inflation is here to stay, what type of investments will provide a hedge against rising prices? Let us make absolutely clear at the outset a strategy that must *not* be pursued. The authors have witnessed many cases where professionals, in their frantic desire to beat inflation, have selected investment alternatives promising very high (14 to 20 percent and higher) rates of return. These investors seem to be oblivious to the facts we presented in Chapter 9: These high yields must be accompanied by high— sometimes enormous—levels of risk. In the majority of cases, the investments have turned sour; the investors have suffered large losses of investment capital, and their frantic efforts to beat inflation have resulted only in their getting hammered both by the market and by inflation. This is a double dose of trouble that no one needs.

Risk is not the way to beat inflation

As we have pointed out, such risky investments are not inherently bad, particularly if the risks are well understood and can be intelligently dealt with. You should not, however, speculate with funds—such as pension fund monies—where the preservation of capital is of prime importance. A broker commented to one of the authors recently that commodities future trading was one of the few ways left to stay ahead of inflation! There is about the same probability of staying ahead of inflation trading frozen pork belly futures as there is at the roulette wheel—some will win and some won't.

If you must preserve capital, don't speculate

Be careful, in your desire to stay ahead of inflation, not to assume an imprudent amount of risk for the promise of large returns; that strategy may bring disaster.

The best hedge: accumulate dollars

What investments, then, would be appropriate? It is our experience that for the typical high-income professional person, the sheer accumulation of dollars may well be the most attractive inflation hedge available. A tax-qualified corporate retirement plan, started early and funded faithfully, creates the potential of accumulating millions of dollars over your lifetime. Because of the deductibility of plan contributions, Uncle Sam matches your contributions dollar for dollar in tax savings. And because of the tax-deferred status of the plan, a conservative 8 percent return on plan investments is equivalent to earning 16 percent on investments outside the plan. You may not be aware of it, but there are very few 16 percent investments hanging around on trees waiting to be picked. Should you be lucky enough to find one, the risk would almost certainly make it an unacceptable alternative.

And accumulate with a retirement plan

We have to conclude that a tax-qualified retirement plan is the almost unbeatable hedge against inflation. To be sure, the dollars in that plan are eroded by inflation. On the other hand, it is possible to amass such a large number of those dollars that your future goals are still assured.

As a final comment, we must point out that a conservative approach to hedging against the effects of inflation does not limit us to 8 or 9 percent yields in high-quality corporate bonds. Stock market performance over the past 10 years suggests that common stocks have not been a very good hedge against inflation in the short run—that is, when the investment horizon is only a few years. However, if a portfolio of sound, blue-chip stocks are held over a long period of time, say 20 to 30 years, one can reasonably expect an 11 to 14 percent average rate of return in spite of the short-run, year-to-year variations. As a result, a well-diversified portfolio of blue-chip common stocks is entirely appropriate as a retirement fund investment, particularly if you are optimistic and confident about the future of the companies concerned and the overall strength of the United States economy.

Blue-chip common stock—a good hedge

Although there is a measure of increased risk in these equity investments, their average yield, particularly in the long run, will probably exceed that of fixed-income securities. The same kind of arithmetic we did above turns those 11 to 14 percent, tax-deferred yields into 22 to 28 percent yields in investments made outside the plan. Need we say more?

Inflation and Retirement Planning. Since the provision for retirement income requires contributions throughout your entire working life, inflation will certainly have a dramatic effect on the real value of your ultimate accumulation and the retirement annuity it will provide.

The tax deductibility of plan contributions and the tax-free accumulation of plan earnings already provide a significant hedge against inflation in the plan, as we have pointed out. In addition to this hedge, however, the plan can keep pace with inflation if you increase plan contributions annually at the current inflation rate. The obvious result is a stream of contributions increasing at about the same rate as

How to maintain constant real value

prices, thus ensuring a constant real value in the retirement fund accumulation.

Understanding constraints on contributions

Constraints on plan contributions—whether legal or self-imposed—do not preclude this course of action, as is sometimes believed. For example, the contribution limits in a defined-contribution, corporate pension plan are 25 percent of income, or $25,000, whichever is less. If 25 percent is the binding constraint, your annual increases in salary will automatically allow annually increasing contributions. If $25,000 is the binding constraint, that limit is designed to increase annually according to increases in the cost of living. Thus, neither of the constraints are binding—that is, annual increases in the cost of living make possible annual increases in the size of your plan contribution.

If the size of your plan contribution is self-imposed (by budgetary exigencies, for example), increases in the fees you charge for your professional services should increase to keep pace with inflation. As your income increases you are able to make ever greater plan contributions.

Increase contributions with increased income

In short, if you want to be certain that your accumulation in a retirement plan will provide—in real terms—the retirement benefits necessary to maintain your current standard of living, you must pursue the disciplined practice of increasing your plan contributions annually at a rate roughly equivalent to the inflation rate.

Summary

Since we have agreed that inflation is one of the certain economic facts of life, we must understand it and assess its impact on our long-range financial plans. Rapid inflation, hyperinflation, could destroy at once all our best-laid and well-intentioned plans, and each of us finds that possibility disconcerting. It would be foolish, however, for you to postpone financial planning, or avoid it entirely, because of that possibility. Rather, you must anticipate a reasonable level of inflation and amend future plans and strategies to account for its effects.

In making your plans, remember that the monthly computation of the CPI as reported by the Department of Commerce, is subject to some statistical variation. You can get a much clearer picture of the underlying level of inflation, therefore, by studying the trends of several months' data rather than taking one month's observation. It would be a mistake, thus, to panic at the announcement of a very high inflation rate during last month. There are any number of factors that could account for large monthly fluctuations around a much more modest long-term trend. Since your decisions relating to insurance needs and pension planning are long-term in nature, be careful that you don't overreact to the short-term environment. In other words, don't be too hasty to alter your investment strategy until you are sure that economic reality warrants it.

Don't overreact to short-term inflation

Lest you get an unwarranted feeling of despair as you contemplate the effects of inflation, you must remember that bad as it is, our infla-

U.S. inflation rates will stay comparatively low

tion rates are modest compared to many industrialized countries. England has in recent times found it difficult to maintain inflation rates below 20 percent, and in South America annual rates of inflation of 300 percent are not unheard of. In these inflationary environments, there is such constant pressure on social and political institutions that the task of long-range financial planning becomes almost impossible. Whereas the 6 to 10 percent rates we are used to are certainly a nuisance, it is unlikely that we will face the problems of hyperinflation in the future. If you think we are wrong in that prognosis, then there is only one short bit of advice we have for you—SPEND IT ALL NOW!

If you think we are right, on the other hand—we certainly hope we are—then take our last and best advice on how to hedge against inflation: Put your dollars, faithfully year in and year out, into consistent and increasing contributions to your tax-deferred pension plan. This strategy is safe and it's profitable—and you will be assured of a comfortable retirement income. If, in the long run, it turns out that you haven't beaten inflation, you can still be certain of one important fact: It won't have destroyed you.

Good luck. We're rooting for you.

BIBLIOGRAPHY

Alchian, Armen A., and Kessel, Reuben A. "A Redistribution of Wealth Through Inflation," *The Investment Process*, Scranton, Pa.: International Textbook Co., 1970.

Homer, Sidney. "Exploding a Myth: Inflation, Observes One Authority, Is Not Necessarily Bullish." *Barron's*, January 30, 1967, p. 3.

Bolton, Stephen E. *Securities Analysis and Portfolio Management*, Chapter 10. New York: Holt, Rinehart, and Winston, 1972.

Christy, George A., and Clendenin, John C. *Introduction to Investments*, 7th ed. New York: McGraw-Hill Book Co., 1978.
Several of the chapters include a discussion of the effects of inflation on investments of various types.